Historians Debate the Ris

How and why did Europe rise to world preeminence? Providing an overview of this central historical conundrum of modern times, *Historians Debate the Rise of the West* enables students to grasp major scholars' evaluations of the biggest picture of all: how Western civilization fits into modern world history.

Most historians who write in this area subscribe to a combination of interpretations set forward by scholars of the field, like David Landes, Jared Diamond, or Kenneth Pomeranz. But it is often difficult to understand the position they are coming from, and for readers to understand clearly how Europe made the transition from merely one of many developing civilizations to the world's first industrial power. In this volume, Jonathan Daly introduces us to the main interpretations of Europe's rise that have been proposed over the past half-century and presents the views of these historians and schools of scholarship, advocating for each point of view and letting each author speak for him or herself through the inclusion of brief textual selections.

Also included are interesting biographical details for each scholar, as well as a list of further reading for each chapter and a collection of maps. An ideal introduction for students of world history.

Jonathan Daly is Professor of History at the University of Illinois at Chicago. His publications include *Autocracy under Siege* (1998), *The Watchful State* (2004), and *The Rise of Western Power: A Comparative History of Western Civilization* (2014).

Historians Debate the Rise of the West

Jonathan Daly

Routledge
Taylor & Francis Group

LONDON AND NEW YORK

First published 2015
by Routledge
2 Park Square, Milton Park, Abingdon, Oxon OX14 4RN

and by Routledge
711 Third Avenue, New York, NY 10017

Routledge is an imprint of the Taylor & Francis Group, an informa business

British Library Cataloguing in Publication Data
A catalogue record for this book is available from the British Library

Library of Congress Cataloging-in-Publication Data
Daly, Jonathan W.
Historians debate the rise of the West / Jonathan Daly.
Includes bibliographical references and index.
1. Civilization, Western–History. 2. Civilization, Western–Historiography.
3. World history–Historiography. 4. Europe–Civilization. 5. Europe–
Civilization–Historiography. 6. Civilization, Western–Study and teaching.
I. Title.
CB245.D26 2014
909'.09821–dc23
2014021706

ISBN: 978-1-138-77480-3 (hbk)
ISBN: 978-1-138-77481-0 (pbk)
ISBN: 978-1-31577-353-7 (ebk)

Typeset in Sabon
by Taylor and Francis Books

Printed and bound by CPI Group (UK) Ltd, Croydon, CR0 4YY

For my Sofia
You are like the air I breathe.

Contents

Acknowledgments

I am grateful to my colleagues Joel Mokyr and Deirdre McCloskey for wise counsel, to Mark Liechty, Kirk Hoppe, and James Searing for valuable references, to Immanuel Wallerstein for insight into his scholarship, to my editor Eve Setch and her team for professional excellence, to the students in my "The Rise of the West in Global Perspective" (History 410) course at the University of Illinois at Chicago for years of enthusiastically discussing many of the texts presented here, and to my wife Sofia for inspiration in all things. I dedicate this book to her.

Maps

Introduction

One thousand years ago, travelers to Baghdad or the Chinese capital Kaifeng would have discovered vast and flourishing cities of broad streets, spacious gardens, and sophisticated urban amenities. They would also have marveled at the extraordinary achievements of these civilizations in the arts, technology, science, and commercial life. The Chinese had invented paper, the mariner's compass, woodblock printing, the blast furnace, paper currency, and gunpowder. Muslim scholars and thinkers had accomplished history's first great cultural synthesis, bringing together ideas and technologies from ancient Greece and Rome, from Persia and India, and from China and the ancient Near East. Europe, by contrast, was a backwater, and Paris, Rome, and London were cramped and unhygienic collections of villages. How, then, did Europe – and the rest of what we call "the West" (North America, Australia, and New Zealand) – rise to world preeminence over the next several centuries? This is the central historical conundrum of modern times.

My goal in writing this book has been to represent the views and arguments of a wide range of scholars seeking to explain the West's ascendancy so faithfully that not even the most perceptive reader can discern my own views.[1] Obviously, the interpretations that I summarize are in some cases so widely divergent that it would be impossible for any clear thinking individual to affirm them all simultaneously. The interpretations summarized in this volume cannot possibly all be right, though there is surely some truth in each one. The scholars who defend them are highly persuasive, however, so students will need all of their critical faculties in order to sort through their arguments. One should be on the lookout for logical fallacies, in particular the straw man argument, whereby a position one wishes to refute is caricaturized or otherwise exaggerated.

Before discussing contemporary authors, it is worth briefly introducing readers to several thinkers who first tried to explain the rise of the West. Scholars and thinkers in medieval Europe generally looked for signs of the unfolding of a divine plan without reference to the other continents and civilizations. Mystics like Joachim de Fiore (1132–1202), for example, speculated about the historical stages leading to the Second Coming of Christ. Many authors during the Renaissance viewed Europe (usually still their only frame of reference) as having declined since ancient times.[2] Yet a few thinkers, including Francesco Guicciardini (1483–1540), began to realize that the discovery of the New World required a new interpretation of European history. Indeed, the proliferation of knowledge about other cultures and peoples, along with an explosion of technical and scientific information and advancements, made it difficult to fathom Europe's own historical development, much less its place in the wider world.[3]

Geography and climate favored Europe (Montesquieu)

Among the first to try was Charles-Louis de Secondat, baron de La Brède et de Montesquieu (1689–1755), the highly influential political thinker who conceptualized the separation of powers theory. Drawing on ancient Greek thought and a vast reading of ancient and modern primary sources, he argued in his masterwork *The Spirit of Laws* (1748), that "People are therefore more vigorous in cold climates," which imparts to them "a greater boldness, that is, more courage; a greater sense of superiority, that is, less desire of revenge; a greater opinion of security, that is, more frankness, less suspicion, policy, and cunning." In hot regions, by contrast, one finds "no curiosity, no enterprise, no generosity of sentiment; the inclinations are all passive; indolence constitutes the utmost happiness."[4] In such climes, he argued, people bear servitude much more easily than people in northern regions. Women also enjoy greater freedom in temperate countries, because hot weather stirs the passions and the imagination, making it necessary for men to hide their wives and daughters from other men. Civilization of course first emerged in southern lands, but in the long run the greater vigor of northern peoples enabled them to triumph.

Europe's political fragmentation, also caused by its distinctive climate, created an excellent geopolitical environment to foster incessant competition among the various countries. He develops his argument thus:

> Asia has properly no temperate zone, as the places situated in a very cold climate immediately touch upon those which are exceedingly hot, that is, Turkey, Persia, India, China, Korea, and Japan.
>
> In Europe, on the contrary, the temperate zone is very extensive, though situated in climates widely different from each other; there being no affinity between the climates of Spain and Italy and those of Norway and Sweden. But as the climate grows insensibly cold upon our advancing from south to north, nearly in proportion to the latitude of each country, it thence follows that each resembles the country joining it; that there is no very extraordinary difference between them, and that, as I have just said, the temperate zone is very extensive.
>
> Hence it comes that in Asia, the strong nations are opposed to the weak; the warlike, brave, and active people touch immediately upon those who are indolent, effeminate, and timorous; the one must,

therefore, conquer, and the other be conquered. In Europe, on the contrary, strong nations are opposed to the strong; and those who join each other have nearly the same courage. This is the grand reason of the weakness of Asia, and of the strength of Europe; of the liberty of Europe, and of the slavery of Asia.[5]

In consequence, Montesquieu suggests that conquering Asian countries was relatively easy for more than a dozen warrior peoples from the Scythians to the Ottoman Turks, whereas parts of Europe were conquered since ancient Greek times by only four powers – the Romans, the barbarians who overthrew the Roman Empire, Charlemagne, and the Vikings, and of course the latter two were European.

Montesquieu also develops a geographical interpretation of the divergent evolution of Europe and Asia. The massive plains of Asia proved relatively easy for conquerors throughout history to control. In Europe, by contrast,

the natural division forms many nations of a moderate extent, in which the ruling by laws is not incompatible with the maintenance of the state: on the contrary, it is so favourable to it, that without this the state would fall into decay, and become a prey to its neighbours.

It is this which has formed a genius for liberty that renders every part extremely difficult to be subdued and subjected to a foreign power, otherwise than by the laws and the advantage of commerce.[6]

For Montesquieu, involvement in commerce makes people more peaceful and less fierce, as well as more prosperous and respectful of the law, and he considered it detrimental to refuse to trade with other people. Though China's domestic economy was vast, Europe's, when one added all its external trading relations to its domestic economy, greatly exceeded it. Therefore, as he writes, "Europe has arrived at so high a degree of power that nothing in history can be compared with it."[7]

Montesquieu was far from a pure climatic or geographical determinist. He also believed that religion, traditions, laws, accumulated wisdom, and mores influenced how particular societies develop. Yet oftentimes, he argued, one factor played a more significant role. For example, rites and manners, comprised in China of religion, mores, and laws, were like the genetic code of that civilization. The societies of "savages," by contrast, are determined largely by natural phenomena. Although he does not say so explicitly, Montesquieu seems to have believed that European cultures evolved through a balanced interplay of several factors, just as he believed that their moderate forms of government and political liberties were typically assured by a separation of political powers. He elaborates:

There would be the end of everything, were the same man for the same body, whether of the nobles or of the people, to exercise those three

powers, that of enacting laws, that of executing the public resolutions, and
of trying the causes of individuals.

   Most kingdoms in Europe enjoy a moderate government because the
prince who is invested with the two first powers leaves the third to his
subjects.[8]

Needless to say, in his view most other societies lacked such a balance of
governmental powers.

Europe was no greater than China (Voltaire)

Later Enlightenment thinkers developed a more relativistically global historical
conception. Voltaire (1694–1778) argued in favor of large-scale, philosophically
informed history. The details did not matter so much as the "big picture,"
which involved detaching "universal history" from the story of the Israelites
and Divine Providence and including the great Asian cultures. It also meant
recognizing a progressive development of the human mind from barbarism to
enlightenment.[9] He and many of his contemporaries – including Benjamin
Franklin and others in the American colonies – were great admirers of China –
especially Confucian rationalism, its apparently well-ordered government, and
the meritocratic civil-service examination, to say nothing of its immense population and extraordinary wealth.[10]

Foreign trade holds the key to success (Adam Smith)

Adam Smith (1723–1790), the famous political economist and author of *The
Wealth of Nations* (1776), similarly praised China's vast and prosperous
domestic market, state-subsidized infrastructure, and highly efficient agriculture. In his words, "China has been long one of the richest, that is, one of
the most fertile, best cultivated, most industrious, and most populous, countries
in the world." Yet Smith did not stop at praise. He also discerned a country
apparently no longer progressing. In his words:

   Marco Polo, who visited it more than five hundred years ago, describes its
   cultivation, industry, and populousness, almost in the same terms in which
   they are described by travellers in the present times ... . The poverty of the
   lower ranks of people in China far surpasses that of the most beggarly
   nations in Europe.[11]

What was wrong with China, in his interpretation, was what was right with
Europe – the one neglected or restricted foreign commerce, while the other
pursued it wholeheartedly. China was rich because of its productive agriculture
and vast domestic market, but Europe's economy was growing faster thanks to
continuous exchanges of goods and ideas not only within its own continental
market but also with peoples across the globe.

Political fragmentation fosters innovation (David Hume and Immanuel Kant)

During the same era, Smith's friend David Hume (1711–1776) and the German idealistic philosopher Immanuel Kant (1724–1804) propounded another idea to account for the vibrancy and economic development of their continent – the very political fragmentation in Europe as fostering novelty and innovation thanks to ceaseless competition and the absence of a single, central authority capable of inhibiting innovation and restraining competition.[12]

A "World Spirit" was guiding Europe's ascent (Hegel)

Another influential German idealistic philosopher, Georg Wilhelm Friedrich Hegel (1770–1831), put forward a complex theory that combined Voltaire's secular vision with the earlier providential outlook and purported to unify the totality of natural and human phenomena. According to Hegel, a "World Spirit" had over the centuries achieved greater and greater rationality and freedom through the intermediary of human civilization and consciousness in a progressive evolution culminating in the Europe of his day. Hegel argued further that tradition, despotic systems of government, and geography kept China and other Asian countries from participating in the development of the World Spirit.[13]

Efficient exploitation is the main cause (Karl Marx)

Karl Marx (1818–1883) famously removed the spiritual element from this idea and conceived of human progress as propelled by purely materialistic forces – in particular by class struggle – but still moving inexorably toward a higher goal. He also believed that political fragmentation within Europe and vibrant international trade relations abroad made it possible for the more productive commercial interests gradually to overshadow the hitherto dominant feudal elites. Furthermore, he noted that the rise of capitalism – and therefore of Europe – occurred in progressive stages, where one country after another climbed to ever higher levels of economic success thanks to increasingly sophisticated capitalist infrastructure and practices. He elaborated:

> The different moments of primitive [capital] accumulation can be assigned in particular to Spain, Portugal, Holland, France, and England, in more or less chronological order. These different moments are systematically combined together at the end of the seventeenth century in England; the combination embraces colonies, the national debt, the modern tax system, and the system of protection. These methods depend in part on brute force, for instance the colonial system. But they all employ the power of the state, the concentrated and organized force of society, to hasten, as in a hothouse, the process of transformation of the feudal mode of production into the capitalist mode, and to shorten the transition.[14]

Yet all was not rosy. The original or "primitive" accumulation of capital by which the world came to be divided between rich and poor resulted largely from "conquest, enslavement, robbery, murder, in short, force."[15] The birth of capitalist production itself, according to Marx, also involved "the extirpation, enslavement, and entombment in mines of the indigenous population" of South America, "the beginnings of the conquest and plunder of India, and the conversion of Africa into a preserve for the commercial hunting of blackskins ... "[16] Even so, capitalism was the most progressive economic system the world had ever known, because it was the most productive.

In fact, it radically changed the rules of the game for every other people on earth. Again in his own words:

> The bourgeoisie, by the rapid improvement of all instruments of production, by the immensely facilitated means of communication, draws all, even the most barbarian, nations into civilization. The cheap prices of commodities are the heavy artillery with which it batters down all Chinese walls, with which it forces the barbarians' intensely obstinate hatred of foreigners to capitulate. It compels all nations, on pain of extinction, to adopt the bourgeois mode of production; it compels them to introduce what it calls civilization into their midst, i.e., to become bourgeois themselves. In one word, it creates a world after its own image.
>
> The bourgeoisie has subjected the country to the rule of the town. It has created enormous cities, has greatly increased the urban population as compared with the rural, and has thus rescued a considerable part of the population from the idiocy of rural life. Just as it has made the country dependent on the towns, so it has made barbarian and semi-barbarian countries dependent on the civilized ones, nations of peasants on nations of bourgeois, the East on the West.[17]

In other terms, European capitalists were in the process of completely remaking global economic relations and indeed were actually bringing to life the modern world.

Systematic rationalism set Europe apart (Max Weber)

Marx's younger compatriot, Max Weber (1864–1920), himself also an important contributor to the development of modern social science, approached the emergence of capitalist modernity in Europe quite differently. Capitalism, he argues, was only one facet of Europe's overall transformation of the world, in science, scholarship, the arts, law, theology, and government – thanks to a systematically rationalizing ethos. Other great cultures – and in particular ancient Babylonia, Egypt, India, and China – advanced knowledge and practice in every sphere of human endeavor. Yet only the West applied mathematics to science, developed rational proofs, devised the experimental method, outfitted the modern research laboratory, and built up entire systems of institutions of higher learning. As Weber develops his idea: "A rational, systematic, and specialized pursuit of science, with trained and specialized personnel, has only existed in the West in a sense at all approaching its present dominant place in our culture."[18] This rationalizing mindset was gradually applied to every aspect of life in the West beginning as early as the Middle Ages.

Instead of assuming that this revolutionary attitude emerged according to necessary principles from the materialistic interactions of classes and modes of production, as Marx claimed, Weber sought its origins in the beliefs, values, and behaviors of cultural, religious, political, and business leaders in specific European countries. In particular, he argued, a radical change in religious outlook – from Catholicism to Protestantism – created a necessary condition in Northwestern European countries for the emergence of an economic and political system whose enormous efficiencies were stimulated by the tendency to prefer rational and effective policies over traditional and time-honored ones. Or as the title of his most famous work implied, "the spirit of Capitalism" emerged from a mentality that he called the "Protestant ethic."

Among the more consequential ideas of this ethic were that every job is a divinely sanctioned "calling" to which one should devote oneself tirelessly, that each person should embrace a continuously active life in order to avoid sin, that worldly success is a sign of God's favor, and that usefulness to the community is more important than personal enjoyment or leisure. Taken together, these values "gave every-day worldly activity a religious significance." As Weber elaborated,

> The only way of living acceptably to God was not to surpass worldly morality in monastic asceticism, but solely through the fulfillment of the obligations imposed upon the individual by his position in the world. That was his calling … . It and it alone is the will of God, and hence every legitimate calling has exactly the same worth in the sight of God.[19]

This outlook resulted in the encouragement of constant striving at worldly pursuits and the achievement of enormous material success.

Weber focused in particular on the "spirit of capitalism," which involved the accumulation of wealth for its own sake and not only or even principally as a means to acquire specific material goods. Weber describes this attitude in the following way:

> Man is dominated by the making of money, by acquisition as the ultimate purpose of his life. Economic acquisition is no longer subordinated to man as the means for the satisfaction of his material needs.[20]

Rather, it becomes a sign of one's righteousness, one's devotion to duty, one's selfless pursuit of one's calling. And if one single-mindedly applied one's talents to business – or any other profession – then inevitably one would become more and more efficient, effective, and ultimately successful.

Weber was far from attributing the rise of the West solely to the Puritans' moral energy and passion. He also emphasized a constellation of historical features he considered unique to Europe. Having conducted an extensive and systematic study of the world's other major civilizations, he considered especially important the separation of economic life from kinship and household relations, politically autonomous cities dominated by commercial interests, the heritage of highly rationalistic Roman law, the modern nation-state constitutionally founded on the rule of law and administered by professional bureaucrats, double-entry bookkeeping as a hyper-rational means of organizing commercial finances, and an enormous labor market in which workers must sell their labor in order to make a living. Combined with the "Protestant ethic," these factors brought the West to materialistic preeminence in the modern world.

The decline of the West (Wells, Spengler, and Toynbee)

A revulsion against materialism, Western dominance, and/or the modern world led three gifted writers to author powerful conceptualizations of world history, which veered away from Eurocentrism. H. G. Wells (1866–1946), who along with Jules Verne invented science fiction writing, feared the degeneration of mankind and the destruction of the world in modern times unless we humans should master our egotistical impulses and work collectively within a world state toward the common good. In order to nudge his contemporaries in that direction, Wells, more an amateur than a professional historian, penned *The Outlines of History* (1920), the most popular historical work of the first half of the twentieth century – it sold more than two million copies. Wells conceived of world history as involving greater and greater interconnection among peoples all learning from one another. By contrast, the gloomy German philosopher Oswald Spengler (1880–1936) described the organic emergence and inevitable downfall of a cyclical succession of civilizations – all morally equivalent – from ancient Babylonia to modern Europe in *The Decline of the West* (1918–1923). In his pessimistic vision, there was no hope at all for humankind. Arnold Toynbee's *A Study of History* (1935–1961) followed Spengler in viewing historical development as dominated by a succession of civilizations, though it explained their rise as the product of innovative responses to environmental challenges. Civilizations, he claimed, decline only when they fail to meet the challenges facing them. The West had begun its decline in the sixteenth century, yet salvation remained possible if humankind could just come together and build a world state.[21]

It is interesting that all three writers had authoritarian – if not totalitarian – impulses. George Orwell wrote in 1941 that "much of what Wells has imagined and worked for is physically there in Nazi Germany."[22] Although Spengler rejected the Nazis' racist outlook and political populism, he supported a large portion of their platform and voted for Hitler in April and July 1932 – a führer was needed, he believed. The Nazis courted him assiduously, offering him a professorial chair at the University of Leipzig, though he declined the honor and soon broke with the party.[23] Even Toynbee, who did not relish the idea of a dictatorship, believed that his long-awaited world state would be "imposed upon the majority by a ruthless, efficient, and fanatical minority inspired by some ideology or religion."[24] Such a turn of events might be necessary for the survival of the human race, he thought. One might characterize these views as representative of a pessimistic (or realistic, depending on one's perspective) "European tradition." In general, the adherents of this tradition never made peace with modern life. Spengler feared that even a victorious Germany, which he deeply yearned for during World War II, would degenerate into a "soulless Americanism."[25] Similarly, Toynbee seems not to have valued the modern West's contributions to worldwide improvements in material well-being, technological progress, and human rights.[26]

American optimism and the Western Civ course

If the unimaginable death and destruction of the world wars drove Wells, Spengler, and Toynbee to despair, they inspired scholars across the Atlantic to develop a completely different historical interpretation in order to preserve their optimism (or naiveté). The Europeans might destroy their own countries or bow down before fanatical dictators, yet did not the ideals that had given birth to the American nation live on? At Columbia University in 1919, there emerged an interpretation of the gradual unfolding – from ancient Greece to the present day – of a civilization devoted to liberty, the rule of law, rationality, and the sanctity of the individual. The authors of this interpretation believed that Western civilization had continued its steady progress; only now the United States was in the vanguard. For decades, millions of American students took the obligatory "Western Civ" course, though it never caught on in other countries.[27]

What your Western Civ or World History instructor is not telling you

The many thousands in any given year who continue to take the course, as well as those in world history courses, might wonder how and why Western civilization ascended to preeminence in the modern world, but their aesthetically pleasing and highly informative textbooks rarely answer those questions. Their professors and the authors of their textbooks know perfectly well that dozens of scholars have spilled great tides of ink propounding diverse explanations for the West's ascendancy. In fact, they usually subscribe to one or a combination of these interpretations. But they typically keep that knowledge to themselves.

It is, therefore, difficult for students in such courses to understand clearly how Europe made the transition from merely one of many developing regions into the world's first industrial power. That most undergraduates take only the first or the second half of the Western civilization or world history sequences – and thus miss out on either the beginning or the end of the story – merely compounds this problem. It seems likely that many students come away assuming that Europe had always been the world's greatest power or in any event that there is nothing requiring explanation in the modern West's global dominance.

Overview of the chapters

Chapter 1, "The Miracle of the West," presents interpretations by scholars within the idealistic "American" tradition. Most of these authors use the analytical approach first developed by Max Weber, though the influence of Voltaire and Hegel can be discerned among them as well. They claim that unique aspects of European culture, in particular Christianity, institutions making possible the efficient use of human and natural resources, unprecedented advances in technology, and the gradual accumulation of systematized knowledge, can best explain the West's ascendancy. In general, these scholars place an accent on factors "internal" to Europe and the wider West. That is to say, they argue that the West rose largely thanks to its own unique set of qualities and capacities.

Chapters 2 through 4 bring together scholars who emphasize above all "external" factors. For them, the West rose largely because of geographical accidents, blind luck, historical conjunctures, and learning from other cultures. The historians described in Chapter 2, "World History," remain mostly within the American tradition, yet they write typically under the influence of European universalist thinkers like Toynbee. They emphasize the impact of geography and interconnections among peoples on human development in general and European evolution in particular. The scholars whose arguments are summarized in Chapter 3, "Imperialism and Exploitation," work within the European tradition and follow the critical analysis developed first by Marx. Their interpretations center on how such evils as the slave trade and capitalist exploitation contributed to the rise of the West. Chapter 4 showcases scholars who returned to "The Greatness of Asia" approach of such enlightenment thinkers as Voltaire. Many also trace their intellectual lineage back to Marx. Their main arguments revolve around the ideas that only imitating the far more developed Asian cultures and exploiting non-European peoples enabled Europe to attain preeminence – and only very late in its history.

Finally, Chapter 5, "Why Not China?" addresses what one might consider the dialectical counterpart to the central focus of this book. If for many centuries China was the world's preeminent power, which over the course of its history contributed powerful technologies to world civilization, why did it not continue its trajectory of greatness and bring about the Scientific Revolution and the birth of industrial capitalism? This chapter summarizes interpretations by both generalists and specialists – from many points of view – who shed further light on why the culture seemingly least likely to come to dominate the globe – the West – achieved that feat after all.

What I left out

Since the scholarly literature on these topics is relatively large, I naturally could not survey every available book, much less all existing articles. Those summarized within these pages seemed to me the most significant – the most convincing, renowned, authoritative, or lively. The many other titles relegated to the Further Reading sections at the end of each chapter are often just as valuable for gaining an understanding of one or another aspect of this book's main question, yet limited space made it impossible to include them. Why and how the West rose remain intensively researched – and contested – questions, as ongoing scholarly output attests. So long as historians and social scientists keep debating them, their work will continue to influence the ways in which Western Civ and world history courses are taught, and students will continue to deserve to know their intellectual background.

Further reading

Gress, David. *From Plato to NATO: The Idea of the West and its Opponents.* New York: Free Press, 1998.

Guizot, François Pierre Guillaume. *General History of Civilization in Europe.* Edited by George Wells Knight. New York; London: D. Appleton and Company, 1928.

Pirenne, Henri. *Mohammed and Charlemagne* [1937]. Translated by Bernard Miall from the French of the 10th ed. New York: Barnes & Noble, 1955.

Spengler, Oswald. *The Decline of the West.* 2 vols. Translated with notes by Charles Francis Atkinson. New York: A. A. Knopf, 1926–1928.

Toynbee, Arnold J. *A Study of History.* 2nd ed. 12 vols. London: Oxford University Press, 1935–1961.

Notes

1 The earliest version of this book included large block quotes from each author; unfortunately, most publishers would not grant permission to include more than a fraction of them.

2 Paul Costello, *World Historians and Their Goals: Twentieth-Century Answers to Modernism* (DeKalb, Ill.: Northern Illinois University Press, 1993), 11–12.

3 Patrick Manning, *Navigating World History: Historians Create a Global Past* (New York: Palgrave Macmillan, 2003), 18–19.

4 M. de Sécondat, baron de Montesquieu, *The Spirit of Laws*, with D'Alembert's analysis of the work. New edition, Revised by J. V. Prichard. Translated from the French by Thomas Nugent, 2 vols. [1752] (London: G. Bell, 1914), 1: 239, 241.

5 Montesquieu, *The Spirit of Laws*, 1: 286–287.

6 Ibid., 1: 290.

7 Ibid., 2: 44.

8 Ibid., 1: 163.

9 Manning, *Navigating World History*, 22.

10 William W. Lockwood, "Adam Smith and Asia." *The Journal of Asian Studies* 23 (May, 1964): 347–348.

11 Adam Smith, *An Inquiry into the Nature and Causes of the Wealth of Nations*, ed. C. J. Bullock, The Harvard Classics (New York: P. F. Collier and Son, 1909), 75–76.

12 Mokyr, Joel. "Mobility, Creativity, and Technological Development: David Hume, Immanuel Kant and the Economic Development of Europe." In Günter Abel, ed., *Kreativität. Tagungsband: XX. Deutscher Kongreß für Philosophie* (Hamburg: Felix Meiner Verlag, 2006), 1129–1160.

13 See Jonathan D. Spence, *The Search for Modern China*, 2nd ed. (New York; London: W. W. Norton, 1999), 135–36.

14 Karl Marx, *Capital: A Critique of Political Economy*, vol. 1 [1869], intro. Ernest Mandel, trans. Ben Fowkes (London: Penguin Books, 1976), 915–916.

15 Ibid., 874.

16 Ibid., 915.

17 Karl Marx and Friedrich Engels, *Manifesto of the Communist Party* [1848], in *The Marx-Engels Reader*, ed. Robert C. Tucker, 2nd ed. (New York: W. W. Norton, 1978), 477.

18 Max Weber, *The Protestant Ethic and the Spirit of Capitalism*, trans. Talcott Parsons, intro. Anthony Giddens (New York: Charles Scribner's Sons, 1958), 15–16.

19 Ibid., 80–81.

20 Ibid., 53.

21 Costello, *World Historians and Their Goals*, Chaps. 2–4.

22 Cited in ibid., 43.

23 Ibid., 62–64.

24 Cited in ibid., 91.

25 Cited in ibid., 53.

26 Ibid., 92, 94.

27 See Gilbert Allardyce, "The Rise and Fall of the Western Civilization Course," *The American Historical Review* 87 (Jun., 1982): 695–725.

1   The miracle of the West

Scholars discussed in this chapter believe the West rose mostly because of inherent qualities of its culture. In general, those who emphasize internal factors – as opposed to external ones, like climate, geography, or interactions with other peoples – tend to emphasize cultural values and beliefs, in particular those stemming from the Christian religion, which for centuries formed the core of Europe's value system. Even historians who give the most explanatory weight to institutions or technology in answering the "how" question, typically resort to cultural underpinnings when trying to address the "why" question.

Christian Europe: uniquely dynamic (Christopher Dawson)

In a series of writings beginning in 1922 and culminating with his *Religion and the Rise of Western Culture* (1950), Christopher Dawson traced the rise of the West to medieval Europe when, in his interpretation, the "barbarian" cult of heroism and ideal of aggression fused with the Christian cult of saintliness and ideal of self-renunciation. The elements of this dualism struggled for mastery not merely within society but within people's heart and conscience, creating conditions of extraordinary dynamism, constant soul-searching and self-criticism, and ultimately world-changing innovation. The West rose, according to Dawson, for distinctive cultural reasons.

Christopher Dawson (1889–1970) spent his early years in Hay Castle, Wales, his mother's ancestral home, an ancient ruin dating to the twelfth century. He later recalled: "What I felt most at Hay was the feeling of an antiquity – the immense age of everything, and in the house, the continuity of the present with the remote past."[1] When he was seven, his family moved to his father's estate in Yorkshire. The family prayed together every morning, and both father and mother taught the precocious child a variety of subjects, both spiritual and secular. After a miserable experience at two private schools on account of poor health and athletic inability, Dawson had more success with a private tutor before entering Oxford University in 1908. He fell head over heels in love with a Catholic girl in 1909, converted to Catholicism in 1914, and married her two years later. After brief stints in the law before, and in military intelligence, during World War I, he settled into a life of independent research, freelance writing, and occasional university teaching.[2]

Extremely learned in both the classics and religious subjects but also in sociology, history, and economics, Dawson early on vowed to devote his life to understanding and explaining how cultures flourish and deteriorate. Using an interdisciplinary and cross-cultural approach, he found in each society's religious life the key to understanding its successes and failings, its rising and declining. As he wrote in 1950, "the great world religions are, as it were, great rivers of sacred tradition which flow down through the ages and through changing historical landscapes which they irrigate and fertilize."[3]

He conceived of human history as unfolding in stages across Eurasia over several thousand years beginning with the emergence from 4500 to 2700 BC of isolated river-valley civilizations – in Egypt, Mesopotamia, northern India, and northern China. These societies came to be dominated by priestly castes, centralized economies, and theocratic god-kings. In the next age, from 2700 to 1100 BC, intercultural diffusion and mutual influencing flourished across Afro-Eurasia, as dozens of new societies emerged along the margins of the core areas of civilization. The great classical cultures and most of the world religions appeared next – the third age – from the Athenian city-states and the Roman Empire in the west to the Gupta Empire and Imperial China in the east. In the fourth age, according to Dawson, great cultures flourished across Eurasia – medieval Christendom, Byzantium, the Islamic civilization, and Tang and Song China. Devastating invasions in the 1200s–1400s, however, stunted the development of China, Persia, India, and the Near East, leaving only Western Europe unscathed.[4]

What distinguished Europe from other major cultures, according to Dawson, and made it capable of uninterrupted innovation and development for nearly ten centuries, was an inherent dynamism and tendency to almost continual reform. The essential ingredient in Europe's dynamic culture was an unremittingly missionary form of Christianity. This missionary movement originated in the first century after Christ in Hellenistic cities of the Near East and continued for hundreds of years as apostles and preachers spread the faith further and deeper into Western Europe. After the fall of Rome, scores of charismatic spiritual leaders – like St. Patrick in Ireland and Gregory the Great in England – laid the foundations of medieval European culture. As the intellectual life of the continent fell into decline in the sixth century, the movement reversed itself, with scholars and missionaries from Ireland and England reinvigorating cultural life among the Germanic and Frankish peoples. For the first time in the evolution of human culture, according to Dawson, there emerged in Europe a distinctive form of societal dualism in which political and cultural elites wielded power and influence in separate but complementary and relatively balanced spheres. In all the other great cultures, including Byzantium, one leader and one set of elites dominated both politics and culture. Europe's organic "separation of powers" made it possible for innovators in many walks of life – first in the spiritual realm but gradually also in commerce, urban development, and intellectual pursuits – to transform and to create European traditions and institutions through "a spontaneous process of free communication."[5] Dawson goes on:

> It is only in Western Europe that the whole pattern of the culture is to be found in a continuous succession and alternation of free spiritual movements; so that every century of Western history shows a change in the balance of cultural elements, and the appearance of some new spiritual force which creates new ideas and institutions and produces a further movement of social change.[6]

Europe's tendency to innovation and reform was fostered not only by ruling elites and institutions in competition but also by competing ideals and outlooks – the "cult of heroism and of aggression" of the mostly Frankish tribes that dominated Western Europe after the fall of Rome and the sophisticated theological culture and the ideals of nonviolence, asceticism, and self-denial of the Christian Church and successive generations of religious reformers. Yet these apparently incompatible visions gradually fused into a single, transformative cultural mix (see Map 1.1 and Map 1.2). For example, the Anglo-Saxon warrior-king, Alfred the Great (849–899), translated into Old English the hugely influential late-Roman *Consolatio Philosophiae* by the Christian thinker and saint, Boethius (ca. 480–ca. 524).

It was precisely the high culture and Christianity infused from the Mediterranean and Near Eastern lands by spiritual leaders like Sts. Paul and Augustine and Boethius and Pope Gregory the Great (r. 590–604) that created from the largely undeveloped European interior a unified and vibrant Christendom. This new culture combined the refinement and discipline of the classical world with the raw energy of the "barbarian" cultures but also a radically different view of values and authority. According to Dawson, "a new principle had been introduced to the static civilization of the Roman world that contained infinite possibilities of change."[7] He quotes the popular reaction to St. Paul's preaching at Thessaloniki. He and other Christians "have turned the world upside down … and [they] are all acting contrary to the decrees of Caesar, saying there is another king – Jesus" (Acts, 17:6–7). Never before in history had a rapidly spreading faith justified placing one's primary allegiance in a transcendent deity and relegating earthly authorities to a secondary status. Within a few centuries, moreover, the Roman Church had replaced the Roman Empire as both spiritual and at times even temporal leader of Western Europe.

Yet the key element in the Christian faith that conquered pagan Europe was not the subtle theology of the Church Fathers but the reputedly awe-inspiring supernatural powers of saints and martyrs. For centuries after the fall of Rome, much of Western Europe fell into deep material poverty, extreme lawlessness, fierce exploitation, and barbaric warlordism. The Church offered not "civilization" but a promise of divine judgment and salvation from the horrific depths of earthly depravity into which the world had sunk. The heart and soul of the

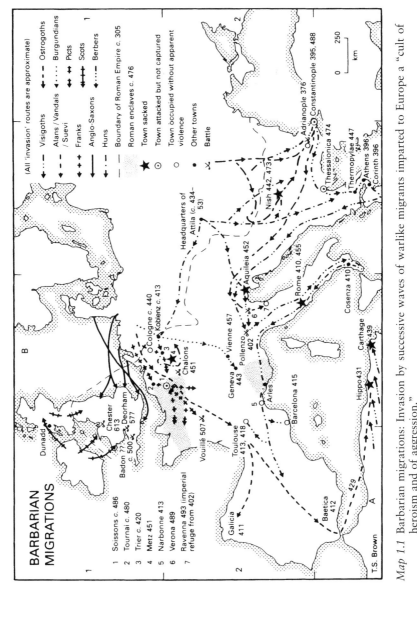

BARBARIAN MIGRATIONS

1
1 Soissons c. 486
2 Tournai c. 480
3 Trier c. 420
4 Metz 451
5 Narbonne 413
6 Verona 489
7 Ravenna 493 (imperial refuge from 402)

(All 'invasion' routes are approximate)

Visigoths ········· Ostrogoths
Alans / Vandals / Suevi ·-·-·-· Burgundians
Franks ┼┼┼ Picts
Anglo-Saxons ━━━ Scots
Huns ·-·-·- Berbers

Boundary of Roman Empire c. 305

Roman enclaves c. 476

★ Town sacked

⊙ Town attacked but not captured

○ Town occupied without apparent violence

● Other towns

✕ Battle

0   250
km

Dunadd
Chester 613
Badon ?? c. 500
Deorham 577
Vouillé 507
Toulouse 413, 418
Galicia 411
Baetica 412
429
Barcelona 415
Hippo 431
Carthage 439
Arles
Geneva 443
Vienne 457
Pollenzo 402
Aquileia 452
Rome 410, 455
Cosenza 410
Cologne c. 440
Koblenz c. 413
Chalons 451
Headquarters of Attila (c. 434–53)
Nish 442, 473
Adrianople 376
Thessalonica 474
Constantinople 395, 488
Thermopylae 447
Athens 396
Corinth 396

B
A
2
2

T.S. Brown

Map 1.1 Barbarian migrations: Invasion by successive waves of warlike migrants imparted to Europe a "cult of heroism and of aggression."

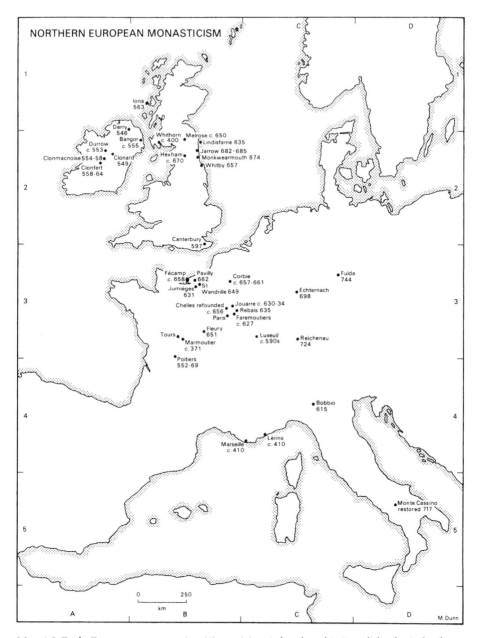

NORTHERN EUROPEAN MONASTICISM

Iona
563

Derry
546
Bangor
c. 555
Durrow
c. 553
Clonmacnoise 554-58
Clonard
549
Clonfert
558-64

Whithorn
c. 400
Hexham
c. 670

Melrose c. 650
Lindisfarne 635
Jarrow 682-685
Monkwearmouth 674
Whitby 657

Canterbury
597

Fécamp   Pavilly
c. 658   662
          St
Jumièges Wandrille 649
631

Corbie
c. 657-661

Fulda
744

Echternach
698

Chelles refounded
c. 656
Paris
Jouarre c. 630-34
Rebais 635
Faremoutiers
c. 627

Tours
Marmoutier
c. 371
Fleury
651
Luxeuil
c. 590s
Reichenau
724

Poitiers
552-69

Bobbio
615

Marseille
c. 410
Lérins
c. 410

Monte Cassino
restored 717

0   250
km

A   B   C   D

M.Dunn

Map 1.2 Early European monasteries: Monasticism infused sophisticated theological culture and ideals of nonviolence, asceticism, and self-denial throughout Europe.

Christian cultural and intellectual life in those centuries was the celebration at mass of the redemption of mankind by the Incarnation of the Divine Word. The mass told a sacred history of human creation and salvation, of the divine purpose on earth and in eternity. In the dramatically rich and beautiful liturgy – full of music and poetry – the people found meaning to life in ways far surpassing the nature myths of the Eleusinian and other ancient mysteries.[8] In such a dark age, one can imagine the fervor with which both rich and poor sought solace within the only stable and continent-wide institution of Western Europe – the Church.

A web of monasteries and monastic orders – often under the nominal authority of the papacy but de facto independent of local prelates – preserved classical culture and spread the Christian faith across Europe. Western monasticism, while deeply influenced by Eastern practices emphasizing asceticism and withdrawal from society, was far more oriented toward building community and developing social order in an environment woefully lacking them. Monastic communities became microcosms of social and economic life where the brothers and sisters followed strictly articulated rules, sharing everything in common, diligently providing for their own upkeep regardless of social status and origin, ministering to the neighboring populations, but above all devoting themselves to the life of the spirit, praying up to eight hours a day for the salvation of the world.

Europe's elites – even many men and women of royal blood – eagerly joined the communities, which to some extent replicated the society of warriors from which they came. One swore absolute obedience to an abbot just as to a chieftain and pledged self-sacrifice and devotion to sanctity instead of to honor and bravery. Both lifestyles aimed at extreme heroism – the willingness to forfeit one's life for a cause. In practice the monastic life involved many arts and sciences necessary to high culture, like reading, writing, calligraphy, music, and – especially important – a proper understanding of the flow of time in order to faithfully observe the complex daily, weekly, and yearly religious offices. Monastic houses in the most far-flung places became centers of learning, teaching, social cohesion, and economic development. Hundreds of able disciples of charismatic abbots gradually established similar institutions in distant lands, implanting the seeds of a new, dynamic culture all across Western Europe. Many of the great monasteries actually served as urban centers north of the Alps until cities began to multiply and grow in the eleventh and twelfth centuries. Basically, European culture was born within monastic walls thanks to what today might be called grassroots activism, albeit often conducted by men and women of the most elevated birth.

The brief Carolingian Renaissance[9] – in learning, music, liturgy, and above all the preservation of classical and Christian texts – developed almost entirely from monastic culture. The very theocratic tradition of the king as representative of God on earth and Christian legislator to the people was formulated and propagated by monastic thinkers surrounding Charlemagne (r. 768–814). When waves of invaders overran the continent in the mid-800s, plunging Western

Europe into brutal lawlessness and leaving even most monasteries either destroyed or exploited and dominated by secular powers, a few monasteries again preserved the foundations of the emerging culture and undertook a wide-reaching spiritual transformation.

Influential new monastic houses established by powerful aristocrats, in particular Cluny Abbey in Burgundy (founded in 910), emphasized selfless devotion to prayer and social consciousness and preached boldly against the oppression of the poor and the corruption and worldliness of the clergy. Many, many other houses and charismatic abbots across Europe – often in frequent contact with each other – followed suit. In the words of Dawson, these monastic centers "were arising like islands of peace and spiritual order in the sea of feudal anarchy."[10] For many lawless nobles, the rebuke of a renowned abbot was more terrible than the threat of the fiercest Emperor; even in death these saints possessed an awesome power for the medieval mind.

From within Europe's leading monasteries emerged in the eleventh century a movement for wholesale Church reform. Monks like Humbert de Moyenmoutier, St. Peter Damian, and Hildebrand of Sovana (Pope St. Gregory VII) demanded the spiritual purity of all men of the cloth, complete ecclesiastical independence from secular meddling, and the spiritual subordination of all secular powers to Church authority. Although many European rulers willingly affirmed themselves "vassals of St. Peter," the more powerful monarchs balked, especially the Holy Roman Emperor, sparking a decades-long bloody conflict. From this struggle there developed, however, key elements of Western political culture: the right of conscientious objection to political authority, a theory of social contract as against the principle of the divine right of kings, and a conception of the fundamental spiritual unity of Western Europe. Moreover, the reformed papacy emerged as the sole heir of Roman universalism.

The most destructive marauders – the Vikings – gradually converted to Christianity in the lands they conquered – England, Ireland, Normandy – and then returned home and implanted the new faith in Scandinavia where it put down deep roots and inspired flourishing cultures in the eleventh and twelfth centuries. Heroic Christian rulers like St. Olaf (r. 1015–1028) unified the old tribal kingdoms and built up national monarchies legitimated by an ideal of universal religion. Missionaries from England in particular spread Christian culture and built monastic communities. Missionaries, conquerors, and crusaders also spread Western Christianity throughout Eastern Europe, the whole of which, including Russia, remained in continual political and cultural intercourse with the West until the Mongol conquest of the thirteenth century.

European feudal warriors remained violent and ruthless, but the teachings of religious leaders and representations in heroic poetry gave them ideals to aspire to of holy martyrs for the faith and defenders of the Church and of widows and orphans. Efforts by reforming churchmen like Fulbert of Chartres (ca. 960–1028) – and secular rulers under their influence – to establish leagues of peace dedicated to protect noncombatants may have moved relatively few warriors to lay down their arms. When the ideals of the peace movement were associated with campaigns to eject Muslim conquerors from formerly Christian lands, however, hundreds of thousands of noble warriors and ordinary people fervently heeded the call. Reinforced through a dozen Crusades and many unnumbered military campaigns to expand Christendom, the dualistic ethos of religious knights and militant priests, of "leaders of the monastic reform and robber barons"[11] – often members of the same family – pervaded medieval European culture.

A further tension entered feudal society when troubadours and courtiers returned from the brilliant courts of Muslim Spain with the ideals of chivalry and courtly love. Their emphasis on the enjoyment of life, refined courtship, lyric poetry, elaborate codes of etiquette, and sophisticated entertainment contrasted strongly with the coarse manners and earnest commitment to lofty values of the age's warriors and ascetics. Thus the bitterest enemies of Christendom – the Muslim infidels – worked a powerful influence throughout Europe's aristocratic and regal courts, just as in the same centuries Islamic thought and science became the gold standard for thousands of European scholars.

Another important institution of the Middle Ages, the self-governing town, often emerged under religious auspices and protection. Medieval towns usually developed from voluntary associations of largely egalitarian members – "sworn brethren," frequently under the patronage of a saint – who not only shared in governance and mutual defense but felt a civic pride unknown since the classical era of Greece and Rome. First in northern Italy in the eleventh century, then spreading gradually northward for two hundred years, Europe's towns and cities experienced an economic boom, which linked them by international trade routes to the great commercial centers throughout Afro-Eurasia. Immense prosperity funded the construction of soaring Gothic cathedrals, vast guildhalls, and splendid palaces, along with magnificent patronage of the arts. Above all, every town dweller, as the member of a guild, participated in an integrated life of both secular and religious customs and pageants, a sort of perfect Platonic Republic, at least that is how Erasmus (1466–1536) described Strasbourg in the early 1500s.[12]

This organic conception of medieval society found further expression in other important institutions. The mendicant religious orders – in particular the Dominicans and Franciscans – were founded in the early 1200s to minister to the rapidly multiplying urban-dwellers. Organizations of estates (tillers, prayers, warriors) developed in the same era to represent national and regional populations; parliaments of various kinds arose in which the estates gave voice to local interests. Beginning in the 1300s, Church leaders organized general councils that regularly brought together representatives of all Christendom to decide matters of faith – the world's first super-parliaments and continent-wide representative institutions. During the same era, philosophers like Marsilius of Padua (ca. 1275–ca. 1342) began to devise theories of political life in which the whole of society was conceived as the ultimate source of law and authority.

An educational flowering also stimulated contacts and exchanges of ideas and intellectual innovation. Monastic and cathedral schools proliferated in the early Middle Ages, attracting scholars from across Europe. Brilliant masters like Pierre Abelard (1079–1142) in Paris gained cult-like status, and schools formed around them. Competition among rival schools was fierce. Soon, corporations – the Latin word for which was "universitas" – of students arose in Bologna, and of masters in Paris. Bologna was primarily a law school, a secular institution where the well-connected and influential students basically ran the show; in Paris, the masters – all clerics – were supreme, answering only to a chancellor. These institutions, which were soon replicated by a dozen more across Europe, enjoyed extraordinary autonomy and academic freedom, certainly for their time and by world standards (Map 1.3). Their key hallmark was a tenacious dedication to logical study and meticulous disputation of even the most abstruse philosophical and theological topics.

Important new texts and ideas for analysis came from southern Italian and Spanish cities like Salerno and Toledo, which provided a conduit into the Christian West for Greek and Islamic learning during the twelfth century. Scholars flocked from all over Europe to study with Jews, Muslims, and Christians and then eagerly propounded the new learning in every school and court of Christendom. The papacy sought to exert control over the emerging intellectual synthesis by means of learned Friars – all the leading philosophers and theologians of the age were either Dominicans or Franciscans – yet many of them pursued the most radical adventures of ideas in every direction, often incorporating the thought of pagan Greeks and infidel Muslims, usually without any fear of danger to the Christian faith.

Yet just as Europe was becoming extraordinarily dynamic and open to the outside world, having synthesized ideas and technologies and stories and traditions from across Eurasia, the great ancient centers of civilization were falling into decline. "Now," argued Dawson, "for the first time Europe is forced to follow untrodden ways and to find new goals, and at the same time becomes conscious of its own powers, critical of accepted traditions and ready for new ventures."[13] These ventures included world exploration and intensive and systematic studies of man and nature. The "rise of the West" was underway. On how this process unfolded Dawson does not elaborate, yet he laments that the dynamism of Christian Europe ultimately shattered its cultural unity.

Europe "invents invention" (David Landes)

The shattering of Christendom was not a problem for David Landes (b. 1924), a Harvard University professor of economics and a respected authority on the history of technology and the Industrial Revolution, but rather a further sign of Europe's extraordinary dynamism. His *The Wealth and Poverty of Nations: Why Some Are So Rich and Some So Poor*,[14] a title that plays on the name of the most famous work of classical economics, Adam Smith's *The Wealth of Nations* (1776), ranges boldly across world history. With lively writing full

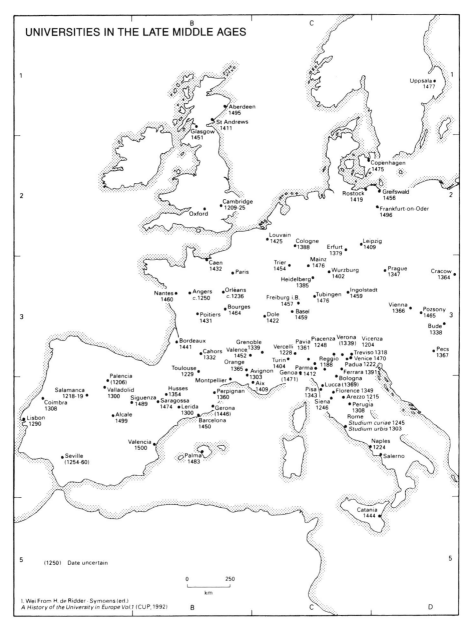

UNIVERSITIES IN THE LATE MIDDLE AGES

B   C

1   Uppsala •
                                                           1477
                    • Aberdeen
                      1495
                   St Andrews
                    1411
                 • Glasgow
                   1451
                                                                    Copenhagen
                                                                    1475
                                                    Rostock • Greifswald
2   1419   1456   2
              • Cambridge   • Frankfurt-on-Oder
                1209-25   1496
            Oxford
                        Louvain
                        1425   Cologne   Leipzig
                                1388   1409
                                      Erfurt
                       Trier   Mainz 1379
              Caen   1454   • 1476
              1432 • Paris   Wurzburg   • Prague   Cracow
                                     1402   1347   1364
                                Heidelberg •
                  Angers Orléans 1385
          Nantes • c.1250 c.1236   Ingolstadt
          1460   Freiburg i.B. Tubingen 1459
                          Bourges   1457   1476   Vienna   Pozsony
                     • Poitiers 1464 • Dole • Basel 1366   1465
3   1431   1422   1459   3
                                                             Bude
                     • Bordeaux   Piacenza Verona 1338
                       1441   Grenoble Pavia (1339) Vicenza
                            1339 Vercelli 1361 1248   • Pecs
                      Cahors Valence 1228   Treviso 1318 1367
                      1332 1452   Turin   Reggio • Venice 1470
                            Orange 1404 Parma 1188 Padua 1222
                  Toulouse 1365 • Avignon Genoa 1412
                  1229   1303 (1471) Bologna
           Palencia   Montpellier Aix   Lucca (1369)
           (1206)   • 1409 Pisa Florence 1349
      Valladolid   Husses Perpignan 1343 • Arezzo 1215
      1300   1354   1360   Siena Perugia
Salamanca Siguenza Saragossa   1246   1308
1218-19   1474 • Lerida Gerona   Rome
Coimbra   1300   (1446)   Studium curiae 1245
1308   Alcale   Barcelona   Studium urbis 1303
Lisbon   1499   1450
1290
           Valencia   Naples
           1500   1224
      • Seville   Palma   • Salerno
        (1254-60)   1483

                                         Catania
                                         1444

5   (1250) Date uncertain   5

             0   250
                  km

I. Wei From H. de Ridder - Symoens (ed.)
A History of the University in Europe Vol.1 (CUP, 1992)
             B   C   D

Map 1.3 Universities in the late Middle Ages: Medieval universities enjoyed extraordinary autonomy and academic freedom by world standards.

of wit and spicy anecdotes and impressively wide learning, Landes investigates the technological and economic development of many of earth's major countries. He notes that one thousand years ago no one could have predicted that Europe – an underdeveloped land plagued by warlordism – would go on to explore the entire globe and then dominate it. China, India, the Islamic world, and other great cultures had flourished in nearly every sphere of endeavor but went into decline when vested interests began actively and successfully to stifle innovation. Once the European societies started to rise, by contrast, it seemed that nothing could hold them back.

According to Landes, the foundations of European success were laid in the Middle Ages by ordinary people, especially artisans and merchants. They established new commercial rules, trade associations, financial instruments, business venues, ever-bigger partnerships, and mechanisms for exchange. In the face of such dynamic innovation,

> The rulers, even local seigneurs, scrambled to keep pace, to show themselves hospitable, to make labor available, to attract enterprise and the revenues it generated … . It was the world of Adam Smith, already taking shape five hundred years before his time.[15]

That world involved increasing labor specialization and a continuously growing market. Such conditions promoted innovation. In the half-millennium before Columbus sailed to America, Europeans invented or perfected and put into widespread use several powerful technologies – water wheels, corrective eyeglasses, mechanical clocks, printing, gunpowder. These breakthroughs were cumulative and dramatically increased productivity and even revolutionized European society. Landes points out that while printing emerged in China – until then the world's most inventive society – "it never 'exploded' as in Europe."[16] (Map 1.4) Plus the Islamic world shunned mechanical printing for religious reasons. Only Europeans developed a continuously innovative society.

Why did the pursuit of novelty enjoy such popularity in Europe? Why were even monasteries across Europe leaders in developing and implementing industrial technology from at least the twelfth century? Landes points to a robust set of attitudes, values, and beliefs, many from the Judeo–Christian tradition. More than in other developed societies of the time, Europeans valued manual labor. Landes finds the origins of this attitude in the Old Testament. For example, God told Noah to build an ark; he did not build it for him. Second, according to the Bible, nature is subordinated to man, who has the right and even duty to develop its every potential. In the third place, the Europeans' sense of time was linear – not cyclical – and progressive – conceived of as heading toward a higher goal. Above all, Landes emphasizes the importance of a relatively free market for stimulating Europeans to try new things, to strive to excel, and to seek power, wealth, and success.

Over the next several centuries, these attributes spurred one European country after another to achieve extraordinary feats. Tiny Portugal, a nation of

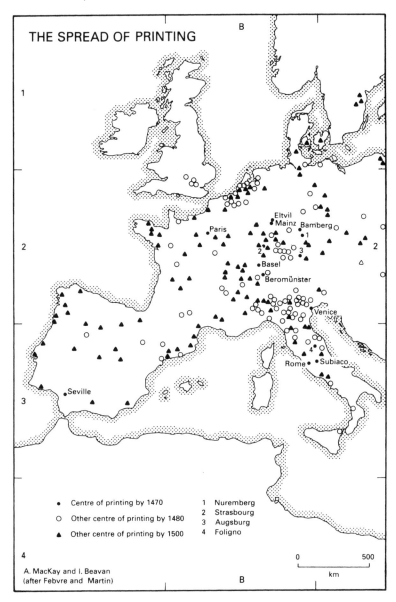

THE SPREAD OF PRINTING

Eltvil
Mainz   Bamberg
Paris
1
2   3
Basel
Beromünster
Venice
4
Rome   Subiac0
Seville

•   Centre of printing by 1470   1   Nuremberg
○   Other centre of printing by 1480   2   Strasbourg
▲   Other centre of printing by 1500   3   Augsburg
                                                    4   Foligno

0   500
km

A. MacKay and I. Beavan
(after Febvre and Martin)

Map 1.4 The spread of printing: By 1500, Europe boasted some thousand
            printing presses, a number that increased dramatically over the
            following centuries.

barely one million people, revolutionized open-sea navigation in the 1400s and
for a century methodically established commercial outposts from Brazil, along
the African coast, across the Indian Ocean, to Japan. In the 1500s, Spain with a
population only 5 percent as big as China's conquered an empire 50 percent

larger in the process toppling two vast and relatively advanced cultures, the Aztec and the Inca. In the 1600s, Holland, only a little bigger than Portugal, forged the world's largest commercial network and dominated international shipping. Over the next hundred years, the English established their supremacy over the oceans. Four centuries, four European countries, four unprecedented achievements. The competitive European state system challenged its members to outdo one another.

Unlike Dawson, who lamented the Reformation's destruction of spiritual unity in Europe, Landes believes that the Protestant values of thrift, diligence, rationality, and orderliness help to explain the extraordinary commercial and scientific advancements in Northern Europe. He also points to the Protestant insistence on the literacy of both men and women, boys and girls, and the fact that Protestants were vastly more time-conscious than Catholics – they made and used clocks more extensively. The Reformation not only promoted literacy, it gave rise to dissent, skepticism, and questioning authority. (The persecution of Jews and Protestants, the Inquisition, book-banning and kindred interferences in Catholic countries impeded scientific and economic progress, he argues.)

In any event, one of history's biggest turning points – the Industrial Revolution – took place in Protestant England. Thanks to the mechanization of production and ceaseless improvements in technology and information, standards of living continuously increased – have continued to increase – for the first time in history, smashing through the "Malthusian trap"[17] and transforming "the balance of political power – within nations, between nations, and between civilizations."[18] Other societies built machines and harnessed fossil fuels and water power, but none as extensively as Europe beginning in the Middle Ages, a trend that increased in intensity century by century. By the late 1700s, many factors came together in England: the ubiquitous use of precision instruments, an abundance of skilled mechanical labor, a high output of coal and iron, the mechanization of dozens of crafts, contagious efforts at innovation, the rapid advancement of scientific and technical knowledge. Per capita British income doubled in one century – something no people had come close to achieving before.

This transformation happened in Europe in general for three main reasons, according to Landes. First, intellectual inquiry grew ever more autonomous, thanks to political and religious fragmentation, expanding personal experiences and observations by world explorers and scholars, and an increasing faith in what we would call progress – Fra Giordano da Pisa marveled in 1306 in a sermon at the ongoing and apparently never-ending increase in human knowledge. Second, new methods of analysis, observation, classification, and definition, often involving quantification – advocated by scholars like Roger Bacon (ca. 1220–1292) – enabled Europeans to advance their understanding of the natural world century by century. The development of the scientific method by Galileo Galilei (1564–1642) and others accelerated this process, as did the invention of scientific instruments like the telescope and microscope (ca. 1600) and the emergence of high-level mathematics – analytic geometry (early 1600s) and calculus (late 1600s). Finally, learned Europeans communicated constantly, cooperated extensively, avidly pursued discoveries, published their results eagerly, and built on each other's advances. The result, according to Landes, was for the first time in world history, "the routinization of discovery."[19]

The Industrial Revolution happened in Britain in particular because it enjoyed several advantages – more highly developed cottage industry, use of fossil fuel, manufacturing technology, agricultural efficiency, and transportation networks than any other country or region of the world. But that was not all. Culture also mattered – and probably accounted for the favorable material circumstances. The people of Britain enjoyed increasing freedom and security from government interference, a rising standard of living and consumer culture going back to the 1400s, an expanding and largely unfettered domestic market, an openness to (often dynamic, moneyed, well-connected, and talented) religious refugees beginning in the sixteenth century, a thriving entrepreneurial spirit, and a widespread and abiding respect for commercial activity.

English individualism and sociability explain Europe's rise (Alan Macfarlane)

Where did these qualities come from? Landes does not really explain, but an eminent English historical and social anthropologist has put forward an explanation in a series of books and articles beginning in 1978.[20] Alan Macfarlane's basic thesis is that

> the majority of people in England from at least the thirteenth century were rampant individualists, highly mobile both geographically, socially, economically 'rational,' market-oriented and acquisitive, ego-centred in kinship and social life.[21]

Most historians of medieval England dispute some of his terms and deny that thirteenth-century English cultivators farmed primarily for the market, but most would accept several of his key claims. First, that large numbers of English men and women owned – and bought and sold – land relatively freely. Second, that petty landowners could leave their property to whomever they wished (and not to specified heirs as in most other known societies). Third, that most people married late, did not form extended families, enjoyed significant geographical and even social mobility, and exhibited something we would call "individualism." Or in Macfarlane's words, "within the recorded period covered by our documents, it is not possible to find a time when an Englishman did not stand alone. Symbolized and shaped by his ego-centred kinship system, he stood in the centre of his world."[22] Macfarlane's ultimate point is that the emergence of individualism in England cannot be explained by the rise of Protestantism or the market economy. England was, in other words, ripening over the course of several centuries for the extraordinary role it played in modern times.

In another work, Macfarlane argues that what made the English particularly successful in the modern age was not individualism alone, but also the ability to work in concert better than other peoples of the world.[23] From medieval times, for example, the English common law allowed groups of people to create institutions, businesses, and organizations as unincorporated bodies, or "trusts." Unlike corporations, which were grounded in Roman law, trusts required no official approval and therefore promoted free association and social autonomy. Many influential English institutions emerged as trusts, including the Inns of Court (where all barristers of England and Wales received their training), the London Stock Exchange, the Universities of Oxford and Cambridge, and many big insurance companies. Trusts also fostered religious pluralism, since dissenting churches could easily establish themselves as trusts. Macfarlane, as a further example of English associativeness, considers it significant that most team sports – rugby, soccer, cricket, and rounders (a forerunner of baseball) – were invented or developed in England from the later Middle Ages.

Where exactly modern cultures come from – how far back one needs to dig in order to find their origins – has never been satisfactorily investigated, mostly because the documentary evidence gradually dries up, and that's true even for societies whose records, like Europe's, are generally well preserved. Macfarlane speculates that English individualism – and many aspects of English law and politics – stems ultimately from the traditions of ancient Germanic societies.[24]

A shift in values caused it (Deirdre McCloskey)

The eminent economic historian, Deirdre McCloskey, personally experienced the kind of mental transformation that she believes led to the most radical economic shift in world history. For the first 52 years of life, she had lived as Donald, had married and fathered children. Then, at age 52, he became she. Repeatedly in her memoir, *Crossing*, McCloskey talks about a psychological dam bursting: for 52 years, she had built up powerful defensive mechanisms against perceiving her true self. Then one day, driving on a highway in northern Illinois, "on the twentieth day of August 1995 a little after noon the dam broke and the water of his life swirled out onto the plain. He knew himself. Herself."[25] McCloskey conceives of the eruption of modern economic growth in a similar way. The forces of technological, scientific, and economic advancement had been building up for centuries – as they had several other times in history. Yet a psychological dam had always thwarted further development, until in early modern Europe when a critical mass of educated and powerful elites gradually reached a positive consensus about business innovation and entrepreneurship. Ceaseless innovation and therefore extraordinary and continuous wealth-creation could then ensue.

McCloskey elaborates this interpretation – the purest version of the cultural explanation for the rise of the West – in a magisterial investigation intended to encompass three big volumes. Volume one analyzes the relationship of seven traditional virtues – four pagan (prudence, temperance, courage, and justice) and three Christian (faith, hope, and love) – to the rise of the West. In brief, a specific ethic undergirded and made possible rapid economic growth in the modern period. Entrepreneurs and merchants did well for themselves by doing good for society, she claims. They could not be successful merely by looking out for their own interests; only by serving their customers and providing social value could most entrepreneurs and businesses prosper.[26]

In volume two, she points out that people in developed countries earned, on average, only 3 dollars a day in 1800 but well over 100 dollars (adjusted for inflation) each day in recent years. Standards of living in these countries, in other words, increased by a factor of at least 16 – that is, 16 times – at the very least – more food, clothing, shelter, and other stuff than our ancestors had just two hundred years ago.[27] In those days women typically had only two dresses; nowadays, in America, they might have 50 different outfits – or more. And that is not counting inventions now widely used that had not even been conceived of back then, like electric light and air travel.

What was necessary for these extraordinary changes were bourgeois dignity and liberty – that is, admiration and noninterference with regard to entrepreneurs seeking to bring to life new ideas, often crazy ideas, like moving pictures or hybrid cars or hand-held computers. Our world was revolutionized not by material forces but by unleashed creativity inherent in all human beings – and only when societies, first in northwest Europe, came to recognize such human creativity as extraordinarily benevolent and therefore worthy of encouragement and imitation. Innovation – and modern prosperity – came about when business people and inventors in vast numbers grew ever more alert to opportunities to improve the way we do just about everything materially, intellectually, culturally, economically, politically, socially; in brief, our ever-changing modern world.

How did this happen? The specific and mutually enforcing array of bourgeois virtues she examined in her first volume gained respectability and acceptance, and therefore the innovative entrepreneurial people who embraced them multiplied and flourished beginning in the late seventeenth century. For most of history, elites and other beneficiaries of vested interests, devoted enormous energy to disparaging and impeding economic innovation. They imposed tariffs, taxes, price controls, regulations of all kinds, and in general castigated as vulgar, deplorable, sinful, or undignified the idea of engaging in commerce, pursuing "filthy lucre," exhibiting unbridled economic ambition, devising newfangled ways of making things or doing business, and undermining traditional conceptions and practices of "social justice." Only when business – and the ethical system that made it successful – won widespread and explicit affirmation in Western societies could those societies begin to "take off" economically. When entrepreneurs and economic innovators could feel as proud of themselves as lords, officers, priests, or officials, then the ambitious flocked to join their ranks. Or as she writes,

> I am claiming, in other words, that the historically unique economic growth on the order of a factor of 10 or 16 or higher, and its political and spiritual correlates, depended on ideas more than economics. The idea of a

dignified and free bourgeoisie led to the ideas of the steam engine and mass marketing and democracy.[28]

She spends much of her book refuting preconditions and causes put forward by other scholars trying to explain why modern economic growth exploded in the West beginning some two hundred years ago. Scientific investigation, educational institutions, printing, monotheism, long-distance trade, the rule of law, sophisticated financial institutions, and many other allegedly crucial preconditions were in place and flourishing in many places across Eurasia for hundreds of years before the astounding emergence of what McCloskey calls the Great Fact, which made the modern world. Likewise, as regards specific causes, humans had always engaged in foreign trade, accumulated capital, and invested in literacy and other forms of human capital. Coal is easy to move, if one is motivated. Europeans actually reaped few lasting profits from their empires, and imperialism is as ancient as trade. Property rights were widespread around the world, and even stronger in China than in Europe, so they couldn't have made industrialization possible. People in the West did not invent greed or take it to a higher level than anyone else. All other conditions being equal, Catholics, Hindus, Buddhists, Muslims, and Confucians were just as successful at commerce as Protestants and every bit as rational about economic thinking. Population growth had been explosive in previous times yet never before led to modern economic growth. The rest of the countries in Europe had until the eighteenth century in various places and at various times seemed on the cusp of achieving dramatic innovation, yet they failed to achieve liberty and dignity for the bourgeoisie—the crucial ingredient. Science in China and the Islamic world until the seventeenth century was more sophisticated than in Europe. Nor, anyway, did this science greatly influence technology until the twentieth century.[29]

Professor McCloskey thus enumerates many of the principal explanations propounded by scholars as shedding light on the Great Fact. She then systematically rejects these – and other – arguments over the following three hundred or so pages.

Consider several other arguments she refutes. Political fragmentation was unlikely to explain an explosion of innovation, since the German lands were highly fragmented before 1871 yet achieved little technological advancement during the two centuries prior. A high savings rate has been widespread throughout history but never sparked a 16-fold economic expansion. Similarly, increasing the quantity of existing technology cannot precipitate such an increase. Only constant, intensive, multifaceted, all-encompassing *innovation* can achieve this. For example, not more scythes and pitchforks, but

clay-pipe underdrainage and plant breeding and forward markets and mechanical reapers and experimental stations and diesel tractors and railcar delivery systems and hybrid corn and farm cooperatives and chemical herbicides does the job better.[30]

Likewise, improved efficiencies or better institutions are insufficient. In fact, she argues that purely economic incentives changed little from 1000 to 1800.[31] The same was true of contract law and the rule of law generally.

Nor are more and more educated people sufficient to cause modern economic growth to burst forth; not, at least, without a more favorable attitude toward innovation. Russia and Cuba have extremely high rates of college completion; neither is much of an innovator. Even a handful of brilliant scientists in ancient Greece or the medieval Islamic world or early modern Europe did not radically transform the economy or enrich the poor. The transportation revolution in Britain from 1780 to 1860 conserved roughly 1.5 percent of national income. A nice little savings, as McCloskey remarks, but "not by itself the stuff of 'revolution.'"[32]

Nor did exploitation and imperialism cause the Great Fact. Free workers can and have picked cotton or coffee beans. Mutually beneficial trade enriches merchants and societies more than one-sided colonial trade: Switzerland and Denmark became rich without colonial empires, and Japan became far richer when not pursuing imperialist ventures. The key decade of industrialization in Britain was the 1780s, precisely when they lost their first empire and had not yet acquired a new one. Imperialism, she argues, is morally wrong and "economically stupid."[33]

No, some specific laborsaving device, some new source of energy, some spurt of imperialism, some new way of organizing production, even a highly exploitative method like the slave trade or the plantation economy – by itself – can never be sufficient. As McCloskey argues, neither railways, nor foreign trade, nor cotton mills led directly to industrial change and indeed contributed insufficiently to any pre-modern economy to so much as double its size, much less multiply it by a factor of 16.[34]

Only an environment conducive to constant and multifaceted innovation could possibly bring about the dramatic improvement in standards of living in developed countries, and even in developing countries, over the past two hundred years. What mattered above all was not greed or connivance or corruption but alertness to possible opportunities for new ways of building things, doing business, organizing societies, and thinking about life itself. Suddenly the Dutch in the seventeenth century and then the English, Scots, and Americans began to see the world differently, to envision constant change and commercial enterprise as worthy and dignified. This made alertness "explode."[35]

Material economic factors mattered far less, she insists, than what people believed and how they thought.[36] Hard, painstaking, work counted enormously also – far more than any heroics. Devotion to work, to one's profession, to improving everything one was involved in was the quintessential attitude of the Dutch and later of the English, Scottish, and Americans. This was what it meant to be bourgeois.[37]

Ideas – "the dark matter of history"[38] – and attitudes made an extraordinary concatenation of innovation possible in the modern West. This innovation flowed directly from the bourgeois values – including faith, hope, and love – of merchants and entrepreneurs. She repeats: not prudence or routine made the modern world possible. Those qualities had existed in abundance for all of human existence.[39] So had background conditions like high levels of urbanization and trade and transportation routes and secure property rights. In 1700, they existed in all the great cultures of Eurasia. But only in northwest Europe did the dignity and liberty of the bourgeoisie emerge.

Institutions made the difference (Nathan Rosenberg)

Scholars who credit inherent qualities in Europe with making possible the emergence of the modern world typically emphasize either culture or institutions. Culture exists in the mind as values, habits, ideals, and beliefs. Institutions, by contrast, are relatively constant ways to organize people, for example, large-scale associations like governments, religious organizations, armies, businesses, and schools, as well as stable relationships with many instances across societies like marriage, friendship, and the family. (Laws, customs, rules, and traditions, as relatively constant ways to coordinate people's actions, are a species of institution.) Naturally, culture influences the emergence and functioning of institutions – though exactly how is open to controversy. Certainly, most scholars would agree that institutions crystallize according to the values and circumstances of a people. Yet according to many well-respected scholars, the existence of key institutions in the West best explain its rise to preeminence.

The most thorough exposition of this point of view has been advanced by Nathan Rosenberg, an eminent professor of economics and public policy and an expert on the history of technology. (His former student, L. E. Birdzell, Jr., a lawyer, transcribed Rosenberg's lecture notes to produce a successful monograph.)[40] They both agree with Dawson, Landes, and others that political and economic actors enjoyed an unusually high degree of autonomy in medieval Europe but contend that it resulted from a decrease not only in political but also in ecclesiastical control over society. The key actors in Europe's rise were not reforming saints or crusading knights imbued with spiritual fervor but hard-headed, practically minded entrepreneurs constantly seeking out new commercial opportunities – new commodities, new production methods, new financial instruments, new business arrangements. They argue that gradually emerging institutions, laws, and practices made this shift possible and resulted in the decline of the unitary medieval worldview, an increasing pluralism of sources of authority and centers of power, and significant gains in efficiency, productivity, and wealth-production.

Rosenberg and Birdzell enumerate and analyze numerous institutions they believe fostered the rise and acceleration of commerce in late medieval Europe. They begin with the legal enforcement of contracts and property claims. Above all, magistrates had to abandon their power to impose arbitrary justice and rulers their claims to confiscatory taxation. As the rule of law evolved gradually in Europe, merchants and entrepreneurs – even those from foreign countries – could plan their business operations without fear of unexpected rule changes.

The authors next discuss four powerful financial institutions and methods born in Italy during the Renaissance. Financing an overseas shipping venture was risky, so clever Italian merchants in the late twelfth century invented a means to spread risk among numerous underwriter-investors. Marine insurance made it possible to separate commercial risk from the hazards of the open seas, so that entrepreneurs could specialize in one or the other field. A second innovation, bills of exchange, which emerged several decades later, enabled merchants to conduct long-distance trade more efficiently and therefore more profitably. Again, it became easier to specialize in the financing of international trade, leaving the transportation of goods to other merchants. Over the following centuries, a brisk trade in these bills, which had something like cash value, financed an expansion of international commerce. Merchants who began to accept deposits of such bills – and to lend a portion of them out to customers – by definition founded banks, the third Italian business innovation. Bills of exchange also made it possible to keep assets liquid and therefore mobile and concealable, enabling merchants to avoid heavy taxation and to migrate to regions more favorably disposed toward business. Fourth, as firms grew in size and scope, Italian bookkeepers devised a means to accurately assess their value in strictly numerical terms and to separate companies from the families that founded them. Double-entry bookkeeping led to the reconceptualization of business firms as independent actors.

These institutions required a new ethos or set of ethical principles to function properly. Other hierarchical and organizational models – familial, feudal, and ecclesiastical – were unsuited for commercial success. For one thing, nepotism was often bad for business. For another, aristocrats and the clergy held merchants in contempt. Third, investors had to learn to trust the managers of companies, to whom they had no blood ties. As Rosenberg and Birdzell argue, commercial capitalism's complex trading and lending relations

> needed a morality epitomized in such terms as "honest dealing," "promise keeping," and "punctuality," and (in the case of employees) "industry," "diligence," "honesty," and "fidelity."[41]

Where did this new morality come from? Did Protestantism engender it, as Weber argued, or did the flourishing commercial life, where "individual choice and bargaining had superseded custom as the basis of exchange,"[42] help spark the Reformation? The authors put forward evidence for the impact of Protestantism on the rise of capitalism. First, John Calvin highly valued the work of merchants and artisans and rejected the pursuit of frivolous pleasures. Second, Protestant clergy, emphasizing personal responsibility, gradually left merchants to govern their own affairs, which attracted many entrepreneurs to Protestant countries. Third, the confiscation of Church land in Protestant countries opened it up to more productive use. Finally, in medieval times rich people often left huge endowments to the Church hoping for favorable treatment after death; the Calvinist doctrine of predestination made such thinking pointless.

Rosenberg and Birdzell emphasize not values in and of themselves, like McCloskey, but values built into, and reinforced by, institutions, including the Church and state governments. In the seventeenth century, for example, several European rulers, adopting the mercantilist philosophy, established national economic policies. Adam Smith later demonstrated that many were counterproductive, but on the positive side, according to our authors, rulers came to appreciate the value of merchants and trade to national well-being.

An even more important way that European states promoted commerce and innovation was by being weak. Feudal relations divided allegiances both vertically and horizontally and undermined the sovereignty of rulers. Within this context, members of various communities

> carved out, by custom, usage, and charter, definitions of their obligations to their overlords and statements of their own rights and privileges, akin to the charters which defined their immediate lords' own relationships to their feudal superiors.[43]

Sustained urbanization beginning in the twelfth century was both a consequence and a cause of the intensification of commerce. European cities gained power, wealth, and the right to self-government thanks to their critical mass of population, mercantile activity, available capital, and means of communication. After the Black Death (1347–1351), a cash-based agricultural arrangement replaced feudal relations, further dispersing authority. The resultant political fragmentation – augmented by the establishment of overseas colonies – provided almost inexhaustible opportunities for experimentation and refuges for innovative thinkers and doers. Even many rulers felt they had to compete to attract and protect merchants and commercial enterprises.

Thanks to political fragmentation, there gradually emerged in Europe a pluralistic society with "comparatively autonomous spheres of industry, trade, finance, science, politics, education, art, music, literature, religion, and the press." Thus, in Western society the powerful benefits of the division of labor and specialization increased efficiency and creativity in nearly every aspect of life.[44] The resultant social and economic openness to change culminated in the Scientific Revolution, large-scale business and financial institutions like limited liability companies and stock exchanges, the Industrial Revolution, modern economic growth, and the unrelenting technological and scientific advancements of the past hundred or so years. Innovation, according to the authors, "is itself a form of revolt against convention,"[45] so throughout history most people and authorities have fought against it. What was different about Europe, and ultimately the wider West, were the many sturdy but autonomous institutions that enabled individuals and groups to innovate relatively freely. The authors conclude that the invention of key institutions was probably just as important to the rise of the West as technological innovation.

Many other scholars disagree, placing a far higher importance on technological innovations. Before exploring their views, one more aspect of institutional development requires comment. A huge scholarly literature investigates the institutions discussed by Rosenberg and Birdzell, but one – property rights – deserves special mention because it provided the foundation for all the others, according to some academics.

Above all it was property rights (Douglass North)

Douglass North, according to Deirdre McCloskey, was an amazing scholar who has led a brilliant and colorful life. He inherited considerable wealth, was a Marxist in his youth, served in the merchant marine during World War II, was an apprentice to the famous Depression-era photographer Dorothea Lange, and went deep-sea fishing with the celebrated crooner Perry Como.[46]

He also received the Nobel Prize for his work in economic history. He and his co-author, Robert Thomas, a professor of economics, concluded that "economic growth will occur if property rights make it worthwhile to undertake socially productive activity."[47] The rights they have in mind are to possess property, to see contracts honored, not to suffer confiscatory taxation or excessive government interference in one's economic affairs, to enjoy security from robbery, and to benefit exclusively from innovation, thanks, for example, to patent law. In fact, they argue that for most of human history, the lack of such protections strongly impeded progress. What would be the point of inventing anything if one's competitors immediately gained access to its design? This is why medieval Europeans perfected many technologies invented elsewhere but devised relatively few themselves. "Innovation involving significant research costs," North and Thomas claim, "would seldom, if ever, be worth the risk without some form of protection to internalize a significant share of its gains,"[48] that is, to profit from it. Only around 1500 did some European governments – in particular those of the Dutch Republic and England – begin to institute the world's first truly favorable conditions for economic innovation and growth. In this way, they conclude, "the differences in the performance of the economies of Western Europe between 1500 and 1700 was in the main due to the type of property rights created by the emerging states."[49]

No freedom without property (Richard Pipes)

Richard Pipes – a refugee from Nazi Germany and the historian of Russia who has written more broadly on his subject than any other scholar in the English language but also an expert on Soviet politics who served in the Reagan administration – goes further. The idea and practice of modern democracy, civil rights, political liberty, personal freedom, and free enterprise, he argues, all had their origins in the medieval city, whose key feature was the right of ordinary people to control property.[50] Pipes shows that, at many turning points in the development of representative government and political liberties in European history, the defense of property (in particular the rejection of arbitrary or unjust taxation) proved the essential motivating factor.

As instances of such actions, he cites the emergence of Parliament in England, the execution of King Charles I and the subsequent English Revolution, the Glorious Revolution of 1688, and the American Revolution. Pipes summarizes his argument:

> The notion of "inalienable rights," which has played an increasing role in the thought and practice of the West since the seventeenth century, grows out of the right to property, the most elementary of rights. One of its aspects is the principle that the sovereign rules but does not own and hence must not appropriate the belongings of his subjects or violate their persons – a principle that erected a powerful barrier to political authority and permitted the evolution first of civil and then political rights.[51]

Only in Europe and the modern West, he argues, did private property rights become sufficiently developed and entrenched to limit the coercive power of government and thus to provide a favorable environment for the emergence of individual liberty and free enterprise.

Attentive readers will have noticed that all of the authors so far discussed place a great deal of emphasis on factors limiting government, in particular political fragmentation, as a way to account for the extraordinary inventiveness and dynamism of European societies beginning in the Middle Ages. Most other flourishing civilizations either had central control of both politics and culture – like China and Byzantium – or unified though dispersed political and religious authorities, as in the Islamic world. Political and economic change, while potentially beneficial to society, is usually viewed as threatening to established authorities, which therefore resist them. When those authorities monopolize power, they can thwart innovation. According to many scholars of the "Miracle of the West" outlook, the absence of such society-wide cohesiveness of the European ruling elites made them less able than those in other cultures to preserve the status quo.

The key factor was political fragmentation (John A. Hall)

It is not to say that the European states were weak, but rather that they were very numerous and in constant competition with each other. In fact, according to John A. Hall, a professor of comparative historical sociology, by the end of the Middle Ages most European states – unlike those in the Islamic world – were strong enough to protect commercial interests and commoners in general from aristocratic predation.[52] At the same time, many European societies were sufficiently well organized and assertive to demand – and to receive – infrastructural services in exchange for tax payments. There resulted a constant tension, a relatively balanced give-and-take among a multitude of social actors. In the Chinese, Indian, and Islamic civilizations, he writes:

> the powerful influenced economic relationships, through bureaucratic interference or predatory rule, so much that it is misleading even to talk of

a separate "economic" realm working according to its own principles. In contrast, Christendom allowed for strong and autonomous power sources. Remarkably these power sources did not then block each other but rather went in the same direction. The presence of liberties ensured the creation of organic polities which eventually became translated into liberal systems of rule. We can rationally reconstruct how this occurred, but it is all too easy to imagine things happening otherwise. It was the European miracle.[53]

Europeans were more productive, inventive, and ultimately wealthy and powerful, according to Hall, because they accomplished more things through social agreement and comparatively fewer things through coercion.

One might suggest that Hall's analysis pulls together the main arguments of scholars emphasizing culture and those focusing on institutions – only the extraordinary political fragmentation and competition among centers of authority, he might reason, made possible the emergence of such a dynamic culture and protective institutions.

Europeans valued technology more (Lynn White)

Other scholars put less emphasis on culture and institutions and more on tools, methods, and machines that humans design and use to improve their lives – in a word, technology. The first scholar to argue forcefully and persuasively that technological development can best explain the rise of the West – and that it began in medieval times – was the American historian Lynn White (1907–1987).[54] Commanding a dozen languages and a wide array of scholarly disciplines, he shows that from the early Middle Ages Europeans were ready and able to adapt and improve available technologies.

In the early 700s, for example, the horse stirrup appeared in Europe and over time brought about a radical transformation of politics and society. Once Charles Martel, the grandfather of Charlemagne, realized the new technology could enable mounted knights to charge with lances extended, he seized extensive church lands and distributed them among his followers, laying the foundation of feudalism. For over six hundred years, the feudal knights dominated every battlefield in Europe. "Antiquity imagined the Centaur," he wrote, but "the early Middle Ages made him the master of Europe." Or as White develops this idea further:

> Few inventions have been so simple as the stirrup, but few have had so catalytic an influence on history. The requirements of the new mode of warfare which it made possible found expression in a new form of western European society dominated by an aristocracy of warriors endowed with land so that they might fight in a new and highly specialized way.[55]

Technologies like the stirrup (and paper, the compass, gunpowder, and printing) may have been invented elsewhere, but no other culture experienced greater technological transformations because of them than Europe.

Building on evidence presented by Marc Bloch in 1931, White also argues for the eruption of an "agricultural revolution" during the early Middle Ages thanks to the invention or adaptation of a concatenation of new technologies, including a heavy plough, horseshoes, the horse collar, and three-field crop rotation, leading to far greater output, dramatically increased population, intensified manufacturing, the specialization of labor, the rise of towns, and an explosion of commerce – making possible the cultural flowering we call the Renaissance.

From relatively early medieval times, according to White, Europeans innovated with many forms of power generation and mechanization. Harnessing animal power was a start. The ancient world had known water wheels, but medieval artisans deployed them all over the continent. Windmills were first put to extensive use in the late twelfth century in Northern Europe and then spread quickly. By the high Middle Ages most settlements in Europe had at least one or other of these complicated devices, which must have dramatically increased productivity and familiarity with mechanical processes. Among the further devices that emerged in this environment was the crank, which makes it possible to convert reciprocal to circular motion and vice versa. White believes this European invention to be the greatest mechanical breakthrough since the wheel and presents it as evidence of an obsessive pursuit of mechanical innovation, leading to a "medieval industrial revolution."[56]

White also investigates the revolutionary application of power to military prowess. He argues that experimentation in both Europe and China yielded independent discoveries of gunpowder but that Europeans devised the world's first effective cannon – an extraordinary advance in military technology. In fact, several scholars have emphasized the role military technology played in the rise of the West (see later).

First, however, how does White explain European dynamism and ingenuity? He points to the Christian religion (though he does not elaborate as much as Dawson) and in particular Benedictine monasticism. In ancient times, manual labor was considered an activity fit only for slaves. White cites several major classical authors, like Plato and Seneca, disparaging physical labor and even mechanical devices. Only intellectual pursuits were worthy of a freeman, they thought. St. Benedict, by contrast, himself an aristocrat, called on monks to toil in field and shop many hours of the day. Indeed, throughout the Middle Ages, following Benedict's lead, all Western forms of religious asceticism proclaimed that "to labor is to pray." Equally important, Benedict – and nearly every successive Western monastic organizer – intended monks to devote themselves also to learning and intellectual training. White makes a striking assertion:

> for the first time the practical and the theoretical were embodied in the same individuals. In Antiquity learned men did not work, and workers were not learned. Consequently, ancient science consisted mostly of observation and abstract thought; experimental methods were rarely used. The craftsmen had accumulated a vast fund of factual knowledge about natural

forces and substances, but the social cleavage prevented classical scientists from feeling that stimulus from technology which has been so conspicuous an element in the development of modern experimental science. The monk was the first intellectual to get dirt under his fingernails.[57]

Later monks, the Cistercians in particular, avidly used and advanced technological know-how. White notes that some monasteries powered four or five different workshops with water wheels. He considers profoundly significant the Christian view of every human being as valuable; none should be used as a machine, especially when machines can make their jobs easier.

Continuous innovation enabled Europe to rule the seas (Carlo Cipolla)

As noted earlier, according to some scholars, one of the most influential kinds of technology for explaining the rise of the West was military. Among the first to address this issue was Carlo Cipolla (1922–2000), a distinguished and path-breaking professor of economic history at the universities of Pavia, Italy, and California at Berkeley. He notes that Europe had barely escaped Mongol conquest in the thirteenth century and was repeatedly assaulted by the Ottoman Turks from the devastating Battle of Nicopolis (1396) to the invasion of Albania in 1468. Then beginning in the late fifteenth century, European mariners managed to dominate the seas and to establish colonies throughout the world. In a word, what made all the difference was learning how to build artillery pieces, to continuously perfect them century by century and often decade by decade, to produce them in huge quantity, and – especially in the case of the Atlantic powers – to mount them on sailing ships, which became indomitable floating fortresses that no non-European power could withstand by the early 1500s. Cipolla writes,

> Within a few years after the arrival of the first European vessels in the Indian Ocean, it became mandatory for non-European vessels to secure sailing permits if they did not want to be blown up by European guns. The oceans belonged to Europe.[58]

Moreover, European military technology kept advancing rapidly, while the rest of the world kept falling further and further behind. Within two more centuries, the Europeans were invincible even on land.

Rosenberg and Birdzell provide more detail about the development of maritime technology and argue that its advances in the Renaissance period made possible the Age of Discovery. The European full-rigged ship, outfitted with three masts bearing rows of square sails and lateen (triangular) sails fore and aft, could sail up to an angle of 60 percent to the wind. These ships were fast, maneuverable, and sea-worthy. European mariners steadily mastered nautical methods and devices. They studied local magnetic variation; deployed quadrants, cross-staffs, and astrolabes not only for triangulation but also for celestial navigation; and developed sophisticated cartography. In this way, in the fifteenth century, trade and maritime technology developed a symbiotic relationship, each fostering the expansion and improvement of the other.[59]

Military revolution in Europe (Michael Roberts and Geoffrey Parker)

The gradual mastery of land-based warfare, which Cipolla alluded to, is the main theme of a celebrated essay by Michael Roberts, "The Military Revolution, 1560–1660."[60] This transformation involved four major changes in warfare beginning in the sixteenth century. First, highly trained infantry armed with longbows and muskets became the mainstay of European armies. Next, those armies grew dramatically in size – tenfold from 1500 to 1700. Third, military commanders devised complex strategies in order to maximize their martial prowess. Finally, societies became mobilized for war – and to bring this about modern states had to emerge. Two decades later, building on this foundation, Geoffrey Parker showed that this military revolution – which Parker expands to include technologies of fortification and naval warfare – enabled the European powers to conquer some 35 percent of the earth's land surface between 1500 and 1800.[61] A key element in Europe's success, he argues, was the intensity of competition among states that drove each constantly to innovate and to imitate and build on its rivals' advances in technology, tactics, and strategy. No other civilization or region of the world was so dynamic in its embrace of military change.

Military power of a new type (William H. McNeill)

The distinguished world historian, William H. McNeill, whose most famous work will be discussed in Chapter 2, contextualized the European military revolution both from a world-historical perspective and by embedding it in the rich detail of European social and political evolution.[62] European soldiers, he suggests, were less squeamish about shedding blood than their counterparts in other societies because, far more than other peoples, Europeans were used to slaughtering their own livestock. The medieval European commercial revolution fueled a commercialization and professionalization of warfare, as many states hired specialized fighters and mercenary units – one factor in the rapid spread of military innovation across Europe. Gunpowder weaponry provided less destructive power than catapults for at least a century after the first cannons were deployed in Europe around 1326. Yet, according to McNeill, "the explosive suddenness with which a gun discharged somehow fascinated European rulers and artisans."[63] So, more than in other countries, they experimented intensively until their artillery began to play a decisive role in combat. Eurasia underwent a second "Bronze Age," as gunpowder empires emerged in Turkey, Persia, India, Russia, and China. All of these powers adapted gunpowder technology from Europe, though they struggled – generally unsuccessfully, at least in the long run – to keep up with its arms race. Maritime commercial operations, by which Europeans established a commanding presence throughout the world oceans, "acted like the molecules of expanding gas, probing every-where the limits of profitable transactions. And whenever a captain returned with unusually handsome profits, other ships soon followed."[64] By the end of the Thirty Years' War (1648), European armies had reached "the level of the higher animals by developing the equivalent of a central nervous system, cap-able of activating technologically differentiated claws and teeth."[65] Systematic training and drilling of soldiers reconnected them with a sense of solidarity going back to prehistoric times. It was this new kind of army, which McNeill considers as remarkable as the birth of modern science, that enabled Europeans to defeat their opponents throughout the world.

The marriage of science and technology enabled the West to soar (Joel Mokyr)

One other scholar who has focused on Western technological innovation deserves mention. Following Lynn White and others, Joel Mokyr, a professor of economic history at Northwestern University, concludes that of all the cultures in world history only the West managed to turn technological progress "into a sustained and almost self-perpetuating mechanism of continuous expansion."[66] Mokyr means that trends of innovation beginning in the Middle Ages built on each other, accelerated, and eventually led to the explosion of creative inven-tiveness that yielded the first and second Industrial Revolutions. He explains these breakthroughs by emphasizing culture. Medieval Europeans valued prac-tical knowledge and innovation far more than the ancient Greeks and Romans – peoples who conquered vast empires and achieved extraordinary intellectual feats – and were more able to pursue this interest than people in China where for most of its history political centralization enabled elites to hamper innova-tion. Why does Mokyr place such a heavy emphasis on knowledge?

"The rise of the western economies based on economic growth and techno-logical progress is the central event of modern history," Mokyr claims in a detailed study of 2002.[67] While admitting the importance of culture and insti-tutions in this development, he places paramount emphasis on what he calls an increase in "useful knowledge." For most of history, the people who studied nature and those who produced goods and services were distinct social cate-gories. The astonishing reality of modern economic growth stemmed in large part from the blurring of these categories, according to Mokyr. The ground was prepared for this development beginning in the Renaissance with the printing revolution, but it began to come to fruition in the eighteenth century thanks to what he calls the Industrial Enlightenment, which brought practical and theo-retical knowledge together, and created a powerful and fruitful symbiosis of scientists and technologists.[68] Its importance was to link science and technol-ogy, the Scientific Revolution and the Industrial Revolution.

These linkages were made possible by a pan-European climate favorable to the pursuit of learning and of acquiring, sharing, classifying, preserving, and using information. Flourishing scientific societies, educational institutions, scholarly journals, encyclopedias, newspapers, and almost numberless publishing ventures made it possible for scientists, engineers, artisans, and educators to learn from one another and ultimately to cross-fertilize the two main kinds of knowledge – pure (what Mokyr calls "propositional") and applied ("prescriptive"). In their efforts to grasp the underpinnings of technical, or prescriptive, knowledge, scientists steadily advanced their understanding of how nature works in general, thus building up more and more propositional knowledge. At the same time, entrepreneurs and inventors continuously ransacked stores of propositional knowledge in their efforts to develop more efficient and powerful technologies. Gradually, the pursuit of technological advancement became more and more scientific in approach – aiming to understand not only how things work but why. The first sector of technology to undergo such a transformation was the synthetic chemical industry, in which by the late 1800s most researchers had graduate degrees. Many others followed.

Technological progress had naturally taken place throughout history and across the globe before 1800. Mokyr seeks to show, however, that from that date a qualitative change occurred: science and technology began to build upon each other in an ever accelerating process of innovation. Before the Industrial Revolution, practitioners of most scientific and technical fields, for example medicine, agriculture, and metallurgy, knew only their very narrow areas of expertise.

> In both Europe and China, techniques worked despite a lack of understanding of why they worked. Normally, it was enough if someone recognized some exploitable regularity. Whether we look at steelmaking, cattle-breeding, or obstetric surgery, most techniques before 1800 emerged as a result of chance discoveries, trial and error, or good mechanical intuition and often worked quite well despite nobody's having much of a clue as to the principles at work.[69]

Over the following decades, more and more people in the West understood both how and why things worked and, putting millions of heads together, set off an explosion of scientific and technological advancement.

Conclusion

The authors reviewed in this chapter argue that key features of social and cultural life enabled Europe to break away from the other regions of the world. Among the features they emphasize are an extraordinary dynamism, an unparalleled willingness and capacity to innovate, unrelenting competition among the societies of Europe, a radical shift in values, uniquely robust institutions for protecting and fostering individual rights, an unprecedented union of science and technology, the lack of a central authority to impose uniformity, and a fervent eagerness to borrow ideas and innovations from others.

Further reading

Culture/religion

Chirot, Daniel. *How Societies Change*. Thousand Oaks, Calif.: Pine Forge Press, 1994.

Duchesne, Ricardo. *The Uniqueness of Western Civilization*. Leiden; Boston: Brill, 2011.

Ferguson, Niall. *Civilization: The West and the Rest*. London: Allen Lane, 2011.

Huff, Toby E. *Intellectual Curiosity and the Scientific Revolution. A Global Perspective*. New York: Cambridge University Press, 2010.

Jones, Eric. *Growth Recurring: Economic Change in World History*. Oxford: Clarendon Press, 1988.

Macfarlane, Alan. *The Riddle of the Modern World: Of Liberty, Wealth and Equality*. New York: St. Martins, 2000.

Nemo, Philippe. *What Is the West?* Translated by Kenneth Casler; foreword by Michael Novak. Pittsburgh, Pa.: Duquesne University Press, 2006.

Roberts, John M. *The Triumph of the West: The Origins, Rise, and Legacy of Western Civilization*. Boston: Little, Brown and Company, 1985.

Stark, Rodney. *For the Glory of God: How Monotheism Led to Reformations, Science, Witch-hunts, and the End of Slavery*. Princeton, N.J.: Princeton University Press, 2003.

Stark, Rodney. *The Victory of Reason: How Christianity Led to Freedom, Capitalism, and Western Success*. New York: Random House, 2005.

Van Leeuwen, Arend Th. *Christianity in World History: The Meeting of the Faiths of East and West*. Translated by H. H. Hoskins. New York: Charles Scribner's Sons, 1964.

Institutions

Acemoglu, Daron and James Robinson. *Why Nations Fail: The Origins of Power, Prosperity, and Poverty*. New York: Crown Publishers, 2012.

Huff, Toby E. *The Rise of Early Modern Science: Islam, China, and the West*. Cambridge: Cambridge University Press, 1993.

North, Douglas C. *Institutions, Institutional Change, and Economic Performance*. Cambridge: Cambridge University Press, 1990.

Ringmar, Erik. *The Mechanics of Modernity in Europe and East Asia: Institutional Origins of Social Change and Stagnation*. London: Routledge, 2005.

Zanden, Jan Luiten van. *The Long Road to the Industrial Revolution: The European Economy in a Global Perspective, 1000–1800*. Leiden: Brill, 2009.

Technology

Allen, Robert C. *The British Industrial Revolution in Global Perspective*. New York: Oxford University Press, 2009.

Brady, Thomas A., Jr. "The Rise of Merchant Empires, 1400–1700: A European Counterpoint." In *The Political Economy of Merchant Empires*, ed. James D. Tracy. New York: Cambridge University Press, 1991.

Cipolla, Carlo M. *Before the Industrial Revolution: European Society and Economy, 1000–1700*. 2nd ed. New York; London: W. W. Norton, 1980.

Maddison, Angus. *Growth and Interaction in the World Economy: The Roots of Modernity*. Washington, D.C.: The AEI Press, 2005.

Mokyr, Joel. *The Lever of Riches: Technological Creativity and Economic Progress*. New York: Oxford University Press, 1990.

Snooks, Graeme Donald. *The Dynamic Society: Exploring the Sources of Global Change*. London: Routledge, 1996.

Knowledge and information

Crosby, Alfred. *The Measure of Reality: Quantification and Western Society, 1250–1600*. Cambridge: Cambridge University Press, 1997.

Goldstone, Jack. *Why Europe? The Rise of the West in World History, 1500–1850*. New York: McGrawHill, 2009.

Mokyr, Joel. *The Enlightened Economy: An Economic History of Britain, 1700–1850*. Princeton, N.J.: Princeton University Press, 2010.

Notes

1 Daniel Callahan et al., "Christopher Dawson: 12 October 1889–25 May 1970," *The Harvard Theological Review* 66 (Apr., 1973): 161–176 (here: 167).
2 Paul Costello, *World Historians and Their Goals: Twentieth-Century Answers to Modernism* (DeKalb, Ill.: Northern Illinois University Press, 1993), 129–131.
3 Christopher Dawson, *Religion and the Rise of Western Culture* (New York: Sheed and Ward, 1950), 12.
4 Costello, *World Historians and Their Goals*, 136–140.
5 Dawson, *Religion and the Rise of Western Culture*, 19.
6 Ibid., 21.
7 Ibid., 27.
8 The Eleusinian Mysteries were initiation ceremonies dating to remotest Greek antiquity.
9 The Carolingian Renaissance flourished from the late 700s to the mid-800s.
10 Dawson, *Religion and the Rise of Western Culture*, 125–126.
11 Ibid., 152.
12 Quoted in ibid., 173.
13 Ibid., 217.
14 David Landes, *The Wealth and Poverty of Nations: Why Some Are So Rich and Some So Poor* (New York: W. W. Norton, 1998).
15 Ibid., 44.
16 Ibid., 51.
17 Thomas Malthus (1766–1834), an influential British scholar, argued that population increase would always outstrip the human capacity to produce more food.
18 Landes, *The Wealth and Poverty of Nations*, 187.
19 Ibid., 204.

20 Alan Macfarlane, *The Origins of English Individualism. The Family, Property, and Social Transition* (New York: Cambridge University Press, 1978).
21 Ibid., 163.
22 Ibid., 196.
23 Alan Macfarlane, *The Making of the Modern World: Visions from the West and East* (Houndmills: Palgrave, 2002).
24 Macfarlane, *Origins of English Individualism*, 170.
25 Deirdre McCloskey, *Crossing: A Memoir* (Chicago: University of Chicago Press, 1999), 51.
26 Deirdre McCloskey, *The Bourgeois Virtues: Ethics for an Age of Commerce* (Chicago: University of Chicago Press, 2006).
27 Deirdre McCloskey, *Bourgeois Dignity: Why Economics Can't Explain the Modern World* (Chicago: University of Chicago Press, 2010), 1–6, 48–50.
28 Ibid., 24.
29 Ibid., 34.
30 Ibid., 133.
31 Ibid., 321.
32 Ibid., 169.
33 Ibid., 231.
34 Ibid., 210.
35 Ibid., 260.
36 Ibid., 351.
37 Ibid., 370.
38 Ibid., 447.
39 Ibid., 393.
40 Nathan Rosenberg and L. E. Birdzell, Jr., *How the West Grew Rich: The Economic Transformation of the Industrial World* (New York: Basic Books, 1986).
41 Ibid., 128.
42 Ibid.
43 Ibid., 62.
44 Ibid., 183.
45 Ibid., 261.
46 McCloskey, *Bourgeois Dignity*, 296.
47 Douglass C. North and Robert Paul Thomas, *The Rise of the Western World: A New Economic History* (Cambridge: Cambridge University Press, 1973), 8.
48 Ibid., 154–155.
49 Ibid., 97.
50 Richard Pipes, *Property and Freedom* (New York: Alfred A. Knopf, 1999).
51 Ibid., 118.
52 John A. Hall, *Powers and Liberties: The Causes and Consequences of the Rise of the West* (Oxford: Basil Blackwell, 1985).
53 Ibid., 142.
54 Lynn White, *Medieval Technology and Social Change* (London: Oxford University Press, 1962). A later work, *Medieval Religion and Technology: Collected Essays* (Berkeley; Los Angeles; London: University of California Press, 1978), catalogues more European technological advances.
55 Ibid., 38.
56 Ibid., 89.
57 Lynn White, Jr., *Machina ex Deo; Essays in the Dynamism of Western Culture* (Cambridge, Mass.: MIT Press, 1968), 65.
58 Carlo Cipolla, *Guns, Sails, and Empires: Technological Innovation and the Early Phases of European Expansion, 1400–1700* (New York: Minerva, 1965), 143.
59 Rosenberg and Birdzell, *How the West Grew Rich*, 81–85.
60 Michael Roberts, "The Military Revolution, 1560–1660," in *Essays in Swedish History* (Minneapolis: University of Minnesota Press, 1967), 195–225.

61 Geoffrey Parker, *The Military Revolution: Military Innovation and the Rise of the West, 1500–1800*, 2nd ed. (Cambridge; New York: Cambridge University Press, 1996).
62 William H. McNeill, *The Pursuit of Power: Technology, Armed Force, and Society since A.D. 1000* (Chicago: University of Chicago Press, 1982).
63 Ibid., 83.
64 Ibid., 104.
65 Ibid., 124.
66 Joel Mokyr, *The Lever of Riches: Technological Creativity and Economic Progress* (New York: Oxford University Press, 1990), 153.
67 Joel Mokyr, *The Gifts of Athena: Historical Origins of the Knowledge Economy* (Princeton, N.J.: Princeton University Press, 2002), 285.
68 Ibid., 35.
69 Ibid., 32. On the linkages of science and industry, see also Rosenberg and Birdzell, *How the West Grew Rich*, Chapter 8.

2   World history

For centuries, authors like Voltaire attempted "universal history," which aimed at encompassing all of humanity's past. Christopher Dawson's work emerged from such efforts. Only many decades of systematic historical research, however, made it finally possible to begin to approach this goal. Scholars who for the past half-century have sought to attain it, have not all ceased to marvel at the rise of the West. They have, however, "decentered" Europe and in more recent decades decried the alleged "Eurocentrism" of most of the scholars discussed in Chapter 1. Instead of internal causes for Europe's preeminence in the modern world, they generally emphasize such external factors as geography, influences from other cultures (in particular cultural and technological borrowing), the interconnectedness of all world cultures, and the exploitation and colonization of other peoples. They also study the West from a much broader perspective.

Human interaction fosters advancement (William McNeill)

The foundational contribution to the emergence of "world history" sports an improbable title. In *The Rise of the West*,[1] William McNeill traces the development of civilizations through five thousand years of recorded history yet devotes fewer than 150 pages out of 800 to the West as such. He obviously still believed that the rise of the West was the central fact of modern history, but he was just as obviously ready to place that fact in a much wider context. The author, as chair of the department of history at the University of Chicago, recruited distinguished scholars specializing in non-Western history.[2] He was thus one of the forerunners of an ongoing and unique trend in American history departments of devoting roughly the same attention to non-Western and to U.S. teaching and research. (History departments in few other countries strike this balance.)

In this extraordinary book, McNeill draws on a vast array of scholarship – from anthropology, archeology, sociology, history, and art history – in the major European languages, both old and obscure and up to date at the time of its publication in 1963, in order to narrate the emergence of the great cultures and civilizations of Eurasia. From the origins of urban civilization in

Mesopotamia, with due regard for others that arose somewhat later in Egypt, India, China, and then Greece, until roughly 500 BC, according to McNeill, the Middle East was the dominant locus of human development. The world's earliest powerful ideas, technologies, beliefs, and institutions arose there, and in many cases diffused to other parts of Afro-Eurasia. Once great cultures developed further east, in India and China particularly, this trend reversed itself, as their achievements found eager imitators back on the eastern shores of the Mediterranean Sea and elsewhere.

In fact, McNeill suggests that much human advancement throughout history was the result of interactions among peoples and cultures. Often this process took the form of the expansion of developed societies upon less developed ones.[3] In other words, the store of knowledge, technology, crops, livestock, skills, institutions, ideas, and artistic motifs, while sometimes and perhaps even often lost under the weight of time, slowly accumulated and gradually raised the cultural level of countless societies across Eurasia. Here McNeill employs a geological metaphor. He likens civilizations to mountain ranges, slowly being eroded by geological forces. Of course, the time frame is far different, but the effects seem rather similar, with one successful culture rising to great heights then gradually receding, as new cultures overshadow them, typically by borrowing and learning from their formerly glorious neighbors.

McNeill then goes on to note that civilizations do not necessarily wither away, except within the frame of geologic time. In the shorter term, the great civilizations persisted. Around 500 BC, the biggest ones were the somewhat eroded Middle Eastern highlands. Next to them were more ragged ridges leading out toward the Aegean and Italy in one direction and toward India in the other. Meanwhile, in the East, the Chinese civilization was still rising. Over the next two thousand years, the cultural "geography" of Eurasia had little changed, except that the principal "mountain ranges" had expanded.[4]

From AD 500 to 1500 Islam was the most dynamic civilization. It expanded to the northern half of Africa, across the Middle East, through central Asia, into the Indian subcontinent, and around East and Southeast Asia. The other great flourishing center was China, which spread its influence in every direction in the region. Significant but lesser cultures emerged in Japan, Western Europe, and Russia. Trade networks thrived across Eurasia. Vigorous cultural exchanges – in particular of the great religions – also took place among the major and minor cultures. Nomadic warriors repeatedly stormed across the same pathways, with often disastrous results for sedentary populations. In this millennium, Eurasia was strongly interconnected, yet roughly balanced, with no one civilization overwhelming the others. Meanwhile, the fruits of civilization spread further and further abroad to outlying regions, and the diversity of cultures across Eurasia were plentiful enough to enable the less developed peoples various choices among the major cultures.[5]

From 1500 to 1700, Europe began to develop faster than any other region and in the process expanded its influence into most inhabited areas of the globe. Only the great ancient civilizations – Islam, India, China – managed to hold their own against the onslaught, while others, like Japan, tried to shut out all foreign influences. Such efforts were doomed to fail, because the continuous transformations of European civilization, especially its technology, empowered Westerners so dramatically that ultimately no other people could withstand them.[6] By the middle of the nineteenth century, when the industrial and democratic revolutions of Europe and America vastly increased their energy and power, the geopolitical balance among the civilizations of Eurasia collapsed decisively in favor of the upstart, Western Civilization.

Why did the West rise? McNeill provides no clear explanation, though he points to some of its peculiarities. For one thing, unlike the other great civilizations – China, India, Islam – the West underwent repeated and at times almost continuous transformations that usually resulted in increased efficiencies and capacities. He considers the West extraordinarily unstable, prone to oscillating from one extreme to another. In this specific trait may have consisted the uniqueness of Western European civilization.[7] Here McNeill is similar to Dawson.

Geography and historical accidents also played an important role, according to McNeill. The Europeans, as their civilization began to rise around the year 1000, had ready access to the classical, Byzantine, and Islamic heritage but without the burden of a flourishing culture within their midst. At the same time, Frankish military prowess and the universalism of the Roman Church gave them the confidence to borrow extensively from foreign cultures without fear of losing their own identity or compromising their own values. Again like Dawson, McNeill emphasizes the fruitful melding of cultures – barbarian, Greco–Roman, and Judeo–Christian – and resultant tensions they introduced into the European hybrid, including between Church and state, faith and reason, violence and law, and nation and Christendom. The result was unique in history:

> Quite possibly Western civilization incorporated into its structure a wider variety of incompatible elements than did any other civilization of the world; and the prolonged and restless growth of the West, repeatedly rejecting its own potentially "classical" formulations, may have been related to the contrarieties built so deeply into its structure.[8]

Europe was a latecomer to civilization and assimilated a vast treasure house of technologies, ideas, concepts, institutions, and learning from every corner of Eurasia and beyond. Perhaps this often incompatible fund of influences drove the West to such astonishing restlessness, so that it has continuously remade and even revolutionized itself.

Yet, according to McNeill, Europe's restlessness and dynamism were not the only powerful ingredients in its success. Probably more important was how astoundingly much the Europeans learned from the other great civilizations of Eurasia. "The ease and eagerness with which they appropriated alien inheritances has perhaps no equal in civilized history," he wrote, save perhaps the ancient Greek assimilation of the great Asian cultural achievements. McNeill argued further that the Europeans' intense focus on borrowing and learning from the established cultures probably enabled them to carry much farther the earlier Asian accomplishments in science, technology, commerce, culture, and other human endeavors. It seems likely that the Europeans were thus able to mobilize vastly more human talent, creativity, and other capacities than peoples of more rigidly hierarchical cultures could achieve.[9]

While continuing to emphasize, like Dawson and the authors considered in Chapter 1, the inherent qualities in European culture to explain the West's rise, McNeill points the way toward an interpretation of world history in which Europe would play a more modest role. In such interpretations, geography and outside influences would play a more potent role. In his preface to the 1991 edition of the book, McNeill expanded on this idea. First, he regretted having failed to understand China's dominance in Eurasia for five hundred years after the millennium. (The available scholarship, he noted, had made this difficult.) He further argued that China's flourishing in this period had depended on borrowing from the Middle East, just as Europe's borrowings from China after 1500 made its own rise possible. Similarly, Japan's rise after 1900 depended on Western influences. Here McNeill believes he has discovered a key historical pattern. This pattern seems obvious, he believes, because no people can rise to great heights:

> without using the most efficacious and powerful instruments known any-
> where on earth; and by definition such instruments are located at the world
> centers of wealth and power – wherever they may be.[10]

Moreover, these powerful mutual influences involved more than culture. A proper world history also requires integrating human interactions with all the elements of their environment, including crops, livestock, pests, and diseases.[11]

Favorable geography gave Eurasia a head start (Jared Diamond)

An eminent American physiologist, ornithologist, historian, and geographer, Jared Diamond, took up McNeill's challenge in a Pulitzer Prize-winning book, *Guns, Germs, and Steel: The Fates of Human Societies*.[12] This fascinating account begins with a conversation the author had in 1972, walking on a beach in New Guinea, where he had spent years studying bird evolution. He was chatting with a local politician named Yali. They discussed many things, Yali plying him with questions. At one point, he asked about the European colonists. Before their arrival two hundred years earlier, the peoples of New Guinea knew only stone tools. The Europeans brought more advanced technology, including steel tools, medicines, and Western clothing, which New Guineans still refer to as "cargo." Yali then asked why the white people had developed and imported to New Guinea so much cargo, whereas the natives had so little.[13]

Diamond hastens to assert that the huge number of people he had known in Yali's country were no less intelligent than Westerners – on the contrary. Moreover, Yali's ancestors had skillfully deployed the earliest watercraft in history, some forty thousand years ago. No, the answer to Yali's question had nothing to do with intelligence or culture. In fact, Diamond is not even satisfied with explanations that focus on science, technology, capitalism, or even germs that caused the death of millions of people in the Americas upon their contact with Europeans. Those, he points out, are proximate causes. His book aims at laying bare the ultimate causes that explain why some peoples developed more guns, germs, and steel than others. These causes were entirely geographic, he claims.

From the emergence of anatomically modern humans beginning some one hundred thousand years ago until the domestication of agriculture ninety thousand years later, all of our ancestors were hunter-gatherers. Then farming became more profitable some ten thousand years ago thanks to the convergence of several factors, including a decline in wild foods, cyclical climate change rendering food crops more plentiful, and the invention of tools like sickles, baskets, and grinders.

Yet food production did not appear in such cornucopias of the modern world as California, Argentina, Canada, and Australia. Instead, it first began to emerge in the Middle East – wheat, peas, olives, sheep, goats – around 8500 BC. and one thousand years later in China – rice, millet, pigs, and silkworms and five thousand years later still in Mesoamerica – corn, beans, turkeys, and squash. And so it went in several places across the globe, though only a relatively small number of regions independently developed agriculture. For the most part, "founder crops" diffused into other regions. Moreover, many peoples inhabiting regions well suited for agriculture remained hunter-gatherers until recent times. Peoples in areas better endowed with founder crops or those living close by thus began their development much farther on "the path leading toward guns, germs, and steel. The result was a long series of collisions between the haves and have-nots of history."[14]

Diamond accounts for this fateful inequality of outcomes with an observation – profound but upon reflection obvious – and some extraordinary data. From years of research in New Guinea he had seen how the hunter-gatherer natives knew every plant, insect, and animal in their ecosystems. They knew their habits, uses, dangers, and potentialities. If there were any domesticable flora or fauna available, they would know about it. Diamond extrapolates from this observation to the doubtless irrefutable assumption that prehistoric peoples everywhere had intimate knowledge of every living thing in their environment. Unfortunately, however, the vast, vast majority of peoples on our planet did not have access to a wide variety of easily domesticable plants and animals. Many had access to none at all. In fact, "Of the 200,000 wild plant species, only a few thousand are eaten by humans, and just a few hundred of these have been more or less domesticated." Yet few of these are really value crops. No, only a dozen species provide more than 80 percent of all the crops produced annually in the world.[15]

[handwritten: certain places had more domesticable crops]

Most of these dozen grew wild only in a few places, in particular in the Fertile Crescent. In fact, of the 56 most productive grass species (with seeds ten times heavier than the average), 32 were native to the Near East – a comparatively small region – and only six native to all of East Asia, four to Sub-Saharan Africa, and 11 to the vast Americas. Moreover, we have not domesticated a single major new plant in modern times. In other words, the failure to develop crops was generally not because of any lack of botanical knowledge or ingenuity; prehistoric peoples presumably had plenty of both. Nature simply was terribly unfair in how she distributed her bounty across the earth.

This unfairness was even more glaring with fauna. Western Eurasia was also endowed with four big mammal species: the goat, sheep, pig, and cow. Altogether, 13 out of all 14 large herbivorous domesticated mammals made their ancestral homes in Eurasia. The only other one on the planet – the llama and alpaca, two breeds of the same species – grew in South America. Unfortunately, few animals can be domesticated. Carnivores eat too much and are too dangerous. Elephants take too long to grow. Some animals, like cheetahs, do not reproduce in captivity; zebras and others refuse to be herded. Deer tend to panic. Solitary species like cats cannot be herded. Antelope do not have a social hierarchy and therefore are not submissive to leaders or herders. The nutritive advantage enjoyed by peoples able to domesticate large animals was compounded by their use as means of transportation and as military vehicles. Indeed, horses and other draft animals revolutionized transportation and warfare and facilitated human migration and the diffusion of technologies. The final – and most unfair – attribute of the Eurasian peoples conferred on them by their livestock was diseases. When Europeans came to the Americas, their Old World diseases decimated the unprotected natives.

[handwritten: Eurasia had more domesticable livestock]

One other geographic feature that powerfully favored Eurasia was its east–west axis. The Americas run 9,000 miles from north to south but only 3,000 miles east to west at the widest point. Africa's longest axis is also north–south. By contrast, one can travel 8,000 miles from the Pacific to the Atlantic Ocean across Eurasia along an east–west axis (see Map 2.1). In prehistoric and premodern times, it was far easier for animals and humans – bearing and spreading technology and knowledge – to venture along paths within, rather than across, climate zones. Thus, not only did premodern Eurasians enjoy the extraordinary benefits of domesticated plants and animals, they were also more easily able to encounter and learn from each other. The major population centers of the Americas in pre-Columbian times, for example, were linked together by relatively few trade routes, unlike densely interconnected Eurasia. And if McNeill is right that intercultural contacts have been one of the principal causes of human advancement – and he probably is – then this was a big advantage.

[handwritten: wider climate zones in Eurasia favored migration + culture-sharing]

Historically speaking, Eurasia boasted vastly more population than the other continents, another advantage. Diamond argues:

A larger area or population means more potential inventors, more competing societies, more innovations available to adopt – and more pressure

[handwritten: = more population = more chance for growth]

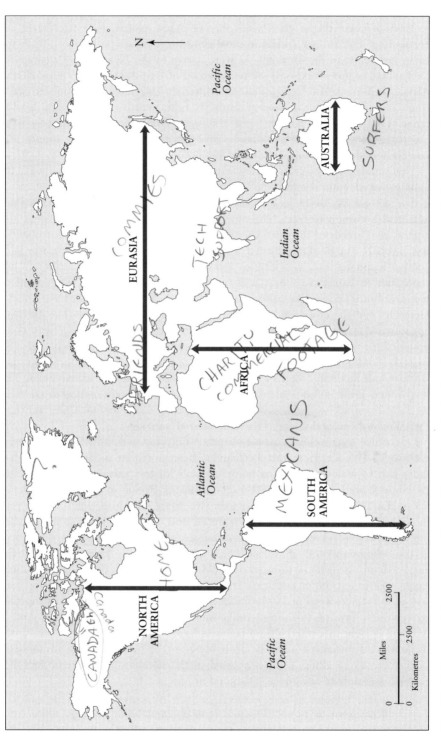

Map 2.1 Major axes of the continents: Goods, ideas, and people circulate far easier along an east–west axis than on a north–south one.

to adopt and retain innovations, because societies failing to do so will tend to be eliminated by competing societies.[16]

Of course, by far the greatest concentration of cultures and peoples have for millennia resided in Eurasia. The Americas, though vast, in premodern times were divided into many separate regions with little communication among them. Those cultures generally could not therefore benefit significantly from each other's breakthroughs.[17] Diamond's main point here is that human beings and their societies are all *on average* highly creative, talented, and innovative. The more heads, the more interconnected they are, the greater the potential for realizing these natural gifts.

Overall, the Eurasian peoples had so many more geographically conditioned advantages that inevitably civilization would first emerge – and then multiply and flourish – there. Other cultures and civilizations would arise on other continents, but unavoidably they would suffer from chronic backwardness in comparison with the Eurasian forerunners.

Diamond also takes a stab at explaining why of all the leading candidates for rapid and powerful advancement only Europe – and not the Fertile Crescent or China or India – broke away startlingly from the rest. The ecology of the Fertile Crescent was fragile, begins Diamond, and over the millennia the societies of the region destroyed much of it. The Europeans and the Chinese were simply very lucky to benefit from more robust environments. China was probably the most technologically innovative country in history and certainly the richest and most powerful from the millennium until 1500. In the early 1400s, they launched giant flotillas of ships 400 feet long and sent them throughout the Indian Ocean. Diamond wonders why the Chinese did not continue onward around the Cape of Good Hope and into the Atlantic Ocean. Their vast wealth and power would have enabled them to colonize Europe nearly a century before Vasco da Gama's tiny ships entered the Indian Ocean. Or why did they not cross the Pacific and discover the Americas? Why, in other words, did "China lose its technological lead to the formerly so backward Europe?[18]

Diamond points to Europe's political fragmentation.

The celebrated Chinese treasure ships were sent out by Imperial edict. When the Emperor decided to end the program, no other authority could step in and keep it alive. By contrast, Christopher Columbus went through four unwilling patrons until the king and queen of Spain agreed to finance his venture. The story was the same, according to Diamond, with subsequent technological advances in Europe: every major innovator eventually managed to find a place or a person willing to sponsor or at least to tolerate the new idea. In this scheme of things, China was overly unified, India was insufficiently unified, and Europe was unified just right.

Again, Diamond believes that geography helps to explain Europe's fragmentation and China's unity. First, Europe's coastline is strongly indented, with many large peninsulas and islands; it has many small rivers and significant mountain

[handwritten marginalia: "docen", "Europe's"]

barriers. China boasts two huge river systems, a relatively smooth coastline, and neither significant islands nor mountain barriers. Thus, for two thousand years China has known enduring centralized authority, whereas Europe has not.

Greater access to waterways made Europe rise (David Cosandey)

Nearly every scholar attempting an explanation of the rise of the West has highlighted geography, though few emphasize it as much as David Cosandey, a theoretical physicist who works in financial risk-management at a Swiss bank. His interesting but not widely known study, "The Secret of the West," has unfortunately not been translated into English.[19] It is worth discussing briefly here because of the significance of one point it makes, which is related to Diamond's argument about Europe's coastline. He begins by stating – in opposition to the "miracle of the West" camp – that nothing about the European peoples as such predisposed them to success: neither religion, nor culture, nor ethnicity. Everything depended instead on a felicitously synergetic political fragmentation made possible by Europe's superabundant access to waterways. By water one could move people and things cheaper, faster, easier, and more freely – with less interference from rulers or other elites. He cites proof that travel by water in the premodern era often cost ten to 40 times less in time and money than by land routes. More means of water transportation also meant more intercultural and commercial communication and exchange.

Cosandey asks what the outline of a continent possessing the greatest advantages for economy growth and fruitful political divisions should look like and then answers his query:

[handwritten marginalia: "complete maritime location"]

> To facilitate commercial activity, the ideal continent should literally "soak" in surrounding waters; that is, it should be "thin," each region lying as close as possible to the sea. Moreover, it should be huge, in order to contain a large population. So as to engender a multiplicity of durable states, it must provide distinct regions, well separated by the sea, while remaining interconnected by isthmuses allowing mutual encounters. To reconcile these somewhat contradictory criteria, it needs a coastal profile that looks contorted, serpentine, with countless peninsulas, gulfs, capes, and islands. We will call this type of coastline an *articulated thalassography*.[20]

The term "thalassography" exists in English and refers to the study of small bodies of water like bays, harbors, and gulfs. Cosandey's point is that a continent or region with the most indented coastline will automatically develop more successfully than other continents or regions. He believes precisely this feature enabled myriad European states to trade thousands of tons of merchandise and raw materials yearly beginning in the high Middle Ages, numbers that increased century by century. A dozen major navigable rivers also provided significant means of communication and transportation and – along with numerous mountain chains – helped define specific geographic regions (see Map 2.2).

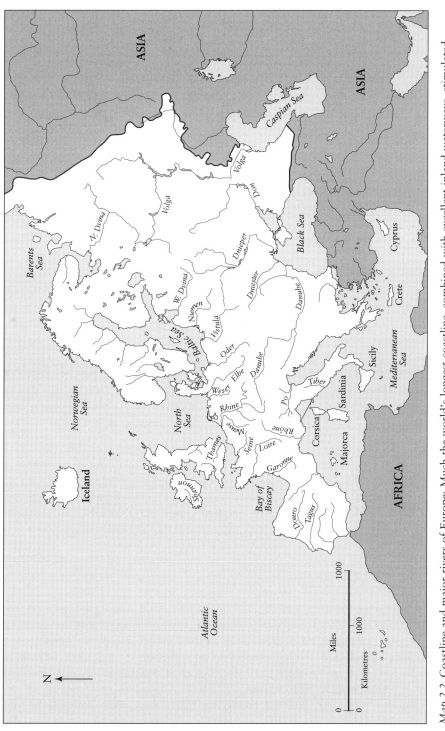

Map 2.2 Coastline and major rivers of Europe: Much the world's longest coastline, combined with excellent inland waterways, stimulated Europe's development.

Cosandey goes on to describe the far less saw-toothed margins of the world's other continents and regions. It was not a coincidence, he argues, that Islam's "Golden Age" coincided with its control over European lands with well-articulated coastlines, like Spain, Sicily, and Greece. The maritime access of India and China was even worse, with ultimately fateful consequences. Japan was the exception that proved the rule. It alone among non-Western countries enjoyed an articulated thalassography, and therefore it alone managed to absorb and successfully deploy Western technology and methods before the twentieth century.

The author provides a plethora of data to undergird his argument. The numbers are remarkable. The percentage of peninsulas and islands as a proportion of overall territory for Western Europe is over 56 percent, but less than 4 percent for India, China, and the Islamic world. One is never farther than 800 kilometers from the sea in Western Europe, as against at least 1,200 in the other three. Finally, the length of Western Europe's coastline dwarfs the others – twice as long as that of the Islamic world (which includes Indonesia), nearly four times longer than India's, and over four times China's.

Cosandey concludes by noting that geomorphology did not predetermine Europe's success or India's "failure" to develop modern science but only made them more probable. Humans act in all sorts of unpredictable ways, yet geography establishes the parameters in which they act, develop institutions, invent, and create social organizations. Thus, it was significant that "Europe is the only continent that boasts both a large territory, welded into one bloc, and an extremely wild and jagged coastline."[21]

Europe's natural endowments favored development (E. L. Jones)

An important earlier work that strongly influenced most geographically oriented studies but that also pushed the boundaries of world history in important directions is *The European Miracle* by the British–Australian economic historian E. L. Jones.[22] Like the scholars discussed in Chapter 1, he considers the rise of the West the central fact of the modern world, but unlike them he attributes that ascension not to inherent cultural features of the European peoples but to geography.

Jones shows that Europe was by far the most favored of continents. He discusses Europe's abundant navigable water routes, and then argues that its location at the far western end of Eurasia was ideal, as well. Europe lay far from most of the great imperial civilizations and was more sheltered than they from incursions of nomadic warriors. It also enjoyed close proximity to the great centers of classical antiquity and to Islam, one of the great Eastern cultures, which had synthesized important technologies and ideas from India and China. Europeans were thus able to receive and adapt achievements from all of history's great civilizations.

Europe, moreover, suffered much less than those other civilizations from natural disasters. Jones deploys abundant statistical evidence for this claim. For example, during the period 1400–1799, thirty Asians died in major earthquakes for every one European.[23] Similarly, flooding and drought were far more devastating in Asia than in Europe. Famines also recurred more frequently and with more disastrous results, nearly one a year in one or more regions of China during the 1,800 years before 1911. These misfortunes sometimes carried away millions of people, like the Bengal famine of 1769–1770, in which ten million died, or one-third of the population. The recurrent famines that struck Europe over the centuries never came close to causing this level of mortality. As for epidemics – like the Black Death – most spread from Asia to Europe because of high population density, irrigation agriculture, human feces used as fertilizer, and a huge concentration of pigs in China. Jones believes that a larger share of population died from pestilence in Europe than Asia, though he admits that further research is needed for a more accurate assessment. Locusts, however, wreaked enormously greater havoc in Asia. He thinks it likely that fires caused less damage in Europe once the peoples there began in the 1200s to build increasingly with stone, brick, and roof tile. Finally, war – that constant scourge – though more frequent in Europe, was more lethal in China, where the Manchu invasion alone killed some 25 million people.

Every disaster cut short lives and demolished capital – buildings, infrastructure, livestock, agricultural improvements – and thus left those still living poorer. If standards of living, technological development, and the advancement of civilization require the accumulation of capital – both human and material – then clearly a region less afflicted by natural and man-made disasters will advance more successfully, all other things being equal.

Crop yields in China and India were naturally far higher than in Europe because of heavy rainfall and longer growing seasons, resulting in huge populations – for centuries the biggest on earth. Even all of Europe taken together could not rival either of them. Of course, geography and climate did not entirely determine this outcome. Surely culture and politics played important roles, though perhaps the cultural bias toward high levels of reproduction in the East stemmed in part from a perceived need to compensate for the inevitable losses from natural disasters. Whatever the causes, population scale and density had significant consequences. Most important, according to Jones, the peoples of India and China could not readily organize themselves, especially when large-scale public works projects were required, like building and manning dykes along flood-prone rivers.

Europe evolved very differently. It was in comparison with the great Asian empires far poorer and for centuries sparsely populated. Much of the continent was covered in forest, with few means of easy communication from place to place, aside from rivers. Jones cites archeologists who try to answer Macfarlane's conundrum: Why did individualism emerge in England? They conclude that small households were more viable than bigger ones. Scattered nuclear families, on this interpretation, settled here and there in isolation and developed the very traits so conspicuous in early modern Europeans – decentralized government, personal autonomy, martial aggressiveness.

The early emergence of the nuclear family in Europe may also explain the adoption in the early modern period of the delaying of marriage. This practice, unique in premodern societies, may have stemmed from the absence of extended families willing and able to supply childcare. Whatever the causes, Jones considers the Europewide policy of keeping the human population low and the animal population high to have been an important factor in the rise of the West. Marrying late made it possible for European families to store up more capital, experience, and skills and therefore to become more productive. They put less effort into reproducing than into producing. For as Jones expresses the idea, Asians "preferred copulation over commodities,"[24] largely in order to ensure against natural disasters and other catastrophes.[25] The results for the Europeans were more creature comforts and a faster accumulation of capital. Again emphasizing environmental conditioning, Jones contends that European peasants would have acted just like Asians in an Asian environment.

Jones goes on to argue that the patchwork quality of Europe's prehistorical landscape persisted with significant consequences:

> Multiple polities had their nutritional and wealth bases in the core-areas, which were separated by mountains, marshlands, or sandy heaths. The extent of land remaining to be cleared as late as the sixteenth century was prodigious. On the modern map the intervening spaces have been cleared, drained, cultivated, and filled up with people, but until the end of pre-industrial times Europe was a succession of population of islands in a sea of forest and heath.[26]

Here Jones is seeking to provide a geographical explanation for the political fragmentation that many scholars emphasize in accounting for the West's rise. As late as the fourteenth century, he notes, Europe was divided into something like a thousand polities, each competing for advantage and collectively pursuing a kaleidoscope of initiatives and experiments in statecraft and in economic life. Empires are more "normal" historically. They can pool far more resources, but because they do not simultaneously seek out best practices in a variety of ways, they are more wasteful of resources. Moreover, a centralized state without threatening neighbors has no incentive to innovate. "State systems" – in which power is delicately balanced among many polities and where ideas and technologies spread quickly – are rare, even miraculous. Europe's enormous geographical diversity meant that many of these states had products others wanted, ultimately stimulating a vibrant intra-continental trade.

Jones investigates one other geographic feature that greatly favored Europe. It was much closer than any other major civilization to the Americas. Moreover, after the first crossing, the Atlantic proved actually less dangerous than some of the waters within the Mediterranean and adjacent seas. Once mariners opened a passage to the New World, the European peoples gained access to extraordinary resources – stupendous mother lodes of precious metals, giant cod, and other single-species fisheries more bounteous than anything in Asia, boreal forests teeming with fur-bearing animals, immense tropical and sub-tropical lands, and vast and abundantly fertile prairies. Suddenly, the territory available to Europeans leaped from 24 to 146 acres per capita – a sixfold increase thanks to what some scholars, including Jones, call "ghost acreage." There was also the "Columbian exchange," most importantly the transplantation of potatoes in Europe and the full range of Old World livestock in the Americas (see Map 2.3);[27] to say nothing of Europeans at home mining deep in the earth for coal – a fuel that powered the Industrial Revolution. In all these ways, Europe – and the wider West – laid the foundations for a powerful economic boom and trading revolution, as they knit all the continents together into one vast market.

Jones refuses to accept the arguments of those who claim that all these advances revealed a kind of exceptional rapaciousness. He points out that the Europeans did not engage in a level of environmental harm never seen before. Asia's terrible history of deforestation and soil erosion completely belies that notion. What was new and unique was Europe's ability to lay hold of – and to put to efficient and powerful uses – an extraordinary ecological bonanza discovered in the New World. "This conjunction of windfall and entrepreneur-ship," he asserted, "happened only once in history."[28] Numerous scholars dispute Jones's interpretation – about which more later.

Jones devotes the final third of his book to the main Asian cultures, in order to suggest why they failed to rise further or keep pace with the West. He provides evidence that only 2 percent of Chinese people worked in occupations other than agriculture as late as the nineteenth century, compared to 15 percent in France, Germany, and Britain as early as the 1300s. Presumably all that talent deployed in higher-order fields in Europe boosted productivity and innovation. It also resulted in a far smaller level of inequality between rich and poor than in the great Asian cultures, as European visitors often noticed. The relatively small better-off classes in China or India stimulated extensive foreign trade in luxuries but nothing like the colossal European commerce in wine, salt, timber, fish, grain, and many other finished products and raw materials. (Again, scholars discussed in Chapter 4 dispute this.)

Europe was a world unto itself, a richly diverse subcontinent united by languages (Latin, Italian, French), culture, religion, and continuous sharing of ideas and technologies. The great Asian states had little in common. From the Ottoman Empire in Western Asia to the Manchu Empire in the East, the great Asian countries were military despotisms. This they had in common, but almost nothing else. They did not share any racial, ethnic, cultural, or religious characteristics. "Asia," writes Jones, "is a collection of subcontinents, themselves divided."[29]

Moreover, unlike in Europe, between the Asian core areas ran not well-defined frontiers but indistinct, often underdeveloped, and continuously contested border zones. Jones is suggesting that Europe's extraordinary diversity and significant unity may have promoted both constant experimentation and competition and cooperation, perhaps something like a "perfect combination." One distinctive feature of Europe was its continuous and intensive adoption of

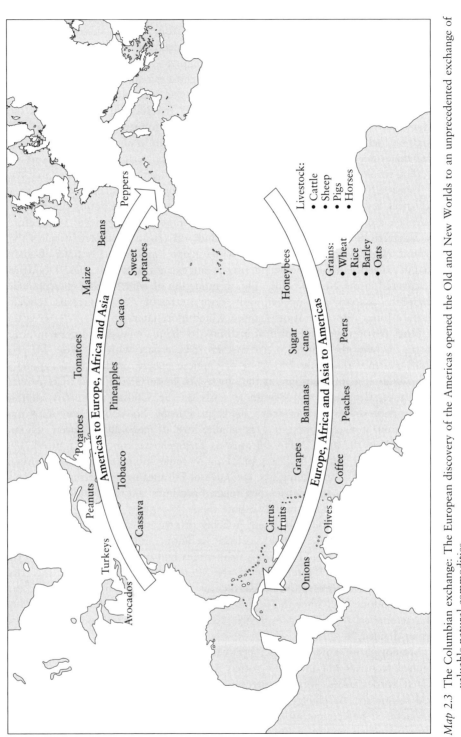

Map 2.3 The Columbian exchange: The European discovery of the Americas opened the Old and New Worlds to an unprecedented exchange of valuable natural commodities.

technical knowledge from other cultures, especially from the great civilizations of Asia. Europe, it is true, was divided into many diverse regions, yet contrary to Asia, they were all united into one community of intellectual and technological innovation whose members avidly and ceaselessly collaborated and learned from each other. The competitive states system itself stimulated efforts to imitate and assimilate all the best available advancements and achievements. Everywhere European thinkers and doers proceeded on the assumption that whatever problem could be tackled in one place would pose no insurmountable challenges anywhere else.[30]

Europe rose on foundations laid by other cultures (Marshall Hodgson)

A colleague of McNeill at the University of Chicago and a noted specialist in Islamic history, Marshall Hodgson (1922–1968), argued that Europe owed its rise to influences from other cultures, in particular the Islamic. For some three thousand years, all significant new technologies and ideas filtered across the Afro-Eurasian landmass at a slow enough pace that many societies could adapt them. All the regions and cultures of this geographical continuum fostered the gradual development and diffusion of civilization. All partook in the achievements of other societies.

> Sheer size of the interconnected zone was important in itself, determining the availability of total human resources at any given time; but still more important was the multiplying of the historical components in Afro-Eurasian development ... . The whole of that expansion had effects greater than any of its parts.[31]

Since no society could break away massively via rapid technological innovation, the major civilizations remained at rough parity.

From time to time, powerful technological and cultural movements swept the interconnected developed world. Among the most important were the Iron Age from 1000 BC and what the German philosopher Karl Jaspers called the "Axial Age" beginning around 500 BC, when nearly all the great philosophical and religious systems emerged. These transformations further defined the major cultures but also involved dramatic mutual influences. Hodgson urges focusing more on these interconnections than on individual civilizations or cultures.

The emergence of Islam both fit into this context and radically transformed it. By the first millennium AD, the people of every major and minor culture of Eurasia believed in the power and persuasiveness of universal religion.

> It was into this cultural setting that Islam erupted, claiming to be the culmination of universal religion, and immediately transforming the balance of political power in the Mediterranean, the Indian Ocean, and the Eurasian steppe, where it set bounds to Chinese influence.[32]

Islam engendered a spiritual ideal that infused throughout nearly every corner of Eurasia and posed an unavoidable and vibrant challenge, both politically and culturally, to greater and lesser civilizations. This challenge involved such compelling traditions and ideals as egalitarianism, cosmopolitanism, universal legality, and respect for the values of urban and mercantile life. Just as important – and what made this global cohesiveness possible – was Islam's omnivorous synthesis of previous intellectual, cultural, institutional, and technological achievements, the first in history. (As noted earlier, McNeill suggested that that distinction belonged to ancient Greece.)

The Islamic challenge provoked a response – rather, a series or wave of responses: the Crusades – that plunged Christendom headlong into an exploration of this great civilization. Hodgson suggests that Islam's biggest influence on Europe consisted in expanding the Western outlook and imagination. Toward the end of the Crusades, Mongol warriors devastated Baghdad and other centers of civilization, in what Hodgson considered a last-ditch effort of nomadic peoples of Eurasia to halt the encroachment of sedentary urban culture from every direction. Ironically, these warriors created favorable conditions for interregional contacts for more than a century, and thus stimulated further development of the sedentary societies. The Black Death of the mid-1300s weakened the Mongol and other Asian empires and enabled the latecomers of the West to seize hold of the wealth of the Orient.[33] Even so, the European Renaissance did not precipitate the modern world; it merely raised Europe's cultural level to that of the other great cultures of Eurasia. In fact, Hodgson rejects McNeill's dating of the "modern" era to 1500. The voyages of discovery did not involve a significant technological advance; all the other great civilizations had similar if not superior technology, he argues.

All the great cultures in history – except Europe – were Asian; therefore, world history should focus on Asia, where the vast majority of human cultural resources first emerged. An emphasis on the Islamic world, in particular, leads one to de-center Europe and the West and to develop a more global, diverse, and interconnected concept of world history. For centuries after its gradual emergence from what scholars used to call the Dark Ages (fifth to eighth centuries), Europe slowly established connections to other cultures throughout Afro-Eurasia. Thanks to these connections and borrowings, Europe accomplished something unprecedented: "the culture of a great new area, not a mere minor extension of one of the older cultural core areas, had drawn abreast of the old core areas in independent fullness of cultural sophistication and originality."[34]

Every major society across the Eurasian landmass slowly and continuously adapted elements from the common stock of ideas and technologies. In various periods, wrote Hodgson,

> Greeks, Indians, and Muslims each had their days of splendor, but in the long run all remained at rough parity. This was because over the millennia any really basic new developments had been gradually adopted everywhere

within the space of four or five centuries – or even more rapidly in such a case as gunpowder weapons.[35]

That is, until Europeans changed the rules of the game through what Hodgson called the "Great Western Transmutation." He meant technical specialization in all areas of society, making it possible to achieve previously unimaginable levels of efficiency leading to the Industrial Revolution. The resultant empowerment shattered all the traditional cultures, including those of Europe. Historical change accelerated, he argued. Major new developments emerged in mere decades instead of centuries. Thus, no culture on earth could complacently rest on its great power status or slowly invent or borrow new technologies.

> Very shortly – at the latest by the end of the seventeenth century – all non-Western people were faced with the problem of coping as outsiders with the new order of civilized life as it was emerging in the Occident.[36]

They could no longer follow their own independent development as they had in the past.

The results of this transformation were catastrophic for all the great world civilizations. Their relative or absolute decline was neither organic nor inevitable. It was brought about because Europe had established a new standard, had raised the bar for technological development. Non-Western peoples simply could not keep up in the face of Europe's technological juggernaut. The Islamic world was still at the apogee of its power in the sixteenth century, yet two centuries later it had fallen dramatically, which by the beginning of the nineteenth century opened the door to massive Western intervention.[37] None of the non-Western cultures, despite the excellence of their achievements, which had enabled them to flourish for hundreds and thousands of years, could withstand the unprecedented power and influence of the radically transformed Occident. There is no point in asking why the Muslims in particular fell behind when the crucial question is how the West catapulted itself so far ahead of the rest of the world.[38]

Even so, there was nothing inevitable about the Western Transmutation. If it was going to happen at all, this acceleration of technical capacity had to occur somewhere. Hodgson credited various favorable geographic features to explain "Why Europe?" But he went on to deny that the Western transmutation could have occurred in one limited area. In the same way that urban, literate societies of the first civilization could never have emerged without the gradual building up of habits, customs, technologies, ideas, and conventions, the great Western Transmutation could not have come about except upon the foundation of advances and discoveries brought to life by peoples and cultures throughout the Eastern Hemisphere.[39]

Hodgson then names specifically Sung China and the major Mediterranean societies. If not for their contributions, he argues, the West could never have risen. In fact, he goes further: Whether the Islamic world resulted in any achievements in modern times is a far less important question "than the quality of its excellence as a vital human response and an irreplaceable human endeavor."[40] In other words, the great non-Western civilizations deserve study and have value both for their obvious influence on the emergence of the modern world and for their intrinsic worth as extraordinarily successful cultures.

Furthermore, Hodgson believed that the Transmutation might have happened elsewhere, for example in Sung China, whose extraordinary technological and cultural advances were cut short by the Mongol invasion. Or indeed, modernity might have emerged first in the Islamic world. In that case, according to Hodgson, there might well have developed, instead of the nation-state, some international corps of super-*ulama*,[41] regulating an industrial society on the basis of some super-sharia code. Universalist and egalitarian principles would have been highly prominent in such a world order.

Hodgson refused to blame the decline of non-Western cultures on Western colonization or imperialism. The modern tragedy of the underdeveloped world emerged out of a general historical context, where Western governments played only a minor role.[42] Many other scholars are not so charitable toward the colonial powers, as Chapter 3 will show.

Conclusion

Scholars considered in this chapter view factors external to Europe as essential to its rise. In particular, most see interconnections and mutual influences among people as paramount in accounting for nearly all human advancement, including Europe's. Most also emphasize the rich foundation of Afro-Eurasian culture, ideas, technologies, and institutions, upon which Europeans built their civilization. Others attribute a leading role to geographical and climatic accidents. Eurasia in general and Europe in particular, they argue, were the most favorably endowed regions of the world. Their main point is that Europe and the West were not uniquely creative or innovative. None of these authors denies that the exploitation of resources and peoples outside Europe contributed to some extent to the West's rise. Neither do they place it at the center of their interpretations, as do the scholars considered in Chapter 3.

Further reading

The rise of world history

Jones, Eric. *Growth Recurring: Economic Change in World History*. Oxford: Clarendon Press, 1988.
Marks, Robert B. *The Origins of the Modern World: A Global and Ecological Narrative*. Lanham, Md.: Rowman & Littlefield, 2002.
Snooks, Graeme Donald. *The Dynamic Society: Exploring the Sources of Global Change*. London: Routledge, 1996.
Stavrianos, L. S. *The World to 1500: A Global History*. Englewood Cliffs, N.J.: Prentice Hall, 1970.

Stearns, Peter N. *Western Civilization in World History*. New York; London: Routledge, 2003.

Van Leeuwen, Arend Th. *Christianity in World History: The Meeting of the Faiths of East and West*. Translated by H. H. Hoskins. New York: Charles Scribner's Sons, 1964.

Geography

Chirot, Daniel. *How Societies Change*. Thousand Oaks, Calif.: Pine Forge Press, 1994.

Crosby, Alfred. *The Columbian Exchange: Biological and Cultural Consequences of 1492*. Westport, Conn.: Greenwood Press, 1972.

Morris, Ian. *Why the West Rules – For Now*. New York: Farrar, Straus & Giroux, 2010.

The interconnectedness of world cultures

Clark, Robert P. *The Global Imperative: An Interpretive History of the Spread of Humankind*. Boulder, Colo.: Westview Press, 1997.

McNeill, J. R. and William H. McNeill. *The Human Web: A Bird's-eye View of World History*. New York: W. W. Norton, 2003.

Phillips, J. R. S. *The Medieval Expansion of Europe*. Oxford; New York: Oxford University Press, 1988.

Thompson, William R. *The Emergence of the Global Political Economy*. London; New York: Routledge, 2000.

Notes

1 William McNeill, *The Rise of the West: A History of the Human Community* (Chicago: University of Chicago Press, 1963).
2 He dedicated the book "To the Community of Scholars Constituting the University of Chicago, 1933–1963."
3 McNeill, *The Rise of the West*, 253.
4 Ibid., 249.
5 Ibid., 480.
6 Ibid., 652.
7 Ibid., 411–412.
8 Ibid., 539.
9 Ibid., 558–559.
10 Ibid., xxviii.
11 Ibid., xxiv.
12 Jared Diamond, *Guns, Germs, and Steel: The Fates of Human Societies* (New York: W. W. Norton, 1997).
13 Ibid., 14.
14 Ibid., 103.
15 Ibid., 132.
16 Ibid., 407.
17 Ibid., 407–408.

18 Ibid., 412.
19 David Cosandey, *Le Secret de l'Occident: Du miracle passé au marasme présent* (Paris: Arléa, 1997).
20 Ibid., 271–272. Italics in the original.
21 Ibid., 314.
22 E. L. Jones, *The European Miracle: Environments, Economies, and Geopolitics in the History of Europe and Asia* (London; New York: Cambridge University Press, 1981).
23 Ibid., 27.
24 Ibid., 15.
25 He also explains the ancient custom of favoring boys the same way: boys are stronger and therefore more able to help rebuild after a catastrophe.
26 Jones, *The European Miracle*, 106.
27 On this world-changing encounter, see Alfred Crosby, *The Columbian Exchange: Biological and Cultural Consequences of 1492* (Westport, Conn.: Greenwood Press, 1972).
28 Ibid., 84.
29 Ibid., 161.
30 Ibid., 45.
31 Marshall G. S. Hodgson, *Rethinking World History: Essays on Europe, Islam, and World History*, ed. Edmund Burke, III (Cambridge: Cambridge University Press, 1993), 19.
32 Ibid., 23.
33 Ibid., 25.
34 Marshall G. S. Hodgson, *The Venture of Islam: Conscience and History in a World Civilization*, vol. 2, *The Expansion of Islam in the Middle Periods* (Chicago: University of Chicago Press, 1974), 334.
35 Hodgson, *The Venture of Islam*, vol. 3, *The Gunpowder Empires and Modern Times*, 200.
36 Ibid.
37 Hodgson, *Rethinking World History*, 125.
38 Ibid., 215, 217.
39 Ibid., 67–68.
40 Ibid., 77.
41 The body of Muslim legal scholars and clergy.
42 Hodgson, *Rethinking World History*, 217.

3   Imperialism and exploitation

In 1916, while World War I was raging across Europe, the Russian Bolshevik leader Vladimir Lenin articulated an explanation of the intense competition among the advanced European countries for economic and political control around the globe. In his refuge in neutral Switzerland, he drew on Marx's theory of surplus value – the idea that capitalists must continuously squeeze more output from available labor just to compete with one another. This idea also held an explanation for the rise of the West, as noted in the Introduction: European entrepreneurs and investors in the early modern period figured out how to extract more and more wealth from the only expandable source of value – labor. Instead of merely exploiting labor to make or do things, one could exploit it to make things capable of making and doing things. Machines and other technology, Marx concluded, consisted in "stored up" capital, or wealth. The amount of wealth one could acquire was thus no longer limited by human reproduction, for example, the number of slaves or serfs born on, or imported to, a plantation or manor. Capitalists could reproduce labor itself in ever more creative forms.

Lenin also carefully read scholarly and journalistic descriptions of the recent territorial expansion of the main European powers in Asia and especially Africa. In *Imperialism, the Highest Stage of Capitalism* (1917), Lenin concluded that in the most advanced economies businesses had achieved maximal efficiencies of scale and scope by creating monopolies and cartels. He argued further that the only way for European capitalists to keep racking up increased profits and surplus value was through the exploitation of developing countries. This exploitation occurred typically by means of investments, the export of capital, the lending of money at interest. In backward countries,

> profits are usually high, for capital is scarce, the price of land is relatively low, wages are low, raw materials are cheap. The possibility of exporting capital is created by the fact that numerous backward countries have been drawn into international capitalist intercourse; main railways have either been built or are being built there, the elementary conditions for industrial development have been created, etc.[1]

The capitalists naturally received a hefty return on investment. Their governments also often obtained diplomatic, economic, or military concessions – for example, access to ports or an agreement to purchase weaponry. Ever-larger industrial firms, backed up by vast networks of banks throughout the developing world, had, Lenin claimed, divided much of the world among themselves.

Although Marx scorned capitalists for exploiting the weaker elements of society – including overseas colonies – he considered this tendency progressive. After all, capitalist efficiency led to the greatest explosion of wealth-creation in history, and the accumulated riches would ultimately enable the poorest class of the developed countries to bring about socialism, a phenomenally equitable economic system, in his view. Similarly, Lenin had nothing but contempt for the warring imperialist powers. Yet he too believed that their frenzied struggles for supremacy were leading unavoidably toward a higher stage of social development.

Reverse Robin Hood economics

Whereas Marx and Lenin focused on the causes of capitalist exploitation and imperialism, other theorists beginning in the 1960s developed explanations for the persistent backwardness and poverty of developing countries. They became and remained poor, according to these theories, because of colonial and imperialist policies rendering them dependent and unable to reach their full potential. On the contrary, a large share of their wealth and resources was – and still is – diverted to the most advanced economies. In other words, the developing countries are poor precisely insofar as exploiting them has made the developed countries rich.

The West became rich by keeping others poor (Andre Gunder Frank)

Among the first and most well-known "dependency theorists" was Andre Gunder Frank (1929–2005), a German–American economist who taught all the social sciences at 15 different universities on three continents in a half-dozen languages. A stream of books and articles commencing in 1967 propounded the idea that underdevelopment in the "Third World" is caused not by any internal failings or antiquated institutions or a lack of resources and capital of these countries but rather was and is "in large part the historical product of past and continuing economic and other relations between the satellite underdeveloped and the now developed metropolitan countries."[2] The rise of international capitalism created a global division of labor enabling the "metropolitan" countries to siphon surplus wealth from their "satellites" (colonies). This process enriched the colonizers but condemned the colonies to a status of "underdevelopment," meaning the inability to develop successfully or ever to catch up with the developed world.

The mechanisms of exploitation replicated themselves within those satellite countries, as an indigenous exploitative elite consigned provincial regions to second- or third-class status. These elites thus enriched themselves at the expense of the majority of their people, yet acted wittingly or unwittingly as agents of the main colonizers back in Europe or America, since most of these countries' wealth ended up there. Frank furthermore rejects the idea of so-called "dual" economies – pre-capitalist and capitalist regions existing together – in the developing world. On the contrary, even the remotest hinterlands of the poorest countries, in which the majority of people live at a subsistence level, are integrated into the capitalist economy and remain poor precisely for this reason. Indeed, a chain of dependency and exploitation links the richest centers of the capitalist world and the most isolated rural areas, with the vast majority of benefits flowing up the chain. If the capitalist world is the "ultimate enemy" of humanity in his perspective, then the elites of underdeveloped countries are the "immediate enemy" of his book's subtitle.

Frank conducted detailed research specifically on Chile and Brazil, which in the late 1960s were both highly dependent and relatively underdeveloped countries, though today are Latin America's most successful economies. Frank presents as a counterexample Japan, the modern world's most successful non-Western country, which he believed owed its success to never having been a satellite of the West. In contrast, those countries or regions that furnished to the capitalist centers in colonial times the most fabulous flows of treasure – for example, sugar from the West Indies or silver from highland Peru and Bolivia – became the most destitute and underdeveloped of all.

Subsequently many other writers built upon these Marxist interpretations to explain further why some countries became so rich, while others remained so poor.

African labor fueled the rise of the West (Joseph E. Inikori)

Another line of argument, going back to the eighteenth century and echoed in the nineteenth by Karl Marx, has sought to explain the Industrial Revolution in Britain by pointing to the fabulous profits of the slave trade and the colonial plantation economies in the New World. The most famous early such scholarly exposition was put forward by Eric Williams (1911–1981), who went on to serve as prime minister of Trinidad and Tobago, in his 1944 study *Capitalism and Slavery*. The latest and most powerful contribution to this burgeoning literature is by Joseph E. Inikori, a professor of economic history at the University of Rochester, originally from Nigeria.

In *Africans and the Industrial Revolution in England*,[3] he deploys vast erudition and impressively wide-ranging research to demonstrate that foreign trade played a central role in Britain's industrialization and that Africans contributed far more than previously acknowledged to this process. He does not deny the importance of Britain's population growth and vibrant domestic market to the increase in economic demand and the accumulation of capital available for industrial enterprise. Nor does he slight the role of technological innovation.[4] Rather, Inikori argues that foreign demand for manufactured goods also stimulated the dramatic series of breakthroughs achieved by dozens and even hundreds of inventors and entrepreneurs who built the first modern industrial centers in the English Midlands and North and that African labor, the slave trade, and related economic inputs throughout the Atlantic economy were necessary for the successful completion of the industrialization process.

Inikori's elaborate argumentation and evidence may be summarized in several paragraphs. First, he claims that the Industrial Revolution made it possible for England's entrepreneurs and merchants to follow a policy of "import substitution" – producing goods at home to replace imports – the first successful case in history. Moreover, this process occurred almost entirely through the domestic production of capital goods – the machines and raw materials for industrial manufacture. By increasing wages, it also stimulated further demand for manufactured goods, resulting in a virtuous cycle of development.

Yet a key precondition for this development was the prior expansion of foreign trade: a high level of imports had to precede import substitution. In fact, until the eighteenth century, Britain manufactured few products on a large scale aside from woollen textiles. Inikori shows that from 1663 to 1724, the provision of services related to overseas trade grew much faster than either the export of manufactured goods or investments in industry. This suggests that overseas trade was stimulating the economy of Britain more than any other factor. Thus it seems reasonable to suppose that foreign trade induced in large part the extraordinary series of technological advancements revolutionizing the manufacture of textiles beginning with the "flying shuttle" in 1734. In fact, the handful of regions that drove industrialization in Britain – the West Midlands, Lancashire, and the West Riding of Yorkshire – were linked more directly with overseas markets than with the rest of the country, including London and the prosperous southeast, and grew faster in wealth. And the fastest growing markets for British goods – at first iron products and then textiles – were the British Caribbean, West Africa, and North America. Significantly, the above-mentioned English regions had previously been far poorer than the southeast, which itself declined in relative terms during the industrialization process. Lancashire, England's first main driver of industrialization, for example, parlayed its cheap labor and the great port of Liverpool into powerful advantages (see Map 3.1). Since it was far cheaper to transport goods by sea, these industrializing regions tended to trade abroad more than within Britain, at least until the development of railroads.

Historians have mostly agreed for decades that the Industrial Revolution occurred in England thanks to a series of technological breakthroughs. They have disagreed, however, about what caused them. Some contend that a creative process of inventiveness, linked closely with scientific discoveries, made them possible. Others emphasize market demand. Most of the latter focus on domestic trade, though some, including Inikori, believe foreign trade inspired tinkerers and entrepreneurs to feverishly invest time and energy in discovering methods of production to enable them to outproduce and outsell their competitors. Inikori notes that they were highly practical problem solvers. Abraham

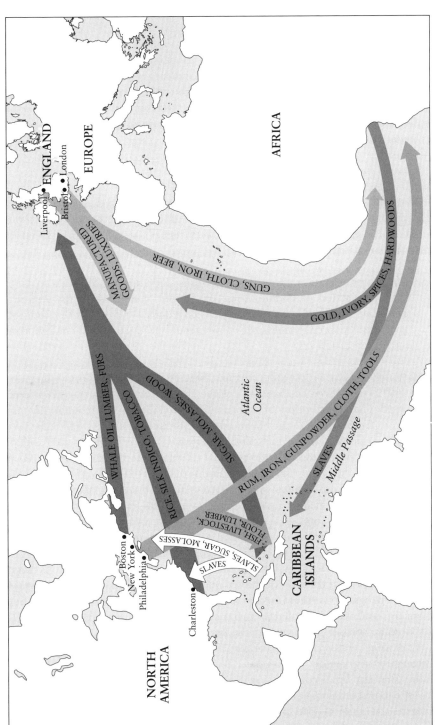

Map 3.1 Triangular trade: Great Britain dominated the "triangular trade" between Europe, Africa, and the Americas in the eighteenth century.

Darby, for instance, devised his revolutionary method for coke-fired iron smelting, in order to produce his cast-iron pots more cost-effectively. Market forces similarly drove Matthew Boulton to develop his world-transforming steam engine. It was indeed precisely entrepreneurs in the economically fastest growing regions of Britain with the greatest need for mechanical devices, like the West Midlands, who proved the most inventive in the country.[5]

But what sources of trade were preponderant – domestic or foreign? Inikori's evidence points to overseas trade. And the main targets of this trade during most of the eighteenth century were Western Africa and the Americas, which consumed just over 70 percent of English manufactured goods, as compared to under 30 percent exported to East India and Europe.

If the Industrial Revolution was driven in England by foreign trade and in particular trade within the Atlantic world, what caused the rapid expansion of commerce in this region from 1500 to 1850? Inikori's research suggests that the main factor was the

> forced specialization of enslaved Africans and their descendants in large-scale production of commodities for Atlantic commerce in the Americas at a time when demographic, socio-economic, and political conditions generally favored small-scale subsistence production by independent, uncoerced producers.[6]

African labor apparently produced some 40 to 50 percent of exports – including gold and silver – from the Spanish colonies in the sixteenth through eighteenth centuries. The contribution of African labor to mining and commodity production in Brazil and the Caribbean during the same period was far higher – at or near 100 percent – and in British America, somewhere in between. Inikori provides data suggesting that the share of all export commodities produced by Africans throughout the Americas increased steadily from 54 percent in the first half of the sixteenth century to 83 percent in the first half of the eighteenth century, but down to only around 69 percent by the middle of the nineteenth century. Thus, he notes in a striking turn of phrase: "In matters of export production for Atlantic commerce, the Americas were indeed an extension of Africa in 1650–1850."[7] Most of these exports ended up in Europe, powerfully stimulating economic activity, especially the gold and silver bullion, which sparked the price revolution of the sixteenth century and enabled the Europeans to consume vast quantities of Asian products. Tumbling prices for commodities from the Americas like tobacco and sugar, moreover, turned them into staples for ordinary people in Europe by the later 1600s.

Exploiting African labor gave slave-owners an edge over their competitors throughout the region and beyond. The British benefited from this advantage more than any other colonial power; their colonies produced roughly one-third of all export commodities in the Americas by 1780, one-half over the following two decades, and over 61 percent by the mid-nineteenth century. Furthermore, thanks to favorable treaties signed with Portugal and Spain, Brazil and, even to some extent, the Spanish colonies in the Americas were, "for purposes of British Atlantic commerce, part of British America."[8] Similarly, even entrepreneurs in the New England colonies took advantage of the African-stimulated Atlantic commerce by developing a formidable shipping capacity – enabling investors in the region to accumulate sufficient capital to fund the New World's first industrialization drive in the early decades of the nineteenth century.

The slave trade, and financial and transportation services allied with it, contributed mightily to the wealth generated in England and its North American colonies. From wide-ranging evidence and meticulous calculations, the author concludes that the British dominated the slave trade in the eighteenth century, until Parliament abolished the practice in 1807, being responsible for the transportation of nearly 4 million people from Africa, in large part to non-British America, the largest share in this grim enterprise of any colonizing power.

By extension, Inikori argues that the slave trade contributed powerfully to the development of English shipping and ship-building, which in turn constituted prime factors in the unfolding of industrialization. He provides statistics showing that English-owned shipping used for foreign trade with Western Africa and the Americas accounted for roughly 30 percent of all English-owned ships in 1663 but rose steadily to nearly 60 percent in 1836. Since a large proportion of Europe-bound ships involved cargos being re-exported to or from the Americas, the actual percentage of English shipping within the Atlantic world must in fact have been still greater. Moreover, the official numbers do not include the transportation of African slaves. Nor do they reflect the much more frequent and costly repair and replacement of ships in the Atlantic trade, subjected as they were to far greater dangers of piracy and shipwreck than those sailing in and around European waters. In other words, although precise data are impossible to track down, trade with Africa and the Americas probably stimulated growth in English shipping far more than all the other trade destinations combined.

Not surprisingly, given the volume of trade involved, financial services related to commerce throughout the Atlantic world also dwarfed those related to other commercial activities. In regard to the marine insurance industry, statistics Inikori has compiled suggest that the value of insurance premiums disbursed for the entire Atlantic shipping commerce, including the slave trade, constituted at least two-thirds of the entire insurance industry in premiums earned in late eighteenth-century Britain.[9]

He tells a similar story about the development of banking, the discounting of bills of exchange, and stock-trading in Great Britain. These elements of financial evolution were crucial for the process of industrialization because they served to channel the immense capital resources of the country toward profitable investments, particularly industrial enterprises, while also boosting the overall national income and creating more high-paying employment opportunities. Moreover, the selection and purchase of slaves in Africa, followed by lengthy periods of upkeep at trading posts and even lengthier transport across the Atlantic, sale in the New World (often on credit), and remittance of part of the proceeds back to England were huge operations, requiring investors – and their creditors – to wait patiently for many, many months. Only a highly sophisticated network of credit institutions could sustain such a huge constellation of intercontinental trading operations over such long periods of time. Since no previous commercial ventures – originating in England or anywhere else – had ever attained the scale of the eighteenth-century slave trade and plantation economies, doubtless only they could have stimulated that network's emergence.

complex institutions

investments

Inikori then assesses the contribution of raw materials produced by Africans and their descendants in both Africa and the Americas to the process of industrialization in England from the eighteenth to the mid-nineteenth century. Statistics he deploys indicate that from the late eighteenth century raw materials coming from those continents dwarfed those from all other regions of the world except Northern Europe, and from the early nineteenth century constituted close to half of all imported raw materials used in British manufacturing. More important, the driving sector of the industrialization process in England, the cotton textile industry, "depended for its raw material almost totally on African peoples in the Americas from its formative years in the eighteenth century to its maturity in the middle of the nineteenth."[10] Imports from West Africa of palm oil for lubricating machinery and substances used to make dyestuffs formed a small but crucial part of overall industrial imports to England.

export consumers

Finally, Inikori demonstrates that in the later 1700s and the first half of the 1800s Africans in both Africa and the Americas consumed a large proportion of England's woollen exports, a majority of its cotton cloth exports, and the vast majority of its linen exports. Moreover, given the central place that cotton textile production occupied in the industrialization of Britain, according to the author, "technological development in the British cotton industry was driven by overseas trade, in particular Atlantic commerce, and not the other way around."[11] Inikori deploys additional evidence showing that the majority of British metal product exports in the eighteenth and the first half of the nineteenth centuries made their way to West Africa and the Americas as well.

Taking into account all of the evidence he has deployed in regard to commercial relations between Britain and overseas trading partners in West Africa and the Americas, Inikori argues that more than anything else the development of Atlantic commerce made possible the industrialization of England. Yet since without the labor of Africans and their posterity the early-modern growth of Atlantic commerce would have been impossible, he considers the conclusion inescapable that this labor "made an invaluable contribution to the Industrial Revolution in England."[12] Naturally, it is impossible to quantify or even adequately qualify this contribution, but the author suggests it was very large.

Eurasian flora and fauna drove Europe's rise (Alfred Crosby)

Other scholars have argued that the European rise to world hegemony stemmed less from intentional efforts to exploit and dominate than from historical accidents. Historian Alfred Crosby recounts the story of how European conquerors wiped out native populations in several huge, underdeveloped territories – the Americas and Australia, in particular – and then migrated by the tens of millions to these lands and built up thriving societies. A half-dozen of these countries today grow more than 30 percent of all agricultural products sold on world markets.

How did these Neo-Europes, as Crosby calls them, rise to such heights of wealth and material success? He believes the answer is partly "biogeographical." Five hundred years ago, the world's biggest exporters today of what were originally Eurasian crops and livestock had no wheat or goats or barley or cattle or pigs or rye or sheep. He then goes on to admit the possibility that the Europeans won out thanks to guns, germs, and steel or perhaps because of their ability to work together or their intense determination, "but what in heaven's name is the reason the sun never sets on the empire of the dandelion?"[13]

As Jared Diamond argued in his bestseller discussed in Chapter 2, most of today's indispensable domesticated plants and animals came from the Middle East and nearly all of them from Eurasia. According to Crosby, these living things – and many, many others, including all sorts of weeds – basically took the New World, Australia, and New Zealand by storm, when the European explorers and conquerors set out and took these lands by the sword.

The European migrants carried with them on their voyages powerful means of transport like horses and oxen, renewable food-producers like hens and cows, all kinds of disease-carriers like rats and fleas, and a vast array of deadly microbes. Europeans happened to be among the few peoples able to tolerate milk after infancy. What a boon the goat therefore proved to mariners and explorers who could take with them reliable suppliers of nutrition into the most unfamiliar climes.

The first European conquerors mostly failed in their efforts, however. Beginning a thousand years ago, Norse wanderers settled in Greenland and what is now eastern Newfoundland, and Crusaders established kingdoms in the Near East. All of these settlements perished, though for different reasons. The former's climate proved inhospitable after the Medieval Warm Period, while the indigenous peoples of the latter had thrived for generations amid ecosystems of flora, fauna, and diseases as advantageous as had the Europeans in their far end of Eurasia – more so, in fact, because native diseases of the Near East proved more lethal than anything the Crusaders carried with them.

The next waves of European migration, beginning in the Age of Discovery, proved vastly different. The first wave broke against the Atlantic islands close to Portugal – the Azores, Madeira, and the Canaries. Their climate was temperate, like Europe's. At first, passing ships "seeded" them with livestock: sheep, cattle, and goats, which multiplied rapidly, providing food to the settlers who came later. Only the Canaries were inhabited when the Europeans arrived. The natives, the Guanches, were fierce fighters but ultimately succumbed to the far more numerous and technologically advanced invaders. As Crosby notes,

The rude process of European conquest began in 1402, a date we might take as the birth year of modern European imperialism. The Moors still held southern Iberia, and the Ottoman Turks were advancing in the Balkans, but Europe had begun to march – or rather to sail – to world hegemony.[14]

Like all human migrants, the European settlers traveled with a portion of their biota (the organisms that populated their local ecosystems). Where it prospered, according to Crosby, the settlers themselves multiplied. In particular, horses and Eurasian diseases facilitated the Europeans' success.

European explorers and conquerors gained valuable experience from these initial encounters. According to Crosby, early modern European imperialism was born in these islands of the Eastern Atlantic, which taught the colonizers powerful lessons that shaped the course of world history. First, they learned that Europeans, along with their flora and fauna, could thrive in places previously devoid of them. Second, native peoples of such lands, no matter how numerous and warlike, could not withstand the European onslaught, however much their original conditions might be favorable. Third, even though the natives should perish from contact with the conquerors, stronger laborers could be brought in from Europe and Africa.[15] In other words, these petty conquerors had acquired the blueprint for the most extraordinary adventures of conquest the world had ever seen.

Three things made all the difference for the European conquerors, argues Crosby. First, they flourished only in foreign lands with a climate and geography roughly similar to theirs. Second, these lands should not be situated on the Afro-Eurasian landmass where diseases and predators had evolved to prey on Europeans and their biota. Third, the conquered peoples should lack the powerful suite of livestock available automatically to Europeans, like horses and cattle, which Crosby considers a greater advantage than advanced military technology. It was, in other words, not just native peoples who were vulnerable to the European onslaught – so were native plants and animals, and for similar reasons. Europeans had developed on the biggest and most populous continent and therefore had gained access, thanks to thousands of years of mutual contacts, to the largest array of technology and innovations – far beyond the capabilities of native peoples outside Eurasia. Similarly, the flora and fauna that had evolved in Eurasia had evolved capacities for survival beyond those of temperate climes on the other continents.

Vast numbers of crops, weeds, diseases, birds, livestock, and parasitic animals from Eurasia, and especially from Europe, ended up flourishing in the Neo-Europes. By contrast, very few living things succeeded in reverse. Crosby notes that nineteenth-century scientists expected a relatively equal exchange of weeds among Europe and its colonies: "Old World crabgrass for American ragweed, for instance." Yet in practice a vast number of weeds from the Old World prospered in the New World, while almost none made the transition in reverse, aside from those lovingly maintained in places like the Royal Botanic

Gardens, Kew, in South West London.[16] Why this should have been so remains something of a scientific mystery, though Crosby suggests that European weeds thrived in the Neo-Europes because the colonizers – and especially the animals they introduced – tore up the environment and thus opened virgin spaces for them to invade.

Much the same can be said of the Old World fauna. Crosby asserts that the Europeans' fast-reproducing entourage of beasts – from cats and rats to dogs and horses – were able to radically alter continental environments more speedily than any machines known to man. Pigs, for example, can eat practically anything and so can be of especial help to colonists during the difficult early stages of settlement. In some environments, like the Argentine pampas, cattle multiplied with such abandon that in a century and a half or so (down to 1700) there may have been 48 million roaming wild. One can tell a similar story of horses on the pampas and in North America. Actually, European livestock thrived vastly better in the Neo-Europes than back in their home countries. What a boon to the settlers. Less welcome, of course, were unwanted stowaways like rats, but they flourished too. As with weeds, however, hardly any New World animals prospered in Europe – only the gray squirrel and the American muskrat, and on a far lesser scale.

The same was true of infectious diseases. Whereas the European explorers and colonists unwittingly brought with them dozens of often deadly microorganisms to the New World and Australia, the latter had developed few deadly pathogens dangerous to people in the Old World. Yet again, the one-sidedness of the exchange overwhelmingly disadvantaged "the peoples whose ancestral homes were on the losing side of the seams of Pangaea [i.e. the oceans]."[17] Tragically, this disparity resulted in the premature death of tens of millions of native peoples in the Neo-Europes.

The totality of this exchange – plants, animals, maladies – was catastrophic for the indigenous peoples. Together with the colonizers themselves, they "made a revolution more extreme than any seen on this planet since the extinctions at the end of the Pleistocene, and the losers could imagine its reversal only by means of a colossal miracle."[18]

Crosby hastens to add that human migrants have always brought with them flora and fauna that have tended to displace local varieties and have always wrought havoc wherever they went. One theory, put forward by Paul S. Martin, that Crosby seems to favor holds that Stone Age hunters at the end of the last Ice Age migrated to the Americas and relatively quickly (in a few thousand years at most) wiped out most large mammals, following a pattern that had struck Australia some forty thousand years ago and Eurasia earlier still. According to this theory, the European conquerors would appear to be only the last in a long line of destructive migratory predators. In fact, Crosby thinks, metaphorically, of the two waves of migrants as "two waves of invaders of the same species, the first acting as the shock troops, clearing the way for the second wave, with its more complicated economies and greater numbers."[19]

Conceptual tools facilitated European imperialism (John Weaver)

The European settlers' more sophisticated culture and conceptualizations also contributed to their successful establishment of colonies. Building on Crosby's idea of Neo-Europes, John Weaver, a Canadian professor of history at McMaster University in Hamilton, Ontario, tells the story of how European settlers seized, purchased, stole, and finagled land from native peoples throughout the main settler societies. The desire for land resulted in frequent collisions between farmers and ranchers, settlers and native peoples, government officials and speculators. As Weaver explains,

> the extraction of wealth from frontiers benefitted from a tension, remarkable and fateful, between defiant private initiatives and the ordered, state-backed certainties of property rights.[20]

Property rights, though largely unknown among the indigenous peoples, were central to the Europeans' self-understanding. Highly developed European legal conceptions undergirded them. According to Weaver,

> In many of the attitudes that underpinned the long, widespread land rush, it is possible to detect the heritage of an aggressive will to possess and alter land that flourished first in England. Planted earliest and strongest in British settlement colonies, this spirit propelled innovations in organizing the material world into tidy assets, elbowed aside indigenous peoples, fostered rule-breaking aggression, led to debates about the distribution of land to small-holders, and helped found today's preoccupation with property rights.[21]

Most important, property rights made it possible to transform land and other natural resources into objects to buy and sell – in other words, commodities.

Government officials of the advanced European societies and their colonizing settlers shared a belief that land and natural resources existed for developing and exploiting. "Improvement or betterment" of the land, argues Weaver,

> is linked to landhunting, squatting, and speculation; often it was also the basis for government acquisition of land from indigenous people and a principle guiding how governments reallocated it. Improvement in a broad sense was common ground for informal and formal processes of occupation. To improve the land meant to apply labor and capital, so as to boost the land's carrying capacity and hence its market value.[22]

In the rush to acquire and make use of the vast natural resources of the British settler colonies, many of the colonizers believed that "virgin" land should go to those best able to make it flourish.

Unfortunately, the native peoples lacked the abundant and diverse domesticable plants and animals available to the inhabitants of the Old World, who mistakenly tended to view most of them as slackers incapable of doing justice to the extraordinary natural resources they happened to live on and among. According to Weaver:

> Ignored in this rationalistic – but mistaken – understanding was the fact that for many indigenous people land was embedded in social arrangements, sometimes through complicated overlapping entitlements to use. Land formations, moreover, often abided in myths and belief systems.[23]

By contrast, especially in North America, the European settlers who flooded the storied pioneer routes like the Oregon Trail conceived of land mostly as a source of livelihood, though in many cases they also developed a sense of ancestral pride. Above all, settlers competed with each other and with first peoples through a variety of means to lay claim to what gradually became a foundation block of the settler societies (what Crosby calls "Neo-Europes").

Government officials in the settler societies nearly always sought to regularize and smooth transactions, ensure the adherence to legal norms, keep meticulous records of title, guarantee something like the fair treatment of native peoples, assert national sovereignty over vast expanses of land, and adjudicate among competing interests. During the nineteenth century, these governments developed technologies and institutions – land offices, public auctions, grid systems, public registries, trig surveys, and improved mortgage law – that dramatically lowered the transaction costs of land acquisitions and sales. Deals that had once taken weeks to complete now took only a half-hour. In the fever and haste of settlement, however, the finer points of civilization and the rule of law were often lost, as "landhunters, grazers, and squatters" discovered and exploited legal loopholes and "by the thousands executed common moves that advanced private property rights in the face of governments' hostility, caution, overwork, and sluggishness."[24] Then, in the second half of the nineteenth century, the settler governments threw their weight almost wholly on the side of "improvement," as they distributed millions of acres through homestead legislation and pushed first peoples into smaller and smaller enclaves.

The way Weaver tells the story, no underlying system or guiding force directed the "great land rush." It was rather the chaotic result of dozens of competing interests pursued by millions of independent actors. The outcome was imperfect, often exploitative, frequently unfair, but no deeper meaning can be discerned beneath the anarchic surface.

A global division of labor centered on the West explains its rise (Immanuel Wallerstein)

Other scholars, most notably Immanuel Wallerstein, have interpreted the rise of the West as a function of exploitation and imperialism not specifically of one or the other continent but rather as a worldwide *system* of plunder. A celebrated sociologist with expertise on contemporary Africa, he found his niche during an international youth congress in Dakar, Senegal, in 1952. As he later wrote,

> I credit my African studies with opening my eyes both to the burning political issues of the contemporary world and to the scholarly questions of how to analyze the history of the modern world-system. It was Africa that was responsible for challenging the more stultifying parts of my education.[25]

He has been showered with honors from his profession and has traveled to "at least three-quarters of the countries on each of the continents: Europe, Asia, Africa, Latin America and the Caribbean, many of them repeatedly." Such abundant experiences of people and their lives, has had, he states, "enormous influence on my scholarship."[26] The key aspect of the theory, for which he drew inspiration from Marxist analysis, is that the main unit of historical analysis was not empires or nation-states or states of any kind, but interconnected systems of historically evolving cultures and economies and societies. From the birth of civilization ten thousand years ago, they evolved here and there in earlier times into self-contained mini-systems and, less frequently and later, into world-empires and, later still, into more fully integrated world-economies. Time and again these more complex systems collapsed or absorbed one another. "Around 1500," however, he argues,

> One such world economy managed to escape this fate. For reasons that need to be explained, the "modern world-system" was born out of the consolidation of a world economy. Hence it had time to achieve its full development as a capitalist system. By *its* inner logic, this capitalist world economy had expanded to cover the entire globe, absorbing in the process all existing mini-systems and world empires. And by the late nineteenth century, for the first time ever, there existed only one historical system on the globe. We are still in that situation today.[27]

The emergence of capitalism thus enabled Europe to rise and to dominate the modern world.

"When scholars claim not to be involved in politics," Wallerstein argues, "they are simply endorsing passively whatever is the established situation and structures in which they are embedded."[28] Like Frank, therefore, he considers his scholarship a contribution to political action and as such an intellectual responsibility. "World-systems analysis," he writes "was born as a moral, and in its widest sense, political, protest."[29] Like Frank, he developed a highly formal social–scientific model, but like Inikori he aimed to found his world systems theory on exhaustive historical research.

The mini-systems Wallerstein posited had a division of labor but a single cultural matrix. They existed among simple agricultural or tribal societies without any relationship to larger entities. They ceased to be self-contained entities as soon as they became tributaries of larger polities, and in general they no longer exist anywhere on the planet. Over time, world systems began to emerge, each with a single division of labor and multiple cultural patterns. Those with a single political system Wallerstein calls world-empires, and those without one he calls world-economies. The great world-empires of the past – Egypt, China, Rome – developed from unstable world-economies and lived from tribute collection and only to a small degree from commerce. "It was only," he argues,

> with the emergence of the modern world-economy in sixteenth-century Europe that we saw the full development and economic predominance of market trade. This was the system called capitalism. Capitalism and a world-economy (that is, a single division of labor but multiple polities and cultures) are obverse sides of the same coin. One does not cause the other. We are merely defining the same indivisible phenomenon by different characteristics.[30]

In a highly influential multivolume work entitled *The Modern World-System* (1974–2011; four volumes so far, six projected), Wallerstein investigates and explains why the specific European world-economy evolved not into a redistributive world-empire but into the capitalist world-economy that still dominates the planet.

He opens the first volume with a succinct presentation of the basic problem: a stupendously original development in Europe.

> In the late fifteenth and early sixteenth century, there came into existence what we may call a European world-economy. It was not an Empire, yet it was as spacious as a grand empire and shared some features with it. But it was different, and new. It was a kind of social system the world has not really known before and which is a distinctive feature of the modern world-system. It is an economic but not a political entity, unlike empires, city-states, and nation-states. In fact, it precisely encompasses within its bounds (it is hard to speak of boundaries) empires, city-states, and the emerging "nation-state." It is a "world" system, not because it encompasses the whole world, but because it is larger than any juridically defined political unit. And it is a "world-economy" because the basic linkage between the parts of the system is economic ... Europe was not the only world-economy at the time. There were others. But Europe alone embarked on the path of capitalist development which enabled it to outstrip these others.[31]

In other words, capitalism, which enabled Europe's elites to extract previously unimaginably big surpluses from the rest of the population, explains the rise of the West.

How did capitalism emerge? Wallerstein argues that the feudal system of exploitation began to break down in the fourteenth century for a constellation of reasons – agricultural technology failed to keep pace with population growth, the tax burdens on agricultural producers became unbearable, the climate worsened, and the Black Death struck. When the population contracted severely, the feudal lords leased out some land to better-off peasants and consolidated other holdings. These new arrangements led to increased efficiencies and bigger surpluses that found their way to market. Yet other factors had to come into play for a more market-oriented economic system to evolve into a world-economy. First, the European world system had to expand, which of course it did during the Age of Discovery. Second, labor productivity needed to increase, which specialization, slave-based plantations, and a labor market ensured. Finally, centralized states capable of promoting the interests of business were required. And indeed such states emerged and conducted themselves in precisely that way, according to Wallerstein, during the early modern period.

Portuguese mariners embarked on their expansion into the Atlantic in pursuit not only of gold and spices, but of fish and lands in which to produce sugar, in other words for food, and of labor to work the land. And the pioneers of overseas conquest were often younger aristocratic sons lacking estates and seeking glory. Obviously the great nutritional sources discovered in the Americas dramatically boosted European standards of living, and not only for the rich. Likewise, the huge influx of precious metals was essential for the development of capitalism.

By the end of the 1500s, a European world-economy linked together a vast region from the British Isles to central Europe and from the Baltic to the Iberian Peninsula, as well as enormous territories in the New World, from New Spain (Mexico) to Chile and from the isthmus of Panama to the Antilles and Brazil (see Map 3.2). Commercial relations within this world-economy accelerated and intensified steadily, as did a gradual division and rationalization of labor. Workers in Northwestern Europe became the most productive and highly paid. They produced manufactured goods from raw materials delivered from less developed regions, like Eastern Europe and the Americas. In Wallerstein's terminology, Northwestern Europe (and the more developed parts of southern Europe) became the core of the world system, to which lesser developed semi-peripheries in Eastern and southern Europe supplied raw materials, foodstuffs, and above all cheap, unskilled labor. Both of these regions, especially the core, were served by still lesser developed regions – the periphery: the Americas, the Atlantic islands, outposts along the African coast, and in time, further-flung territories.

This system involved a much greater diversity of dominant and subordinate relationships than the tripartite division would suggest in itself. Wallerstein writes,

> Thus, concretely, in the sixteenth century, there was the differential of the core of the European world-economy versus its peripheral areas, within the European core between states, within states between regions and strata, within regions between city and country, and ultimately within more local units.[32]

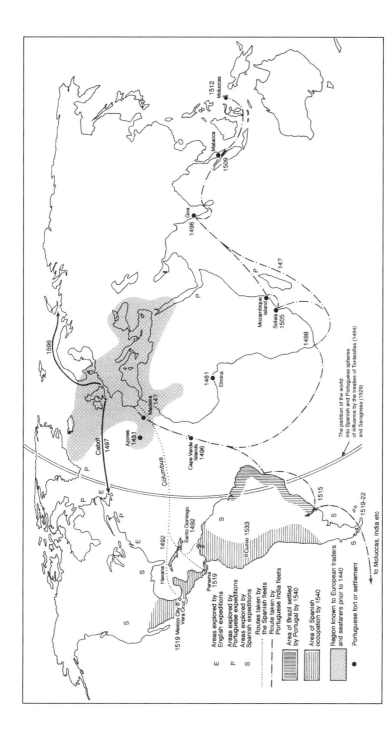

Map 3.2 The age of European discovery: By the early 1500s, a Europe-centered world-economy began to emerge.

This interpretation is similar to Frank's but more complex and explanatory. The various dominant regions did not just exploit their peripheries and semi-peripheries gratuitously. Rather, it was the extraordinary efficiencies achieved through labor specialization that enabled the core areas to thrive economically beyond anything previously achieved in history.

Labor specialization manifested itself in a variety of methods of controlling labor. In urban areas within the core, where sophisticated skills and technology were most developed, labor was to a large extent unfettered, which fostered individual initiative and creativity. In much of the periphery, by contrast, slave labor was employed, as were other forms of coerced and partially coerced labor. Labor in Eastern Europe and other semi-peripheral regions was more coerced than in the core, but less than in the periphery. Employers throughout the European world system – hard-nosed entrepreneurs pursuing the greatest possible returns on their investments and property – imposed or allowed precisely those labor regimens yielding the greatest increases in efficiency and productivity. Sharp competition between producers kept them constantly searching for the most profitable arrangements. In England, for example, many landed aristocrats consolidated their holdings into highly efficient large-scale farms, while others sold or rented their land to relatively free yeoman farmers. This process tended to push the less successful peasants into urban areas where they provided cheap labor for industry. Again, the name of the game was squeezing as much profit and efficiency from workers as humanly possible.

Exploitation and domination were pervasive, and how they manifested themselves was obvious in the case of the core and the periphery. Yet what about within the core itself, which was very large?

> Did Genoese merchants and bankers use Spain or did Spanish imperialism absorb parts of Italy? Did Florence dominate Lyon, or France Lombardy, or both? How should one describe the true links between Antwerp (later Amsterdam) and England?[33]

Wallerstein argues that the key factors in understanding these relations were the abilities and willingness of the various European states to promote the interests of merchants and entrepreneurs. Stronger and more centralized states in the core areas translated into greater backing for them and therefore more commercial success, greater profits, and ultimately the emergence of capitalism.

How did European states in core regions become strong? They built up bureaucracies to administer territory and collect taxes, expanded and continuously reformed their military forces, developed philosophies and practices of political legitimacy (like the concept of absolutism and the "divine right of kings"), and homogenized their subject populations (for example, by expelling Jews under pressure from Christian business interests who resented the competition). In general, strong states often enabled dominant economic and political interests to achieve goals that popular movements or tradition might otherwise oppose.

The first strong and stable European state capable and willing to promote the commercial interests of its realm was Portugal, which in the fifteenth century launched Europe on its discovery and exploitation of foreign lands. With the help of Genoese financiers and navigators, Spain, another strong and centralized state, then catapulted itself to the dominant position in the Atlantic world, the volume of its transatlantic trade growing elevenfold during the course of the sixteenth century. Yet Spain squandered vast wealth on constant warfare and failed empire-building in Europe. Despite controlling three of the four principal Italian city-states, fabulously wealthy merchant-banking houses of southern Germany, and the world's greatest financial center of the time, Antwerp, the Spanish–Habsburg Empire in Europe went bankrupt. Spain failed to thrive because it sought to transform the flourishing European world-economy into a world-empire centered on Castille. The cost of warfare in the early modern period had simply become too great for any one region to afford to subordinate to itself a continent full of economically rising states and regions. Plus, the moneyed interests of the country invested too little of their wealth in industry or other productive activities, aside from land ownership.

In the wake of the decline in Spain, which dragged down a half-dozen states and regions closely allied with it, including northern Italy and southern Germany, the world system underwent a radical restructuring. According to Wallerstein,

> The new system was to be one that has predominated ever since, a capitalist world-economy whose core-states were to be intertwined in a state of constant economic and military tension, competing for the privilege of exploiting (and weakening the state machineries of) peripheral areas, and permitting certain entities to play a specialized, intermediary role as semi-peripheral powers.[34]

The first successful core region of Europe was the Netherlands.

How can one explain the success of the Low Countries in this regard? Most important, the Spanish decline made it possible for the Dutch to win their independence from that colonial master in 1581. The Dutch merchants then established a relatively informal and unhierarchical confederation of local governments without the intrusive state apparatus of the other important European polities, thus enabling the country's bourgeoisie to use the state, such as it was, to maximize their interests. Religious toleration proved a magnet for Jews and radical Protestants, many of them skilled and moneyed international entrepreneurs. Already the Dutch had played a dominant role in the crucial Baltic grain trade. Now Eastern European grain fed the bourgeoning Dutch cities, and timber and other supplies made possible a dramatic expansion of shipbuilding and then a further development of Baltic and international trading prowess. There was another factor: as a former part of the Spanish empire, the Dutch maintained important financial links to the vast Spanish–American imperial sphere. Amsterdam from around 1590 parlayed the wealth streaming through

Dutch hands into a dominant role in Europe's commodities and capital markets and a global shipping business. The Netherlands outperformed the still-prosperous northern Italian city-states thanks to lower-cost skilled labor and access to less expensive raw materials and foodstuffs. These and other cost-savings made it impossible for any other people on the planet to compete with them in international finance and trade.

Also in the second half of the sixteenth century, industrial development began to advance rapidly and to concentrate in Northwestern Europe – chiefly England, Scotland, and the Dutch Republic. The big success story in particular was England, which went from exporting raw materials and grain in medieval times to specializing in the export of textiles in the early modern period. England enjoyed important economic and political advantages. Its industrial sector was less fragmented than Holland's, its tax burden lighter than that of Flanders or northern Italy, and its technology was cutting edge. The system of government was the most unified but limited and efficient in Europe, and the realm enjoyed internal peace – in the age of religious war – without a standing army. Also, the landed interests (as in Holland) managed to transform a large portion of farmland into a mere commodity, to be bought and sold at will. It therefore ended up in the hands of the most efficient, productive cultivators, who naturally increased output and also unleashed from the soil an army of unskilled and therefore cheap laborers available for industry. And precisely in this era industry and industrial technology rapidly developed in England. When an economic depression hit all of Europe from around 1620, England (and to an even greater extent Holland) avoided its full impact. Why? In part because English entrepreneurs had developed new industries and a surging re-export trade.

When England began to assert itself, along with the Netherlands, as the emerging core of the European world system, most of the world lay outside its bounds, as what Wallerstein calls the "external arena." This included, for example, Russia, nearly all of Africa, and – most important – Asia, where:

> The Portuguese arrived and found a flourishing world-economy. They organized it a little better and took some goods home as a reward for their efforts. The social organization of the economy as well as the political superstructures remained largely untouched ... . Hence, a century of Portuguese dominance meant for most of Asia principally that Portuguese rather than Arabs made the profit.[35]

The main impediment to more direct European control in the East was the existence there of strong states. The situation in the New World was exactly the opposite:

> On the one hand, the rewards of American colonization were in some sense greater. On the other hand, the difficulties of colonizing Asia were much greater. The combination of the two meant that the Americas became the

periphery of the European world-economy in the sixteenth century while Asia remained an *external arena*.[36]

The key difference was this: the Asian trade involved importing desired Asian goods. The Americas provided for their part an overwhelming cornucopia of precious metals and lumber and wonder crops (like the potato), along with sought-after commodities like sugar and tobacco – all under the direct production and overall control of Europeans.

Wallerstein devotes the next three volumes of his opus to showing how the European world system evolved over the next few centuries. "The capitalist world-economy," he writes,

> has (a) geographically expanded to cover the entire globe; (b) manifested a cyclical pattern of expansion and contraction ... and shifting geographical locations of economic roles (the rise and fall of hegemonies, the movements up and down of particular core, perhipheral, and semiperipheral zones); and (c) undergone a process of secular transformation, including technological advance, industrialization, proletarianization, and the emergence of structural political resistance to the system itself – a transformation that is still going on today.[37]

In other words, dominant and exploited regions came and went – though very slowly – but the exploitative system persisted and was extended. As a Marxist, Wallerstein presupposes the eventual collapse of the capitalist world system (he expects to analyze this event, "if I can last it out," he writes, in volume 6),[38] yet he recognizes its adaptability; he deplores its frequent inhumanity yet acknowledges its success thanks to an extraordinary increase in the efficiency of labor through specialization and regional divisions.

State support for commerce made Europe unstoppable (Eric Mielants)

Other scholars working in the world system framework have offered revisions, reinterpretations, and new departures. Eric Mielants, an associate professor of sociology at Fairfield University in Connecticut and a research associate at the Maison des Sciences de l'Homme in Paris, who took his Ph.D. with Wallerstein, challenges his mentor on several keys points.[39] First, he argues that Europe began its transition to capitalism as early as the twelfth century, noting for example that during that century the Flemish textile industry became minutely specialized, that by the mid-thirteenth century merchants regularly borrowed and lent at interest despite the religious prohibition against usury, and that in the following century Europe's financial instruments and institutions were functioning robustly. Like Landes, he also emphasizes the technological importance of the proliferation of mechanical clocks by the fourteenth century but adds that one of their chief functions was to control labor.

Moreover, the European warriors who established crusader states in the Middle East beginning in the twelfth century and systematically expelled Muslims from Spain during the Reconquista, Mielants suggests, were conducting "an *identical* form of expansion, subjugation, domination, and exploitation as Spain's conquest of the New World, albeit on a smaller scale."[40] Similarly, between 1150 and 1350, the Italian city-states colonized much of the Byzantine Empire in order to control the extraction and export of raw materials. These merchant-warriors also consciously undermined existing manufacturing enterprises in these colonies. In other words, the process of peripheralization – the creation of an exploitable periphery – was well underway three or four centuries earlier than Wallerstein claims.

The most important feature of the medieval European political economy, according to Mielants, was the European inter-city-state system. The high level of autonomy of European cities ruled by a merchant patriciate distinguished them from cities in the other civilizations. Intense interregional and intercity competition constantly pressed entrepreneurs to seek cost-saving measures. Most responded by striving to keep their labor costs down by hiring children and women and relocating their operations to places outside the control of the urban guilds, such as suburbs and the countryside. In these efforts, they worked hand-in-hand with urban government, which was easy since in many cases they were the urban government. Gradually, the mercantile bourgeoisie in medieval Europe's relatively autonomous cities came to exercise legal, political, and socio-economic power in the countryside – their periphery. The medieval European city-state:

> was essentially a socioeconomic and juridical entity controlled by an oli-garchy of intermarried merchants, wealthy craftsmen, and lesser noblemen, whose interests were intrinsically linked with the successful exploitation of those in the hinterlands (either the immediate rural countryside or a colony/province overseas) and the proletariat living within the city-state.[41]

As such, the medieval European city-state, Mielants concludes, was the main engine of Europe's rise to world preeminence.

Although he acknowledges the significant influences of other cultures on European evolution and rejects the idea that Europe rose thanks only to internal developments, Mielants insists that "one has to be somewhat Eurocentric in order to pin down the specifics that contributed to the qualitative shift on the European continent between A.D. 1000 and 1500."[42] In order to get to the bottom of the peculiarities of Europe's rise, he devotes most of his book to meticulous comparisons of Europe and the other major civilizations.

In the eleventh and twelfth centuries China underwent a commercial revolution, during which it mostly imported raw materials and exported manufactured goods. The Mongol conquest in the thirteenth century, which devastated much of eastern Eurasia, opened trade routes allowing ideas and

technology to flow westward – think: gunpowder – and European merchants to
travel freely to the East. When the Ming overthrew the Mongol (Yuan) rulers in
1368, they reoriented the country inward. The vast treasure fleets sent round the
Indian Ocean in the early 1400s were meant to assert the dynasty's prestige in
the region, not to promote commerce. In fact, the Chinese emperor typically
gave more valuable material goods than he got through the tribute system.
By contrast, the European city-states from the early Middle Ages "systematically designed and implemented a foreign policy of direct conquests, political
control, and commercial exploitation in order to ceaselessly accumulate capital
from a constructed periphery."[43]

Whereas in much of Europe merchants controlled or at least strongly influenced government, and even kings often depended on international bankers and
lenders, in China the government frequently stifled economic development and
harassed domestic and foreign merchants. The emperors feared peasant
revolts – several toppled dynasties – but not commercial interests, which could
not even threaten the power of the scholar-officials. The Chinese Emperor
enjoyed a steady revenue stream from taxes on the land and, therefore unlike
the European monarchs, did not need to promote commerce, especially after
the establishment of the Ming Dynasty. Mielants does not deny that China
was highly commercialized with urban trade networks, huge flows of goods,
divisions of labor, and big cities, but he underlines that the state was more of a
competitor than a support for private enterprise.

The story of South Asia was rather similar. From the eleventh century, India
enjoyed rapid urbanization and commercial development with sophisticated
credit and banking institutions. Indian producers dominated the textile trade
throughout the region. They accumulated enormous capital, yet capitalism
failed to emerge. Why? Again, Mielants argues that merchants lacked the ability
to use the machinery and officials of the state to further their own interests.
They could not even exert control over labor or the production process in the
textile industry. He summarizes:

> It was precisely this variable – the power of the merchants – that ultimately
> transformed Western Europe into a core area within an expanding global
> division of labor. In Western Europe, the combination of merchants'
> growing power over the proletariat due to a highly unusual alliance
> between the state and the bourgeoisie and the *subsequent* increasing rev-
> enues from the financial windfall of overeas colonial conquests – first in the
> Mediterranean and eventually in the New World – explains why specific
> polities were capable of eventually achieving world domination. This
> explanation is not meant to replicate "the image of the eternal East, as a
> counterpoint to the vibrant, dynamic and therefore dominant Occident."
> But it does stress the fact that in South Asia, merchants lacked the institu-
> tionalized political power structures to effectively proletarianize their
> workers at home and effectively peripheralize other geographical areas
> within the Indian Ocean region.[44]

Unlike in Europe, the Indian nobility and bureaucracy could coerce merchants like milch cows. Towns and cities in India enjoyed more autonomy than in China but nowhere near as much as in Europe, again, for the same reasons – the power of the merchants.

Finally, the elites in India devoted all available military resources to fighting nomadic warriors (just as in China), leaving little funding for naval power, a crucial support of European merchant-colonizers, who easily forced the Indian merchants into a subsidiary role and ultimately colonized the country.

Mielants finds the same outcomes in North Africa and the Ottoman Empire. In general, Muslim cities did not colonize the adjoining countryside like the European cities, nor was intercity trade as intensive. The crucial distinguishing feature of European development was the capitalist dynamic of merchants using the state in order to control and exploit cheap labor wherever it could be found. Throughout the Muslim world, extensive slavery inhibited innovation. Mielants writes:

> In a capitalist system where many wage laborers are present, it is inevitable that private capital – controlled by capitalist entrepreneurs – is (continuously) invested in technological equipment and innovations in order to offset the cost of salaries. This incentive is lacking in a slave economy, where more energy will be devoted to overseeing and coercing the slaves.[45]

European wage labor was not "free" in any strict or moral sense; it was simply coerced more efficiently than in the other developed societies of the world.

Europe built on five thousand years of human development (Frank and Gills)

Andre Gunder Frank and Barry K. Gills, an English political scientist, would not disagree with the exploitative nature of European capitalism, yet they argue that the world system of which it was a part did not first emerge in Europe and is vastly older than Wallerstein (or even Mielants) believes. They argue that for at least five thousand years a world economic system has been developing and that therefore the West's ascendancy to preeminence "in this world system is only a recent – and perhaps a passing – event. Thus, our thesis poses a more humanocentric challenge to Eurocentrism."[46]

The world system they hypothesize involved – just like Wallerstein's – continuous capital accumulation, relationships of center and periphery, ongoing rivalries for hegemonic leadership, and cyclical economic growth and decline. It also relied on a

> world wide division of labor even in the distant past some 5,000 years ago. Its form does not necessarily have to be identical with the modern form. Why should it? The labor of the ancient lapis-lazuli miners of Afghanistan and the textile workers in urban Sumeria was surely interlinked in a

"world" economic/system division of labor even in the fourth or third millennium BC.[47]

All such workers were, even if only indirectly, linked together in one enormous commercial nexus. In other words, an interconnected world economic system has existed as long as civilization itself, because humans have constantly invested in tools and human capital and have traded and competed with each other for as long as they have trod the earth.

Their main point is to argue that since Europeans joined the ongoing world system only a few hundred years ago, their achievement comparatively speaking has been relatively minor. This reassessment changes the way all of "Western" history is perceived. As they claim, "A world system framework clarifies that for most of world history, including ancient 'classical' history, Europe was ever 'marginal' and west Asia ever 'central.'"[48]

An Asia-centered economic boom propelled Europe (Janet Abu-Lughod)

Building on Wallerstein's broader model but deepening the idea of an earlier world system, historical sociologist Janet Abu-Lughod describes the simultaneous flourishing of many cultures across Eurasia during the century after 1250. For roughly a century throughout Eurasia, greater economic, technological, and social progress was made than ever before. During the few decades before and after 1300, significant commercial relations were established between even Europe and China. This pan-continental thirteenth-century renaissance went far beyond merely economic development. In fact, she argues, "Never before had so many parts of the Old World simultaneously reached cultural maturity."[49] Cultural and intellectual advancement in all these places was made possible by nearly ubiquitous economic expansion, technological innovation, and increased economic integration.

According to Abu-Lughod, the thirteenth-century "world economy" centered on what she calls the Middle Eastern heartland. Within that story, Europe was a bit player. In fact, Europe was able to rise to world prominence, as the core area of the world system that Wallerstein has posited, only thanks to this earlier knitting together of the Old World into a vast common market by the far more developed Asian civilizations. This polycentric system of exchange (see Map 3.3) involved huge quantities of raw materials and manufactured goods and highly sophisticated commercial practices and technological methods, especially in metallurgy and textile-production. Joining this flourishing set of interconnected world-economies helped Europe to emerge from its "dark age." In fact, since until that point Europe was the least developed of the major civilizations, it had by far the most to gain from such contacts. Abu-Lughod concludes by asserting that the West subsequently rose to preeminence not because of any internal structural advantages but because Asia was in a temporary state of disarray, whereas Europe's economy continued to grow.

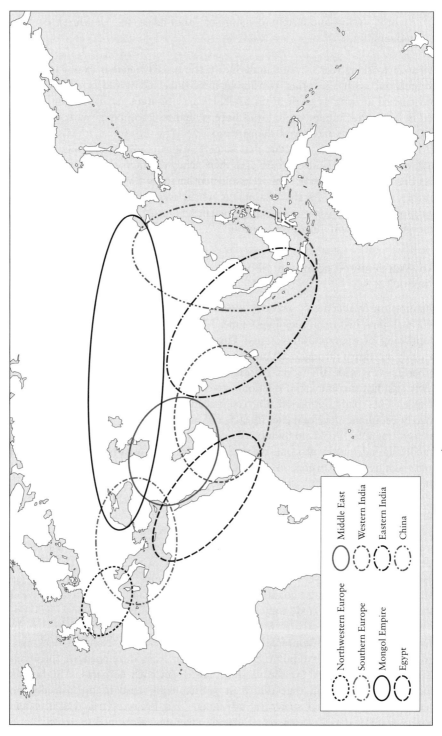

Map 3.3 Eight circuits of the thirteenth-century world system: The major Asian countries forged a polycentric system of exchange in the thirteenth century.

The author divides her book into three parts, focusing on the three main participants in the thirteenth-century world system – Europe, the Islamic world, and Asia, from India to China. She demonstrates that in a host of ways, Europe was the outlier, the upstart, the laggard. Business practices, credit institutions, state structures, and stable currencies had reached far higher levels of refinement and efficiency in the Middle East and Asia than in Europe.

The Crusades, according to Abu-Lughod, reintegrated Northwestern Europe into a world system for the first time since the age of Rome. Europeans discovered a wealth of precious luxuries – spices, porcelain, silk and cotton textiles. Since they possessed or produced few goods merchants in the rest of Eurasia wanted, the Europeans were spurred on to increase their manufacturing abilities, in order to participate in the tempting world market. The Italians had never lost contact with that market, and indeed they introduced the crucial financial instruments and practices, typically acquired from their Muslim trading-partners, to the rest of Europe, thus facilitating the medieval commercial boom. They brought these techniques – along with capital, their "Rolodex" of trading contacts in the Middle East, and business skills – to Northern Europe and thus facilitated the emergence of the great Flemish commercial centers – Ghent, Bruges, and Antwerp.

Abu-Lughod recounts the development of textile manufacturing in Flanders, beginning in the early Middle Ages. This region abutted the sea and had a high population density, which obliged most people to supplement their farming income with cottage industry. Participation in the Crusades opened the eyes of Flemish knights to the appealing wares of Middle Eastern markets. Over the next couple of centuries, textile production soared, peaking in the early 1300s. Some scholars even speak of an industrial revolution. The author herself suggests that

> In some ways it was an industrial revolution (albeit still using primitive technologies of handwork that can still be seen today in the famous lace of Brussels) and a capitalist one at that.[50]

She means that instead of the organically interlocking social relations of the gradually decomposing feudal hierarchy, there was now emerging a more strictly differentiated class arrangement with wealthy patricians in control of the means of production at the top and an aggregate of laborers at the bottom who had only their labor to sell. The business elites, who frequently married their daughters to landless noblemen, so dominated the political system that it was practically an extension of the region's commercial interests.

Meanwhile, merchants from across Europe had been flocking to Bruges, seeking goods from around Europe and the Eastern world, but also to borrow, exchange, and convert money. By the fourteenth century, business there centered more on financial services than on trade. Permanent "nations" of foreign financiers and merchants sprang up in specific neighborhoods – 16 in all from around Europe – to defend their interests. The Italian firms especially sent dozens of agents to represent them. As these companies became more and more complex and far-flung, precise accounting practices became necessary – double-entry bookkeeping, for example. They disposed of more and more capital, and thus needed a capital market. Bruges was Europe's first major one. Even in Flanders, Italians dominated the international financial services business, in particular the issuing of bills of exchange. Moreover, when Bruges began to decline as a manufacturing center in the thirteenth century thanks to the rise of England, the Italian money-men simply moved to Antwerp, the next international business center of Europe. Capital had become highly mobile.

The two great Italian maritime city-states, Genoa and Venice, competed ferociously with each other to penetrate furthest into Asia, to accumulate more and more capital, to increase business efficiency, to gain trading concessions from Byzantium and the Islamic states, and to advance the technology of navigation and war. They also eagerly established trading colonies throughout the eastern Mediterranean. By the later thirteenth century, together they dominated the developing European world-economy and linked it to the Central Asian and Middle East–North African and world-economies – and thence to the greatest economies of the East. Their merchant-convoys of ships crisscrossed the Mediterranean and Black Seas, loading and unloading a vast array of cargo and passengers at dozens and dozens of ports. During the early years of the 1300s, the more developed societies throughout Afro-Eurasia were flourishing economically. To a perspicacious observer of the time, it might have seemed that these less and less isolated world-economies were on the cusp of becoming a single, interconnected world system. In actuality, however, the European players continued to thrive while their Asian and North African partners fell into decline.

Abu-Lughod devotes the remainder of her book to explaining how the advanced societies of Asia had been flourishing during previous centuries and why they then fell into decline. Central to her story is the Mongol Empire, which unified most of Asia, from China to the Middle East and from India to Russia, and thus, despite the horrible destruction they often left in their wake, created the most highly developed and secure pathways for trade until then in world history. Unifying the hundreds and thousands of tribes and polities across Eurasia was an astonishing accomplishment, though it could not survive in the long run on account of being largely exploitative. Only continual expansion could keep the system going, but no empire can expand indefinitely.

Throughout Central Asia and far beyond, Muslims were the dominant traders, with Jews a distant second. They deployed sophisticated accounting, financial, and commercial practices and instruments. In fact, according to the author,

> all the legal and institutional prerequisites for financing and administering "capitalist" production and exchange were in place in the Islamic world long before the Europeans would benefit from them.[51]

The Muslim religion itself promoted commerce and alone among the great religions and public philosophies of Eurasia held merchants in high esteem.

Europeans had practically no clue about eastern Eurasia or its peoples until papal envoys seeking allies for anti-Muslim crusades and merchants like Marco Polo began trickling eastward in the 1240s. The Europeans were, in other words, the last to hear the fabulous stories of extraordinary riches in the East. Polo encountered merchants from "every nation" in Peking. But not other Europeans, since Polo repeatedly points out that he and his family are the only ones. So who were they? It seems obvious that all of the countries he was talking about were Islamic, and indeed Muslims had dominated international trade throughout most of Eurasia for centuries. "For them the Khan's domains are no new discovery; they are a natural and integral part of their world."[52] Europeans in general were obviously very late comers to a flourishing economic sphere.

A tragic consequence of the Mongols' interlinking of the four corners of Eurasia was the spread along Mongol caravan routes of deadly diseases, and most catastrophically the Black Death, which struck China in 1331 and Europe in 1347, apparently ferried along by Mongol military personnel. Moreover, infighting among competing Mongol clans and destructive conquests in the Middle East undermined most of the major economic centers of Eurasia. In particular, the Mongols' vicious sacking of Baghdad in 1258 caused that once thriving, though recently declining, metropolis, to fall on hard times. The long-distance trade between India and China and the Mediterranean world via the Persian Gulf diminished.

In fact, in the West only Europe and Egypt, the locus of a new Islamic Sultanate, remained strong. Italian traders, by supplying the Egyptian elites with a continuous flow of slaves, necessary for the maintenance of the Mamluk warrior caste, both helped keep the system in power and ensured their own access to the Europe–Asia trade that now passed almost exclusively through the Red Sea. The twin cities of Fustat and Cairo, under the Mamluks, who ruled both Egypt and Syria, were the second or third largest urban centers in the world in the early 1300s, with a combined half-million people. Most important, they held back attacks from both the Mongols and the Europeans and by the thirteenth century constituted "a vanguard for the world system."[53] Moreover, Egypt's survival of the Black Death catastrophe enabled Venice, its closest trading partner, to continue to flourish as well. Fustat thrived as both a major manufacturing center, in particular of textiles, and an international commercial hub. Upper Egypt also produced vast quantities of refined sugar and textiles.

Gradually, however, the Egyptian economy slumped, too. European textile manufactures undercut their Egyptian competitors, who began to export more and more unprocessed materials, like flax, raw cotton, and sugar cane. From the later 1300s, the Mamluk government became more oppressive, imposing higher taxes and steeper tariffs on goods transshipped through to Europe and Asia. It was to avoid these increased fees that Portuguese mariners desperately sought – and of course found – a blue-water passage to the East. Once European traders had a new, less expensive means of acquiring the precious spices, silks, and porcelain of Asia, the Egyptian hub went into deep decline.

For centuries, and even stretching far back into prehistoric times, India was the most important commercial hub in the world. It linked all the great civilizations of Eurasia – Mesopotamia, Egypt, China, Southeast Asia, and ultimately Greece, Rome, the Islamic world, and later still Christian Europe. Permanent foreign-merchant communities, first of Arabs and Jews and much later Italians, settled along India's west coast. Traders from India and East and Southeast Asia were constantly traveling between their respective ends of the Indian Ocean, and Indian merchants were a regular presence in Eastern Africa, Egypt, and even Rome from ancient times. In the late thirteenth century, Calicut on the Malabar Coast flourished as the commercial counterpart to Mamluk Egypt. Muslim, Jewish, and Gujarati traders flocked to the port city. Between them, they controlled most of the Indian Ocean commerce – Muslims the western half, Indians and Chinese the eastern half.

Highly efficient textile production in southern India led in the thirteenth century to rapid urbanization. Yet India was highly self-sufficient in raw materials, agricultural produce, and manufactured goods and therefore played a rather passive role in the world economy. This was, as Abu-Lughod notes, more because of a general economic self-sufficiency, rather than a lack of material goods. Indeed, the more India's manufactured goods and commodities were drawn into the increasingly integrated world system, the smaller role its merchants played in handling that trade.[54] Basically, Indian merchants left the Indian Ocean seafaring trade to Muslims in the West and Chinese in East.

By the thirteenth century, China had the most sophisticated and productive agriculture in the world. It boasted a highly developed and populous domestic economy and a strong state that maintained a stable currency (including paper money), ensured the proper functioning of credit markets, built and kept up elaborate transportation infrastructure, and exercised monopoly control over key economic sectors, like salt production. Chinese craftsmen developed the widest array of technological breakthroughs of any people in history until that time. They invented paper two thousand years ago, woodblock printing seven hundred years later, and a process for movable-type printing in the mid-eleventh century. Several decades later, Chinese metalworkers were using refined methods to produce iron and steel at a rate not achieved again anywhere in the world until the Industrial Revolution. Invasions by nomadic warriors over the following century and a half put an end to this production, however. Chinese alchemists invented gunpowder in the seventh century and powerful gunpowder weaponry five hundred years later. Finally, Chinese artisans crafted some of the most beautiful and sought-after wares of silk and porcelain in the world.

Moreover, the capital of the Yuan dynasty, Hangchow, at which Marco Polo marveled, was by far the world's largest city. Its one million inhabitants enjoyed every manner of amenity – pleasure gardens, canals, firefighting services, innumerable teahouses and restaurants, and at least ten markets teeming with abundant produce and wares. Extensive residential neighborhoods catering to foreign merchants and diplomats – mostly Muslims – occupied an entire quarter of the city.

During Sung and Yuan times (until 1368), the most powerful navy in the region was Chinese. Yet apparently rival mariners respected each other's ships and rarely resorted to warfare or piracy. However, the Chinese government closed the country's seaports to foreign merchants in the later 1300s, and after 1433 the Ming dynasty ceased sending its vast treasure fleets throughout the Indian ocean world, leaving a huge power vacuum that ultimately, several decades later, Portuguese merchants "filled with their own brute fire power."[55] The Portuguese, who arrived at the end of the 1400s, were not merely violent, using their heavily armored ships to blast their way into the Indian Ocean markets; they violated the unwritten code of honor by attacking fellow traders. They also enforced a compulsory system of trade throughout the region.

Abu-Lughod rehearses the major explanations for the Chinese withdrawal from the world system, including emphases on the anti-commerce bias of Confucianism and the difficulty for merchants to influence government policy. The Mongol rulers of the Yuan dynasty, by contrast, had drawn China more fully into international relations and commercial expansion than ever before. The author speculates that the indigenous Ming rulers, who took power in 1368, aimed to steer China in the opposite direction. Confucian moral strictures obviously justified this move. Moreover, the epidemics that had visited China regularly from the early 1300s and anti-Mongol rebellions had wrought such destruction that rebuilding the country required a concentration of resources on the domestic sphere. That task mostly completed by the early 1400s, the Chinese government returned to foreign policy. Several fabulous "treasure" fleets, involving vast resources, were meant to demonstrate Chinese greatness throughout the Indian Ocean world. A mid-fifteenth-century economic collapse again reoriented China's rulers toward domestic affairs.

Many historians of China emphasize internal causes for this collapse, including corruption, political infighting, and a decline in tax revenues (see Chapter 5). Abu-Lughod adds a world system interpretation. China's economy fell into a slump because the Mongol conqueror Tamerlane shut down the Silk Road across Central Asia, and the diminished Indian Ocean commercial prosperity meant that the treasure ships proved less profitable than expected. The voyage of 1433 proved the last. The author notes that the treasure voyages had proved economically unprofitable and, in part because of this, that the imperial rulers decided to reorient their focus toward domestic affairs. They also considered the seaports to be "infested with foreigners and their 'inauthentic' commercial pursuits." Thus, she writes, the two-hundred-year anomaly "of southern port centrality to the economy ended, and with it, the chance for world hegemony."[56] Thus, when European explorers opened up deep-water routes across the major oceans, no naval power could rival them.

According to Abu-Lughod, the European mariners and conquerors of the sixteenth century possessed neither financial instruments and institutions nor navigational technology that surpassed those of the thirteenth-century Islamic world or China. The earlier world system integrated peoples of diverse cultures, economic levels, and religions. To some extent, this was the system's strength.

It emerged precisely because these various peoples achieved economic prosperity simultaneously during a more than hundred-year period. Unfortunately, this very integration proved the system's undoing, when epidemics drastically diminished population levels throughout Eurasia and when the Pax Mongolica collapsed.

So, why exactly did Europe "rise" and not those other civilizations? Abu-Lughod considers the dramatic decline of the East crucial to that ascendancy. Yet, the West's rise consisted neither merely in the "takeover" of the already existing system nor in an inevitable triumph thanks to some peculiar hallmarks of European culture.[57] Rather, Europe benefited from the existing network of commercial pathways that it "grew into" and restructured according to its own interests. Also, the Europeans came with a mentality of conquerors and plunderers. They entered a system in which the participants had been relatively equal in strength. By contrast, the Europeans, especially after the decline of China, were able to project far more military power than any other peoples. When they incorporated the Americas into their rising world system, its epicenter naturally moved westward from Asia. Yet, as the authors surveyed in Chapter 4 make abundantly clear, Asian preeminence had long preceded Europe's.

Conclusion

The work of scholars analyzed in this chapter attribute the West's rise neither to alleged virtues of Europeans nor historical accidents but largely to policies and practices of Europeans enabling them to dominate peoples and resources beyond their shores. Many of these scholars describe a global division of labor and a hierarchy of economic control centered on the Northwestern European countries where capitalism and industrialization first developed and to which the peoples of Africa and Latin America and later Asia gave up labor and resources. Not all agree on exactly how and when the system emerged or what exactly other peoples contributed to its emergence. One emphasizes assistance from Eurasian flora and fauna. Another points to conceptual tools like the idea of property rights. Yet another dates the beginning of Europe's rise to the Middle Ages. Still others downplay its importance by positing five thousand years of worldwide economic growth onto which Europe merely grafted itself as an outsider. What all these authors agree upon is that the rise of the West involved exceptional violence, aggression, and exploitation.

Further reading

Reverse Robin Hood economics

Adelman, Jeremy, ed. *Colonial Legacies: The Problem of Persistence in Latin American History*. New York: Routledge, 1999.

Aston, T. H. and C. H. E. Philpin. *The Brenner Debate: Agrarian Class Structure and Economic Development in Pre-industrial Europe*. Cambridge; New York: Cambridge University Press, 1985.

Blackburn, Robin. *The Making of New World Slavery: From the Baroque to the Modern, 1492–1800.* London; New York: Verso, 1997.

Frank, Andre Gunder. *Capitalism and Underdevelopment in Latin America: Historical Studies of Chile and Brazil.* New York: Monthly Review Press, 1967.

Frank, Andre Gunder. *World Accumulation, 1492–1789.* New York: Monthly Review Press, 1978.

Frank, Andre Gunder. *Dependent Accumulation and Underdevelopment.* New York: Monthly Review Press, 1979.

Galeano, Eduardo. *Open Veins of Latin America: Five Centuries of the Pillage of a Continent.* Translated by Cedric Belfrage. New York: Monthly Review Press, 1973.

Moulder, Frances V. *Japan, China and the Modern World Economy: Towards a Reinterpretation of East Asian Development ca. 1600–ca. 1918.* Cambridge; New York: Cambridge University Press, 1977.

Stein, Stanley J. and Barbara H. *The Colonial Heritage of Latin America: Essay on Economic Dependence in Perspective.* New York: Oxford University Press, 1970.

Wolf, Eric. *Europe and the People without History.* Berkeley: University of California Press, 1982.

Environmental imperialism

Anderson, Terry L. and Peter J. Hill. *The Not So Wild, Wild West: Property Rights on the Frontier.* Stanford, Calif.: Stanford Economics and Finance, 2004.

Blaut, James. *The Colonizer's Model of the World: Geographical Diffusionism and Eurocentric History.* New York; London: Guilford Press, 1993.

Chew, Sing C. *World Ecological Degradation: Accumulation, Urbanization, and Deforestation, 3000 B.C.–A.D. 2000.* Walnut Creek, Calif.: AltaMira Press, 2001.

Ponting, Clive. *A Green History of the World: The Environment and the Collapse of Great Civilizations.* New York: Penguin Books, 1993.

World systems theory

Amin, Samir. *Accumulation on a World Scale: A Critique of the Theory of Underdevelopment.* 2 vols. Translated by Brian Pearce. New York; London: Monthly Review Press, 1974.

Arrighi, Giovanni. *The Long Twentieth Century: Money, Power, and the Origins of Our Times.* London; New York: Verso, 1994.

Chase-Dunn, Christopher and Thomas D. Hall. *Rise and Demise: Comparing World-systems.* Boulder, Colo.: Westview Press, 1997.

Sanderson, Stephen K., ed. *Civilizations and World Systems: Studying World-Historical Change.* Walnut Creek, Calif.: Altamira Press, 1995.

Smith, Alan K. *Creating a World Economy: Merchant Capital, Colonialism, and World Trade, 1400–1825.* Boulder, Colo.: Westview, 1991.

Notes

1 V. I. Lenin, *Imperialism, the Highest Stage of Capitalism; a Popular Outline* (New York: International Publishers, 1939), 63.
2 Andre Gunder Frank, *Latin America: Underdevelopment or Revolution: Essays on the Development of Underdevelopment and the Immediate Enemy* (London: Monthly Review Press, 1970), 4.
3 Joseph E. Inikori, *Africans and the Industrial Revolution in England: A Study in International Trade and Economic Development* (Cambridge: Cambridge University Press, 2002).
4 These are some of the arguments put forward in such works as David Eltis and Stanley L. Engerman, "The Importance of Slavery and the Slave Trade to Industrializing Britain," *The Journal of Economic History* 60 (March 2000): 123–144.
5 Inikori, *Africans and the Industrial Revolution in England*, 142.
6 Ibid., 157.
7 Ibid., 197.
8 Ibid., 214.
9 Ibid., 361.
10 Ibid., 381.
11 Ibid., 451.
12 Ibid., 486.
13 Alfred Crosby, *Ecological Imperialism: The Biological Expansion of Europe, 900–1900* (Cambridge: Cambridge University Press, 1986), 7.
14 Ibid., 81.
15 Ibid., 100.
16 Ibid., 165.
17 Ibid., 216.
18 Ibid., 271.
19 Ibid., 280.
20 John C. Weaver, *The Great Land Rush and the Making of the Modern World, 1650–1900* (Montreal; Kingston: McGill-Queens University Press, 2006), 4.
21 Ibid., 43.
22 Ibid., 81.
23 Ibid., 150.
24 Ibid., 264.
25 Immanuel Wallerstein, *The Essential Wallerstein* (New York: The New Press, 2000), xiv–xv.
26 Personal communication to the author via e-mail, September 28, 2011.
27 Wallerstein, *The Essential Wallerstein*, 140.
28 Personal communication to the author via e-mail, September 28, 2011.
29 Wallerstein, *The Essential Wallerstein*, 129.
30 Ibid., 75–76.
31 Immanuel Wallerstein, *The Modern World-System I. Capitalist Agriculture and the Origins of the European World-Economy in the Sixteenth Century* (New York: Academic Press, 1974), 15, 17.
32 Ibid., 86.
33 Ibid., 129.
34 Ibid., 197.
35 Ibid., 333.
36 Ibid., 336.
37 Immanuel Wallerstein, *The Modern World-System II. Mercantilism and the Consolidation of the European World-Economy, 1600–1750* (New York: Academic Press, 1980), 8.

38 Immanuel Wallerstein, *The Modern World-System IV. Centrist Liberalism Triumphant, 1789–1914* (Berkeley; Los Angeles; London: University of California Press, 2011), xvii.

39 Eric H. Mielants, *The Origins of Capitalism and the "Rise of the West"* (Philadelphia: Temple University Press, 2007).

40 Ibid., 27. Italics in the original.

41 Ibid., 157.

42 Ibid., 43.

43 Ibid., 61.

44 Ibid., 101. Italics in the original.

45 Ibid., 131.

46 Andre Gunder Frank and Barry K. Gills, eds., *The World System: Five Hundred Years or Five Thousand?* (London; New York: Routledge, 1993), 3.

47 Ibid., 299.

48 Ibid., 22.

49 Janet L. Abu-Lughod, *Before European Hegemony: The World System A.D. 1250–1350* (New York: Oxford University Press, 1989), 3–4.

50 Ibid., 84–85.

51 Ibid., 224.

52 Ibid., 167.

53 Ibid., 242.

54 Ibid., 285.

55 Ibid., 259.

56 Ibid., 347.

57 Ibid., 361.

4 The greatness of Asia

It is an obvious fact to all of the authors reviewed in the preceding chapters that human civilization first emerged in Asia and northeast Africa, that for most of history Europe was far less developed than the great world civilizations, and that the Europeans learned much from those civilizations during their own rise. Serious Western scholars have held these views for over a century. For example, a prominent foundation stone of the University of Chicago's Haskell Hall, built in the 1890s, displays the inscription: "Lux ex Oriente" – "From the East comes light [i.e. culture]." Marshall Hodgson, who spent his academic career at that university, argued decades ago that all the great cultures in history – except Europe – were Asian; therefore, world history should focus on Asia, where the vast majority of human cultural resources first emerged. At the same time, nearly every scholar discussed so far in this book considers the rise of the West something of a miracle – an accomplishment beyond anything achieved by any other culture in history. Abu-Lughod explicitly argues that the most advanced Asian cultures together prefigured that accomplishment and indeed made it possible. Yet even she still holds that the ultimate rise of the West, beginning in the sixteenth century, was the most extraordinarily singular event in world history and has shaped the world ever since.

By contrast, this chapter investigates scholars who argue either that everything Europe achieved was made possible by Asia or that the great Asian cultures continued to outperform the European economies and societies until well into the nineteenth century – or both.

The first major work along these lines came from the pen of Jack Goody, an eminent British social anthropologist. He points out that in medieval times China outperformed Europe in a host of human endeavors. Yet he questions the received explanations for the West's eventual rise to preeminence. He rejects the idea that the West was uniquely able to innovate; for centuries its peculiar ability was to adapt technologies from elsewhere. Also, whereas Confucianism was once considered an impediment to development, it is now seen as its promoter. In brief, any alleged "uniqueness of Europe" turns out to be a moving target that keeps changing shape over time.

The author begins by seeking to debunk the widespread view, beginning at least with Max Weber, that people in Western societies deployed more powerful forms of logic and achieved a higher level of rationality than their counterparts in other civilizations. True, Aristotle developed a peculiar form of syllogistic reasoning. Yet much research suggests that all peoples on earth think logically in a variety of ways, that certain aspects of logical thinking are universal, that the other great civilizations invented their own sophisticated tools of formal logic, and – most important of all, perhaps – that Aristotelian logic stemmed from earlier Middle Eastern antecedents. After all, he argues, the typical methods of logical inference are quite similar in both Europe and Asia. It may be that all of them had Mesopotamian origins. Goody himself, who has demonstrated how sophisticated thinking emerged from the development of writing systems,[1] believes that was the most likely source of the common logical patterns across Eurasia. Yet even if logical thinking diffused from Greece in every direction, it would have come to India before Western Europe. Thus, he writes, "the East had as much claim to these Greek achievements as the West that was later to become the home for the development of industrial capitalism and of 'modern' knowledge systems."[2] Goody concludes this piece of his argumentation by asserting that the highly artificial form of syllogistic proof – or indeed any other specific mode of thought – would have to be shown to have been both unique and a direct cause of, say, the Scientific Revolution, something no one has ever done.

The most he is willing to concede is that perhaps many Europeans, during the early modern period, did not invent any new forms of rationality but simply extended a rational approach, which was common to many societies, to all of human affairs. There was never any such thing, he argues, as "Western rationality," but rather a variety of fields of learning and understanding, all quite rational. Within these realms, the Chinese were far ahead of the West until the Renaissance. "Rationality," therefore, must be thought of as historically evolving and not culturally anchored.[3] Historically, the peoples of the West simply cannot be considered more rational or less superstitious than other peoples over the entirety of their existence.

Goody next analyzes the practice of double-entry bookkeeping, which many serious scholars, again including Weber, have considered an especially "scientific" form of financial reckoning. Our author questions this assumption. How unique was this European invention? And how did it contribute to the emergence of capitalism? For one thing, just as the alphabet – that powerful technology of communication – first appeared "on the unspecialized and uncluttered periphery of the literate world rather than the institution-bound center,"[4] so the more backward Europe was the home to some important innovations in commerce. Yet their roots, which the author traces back to ancient times, lay elsewhere, in particular in the Islamic world.

Medieval Italian merchants were Europe's great innovators in banking, navigation, commercial law, maritime insurance, and other practices invaluable to business, including double-entry bookkeeping, in which each transaction is recorded twice, once as a debit and once as a credit. Yet Goody shows that neither the Greeks nor the Romans, nor the Chinese, Indians, or Muslims – all consummate trading peoples – used that accounting method, nor did most European firms right down to the nineteenth century. Moreover, merchants in the ancient Near East had for centuries, if not millennia, applied rational accounting practices. The Qur'an, for example, that supremely pro-business text, explicitly urges merchants to keep careful records of their debts and receipts. Indeed, before the invention of double-entry bookkeeping in the thirteenth century, literate merchants around Eurasia had used sophisticated accounting practices that kept track of elaborate business transactions perfectly rationally. Goody stresses that the later European Middle Ages witnessed not so much a birth of techniques but a recovery of them. Of course, this recovery did not involve mere imitation, but rather a rethinking of practices that had grown sclerotic and inefficient.[5]

The author is suggesting that European innovators enjoyed the best of all possible worlds: on the one hand they had myriad ideas and technologies to borrow from right next door, as it were; on the other hand, their cultures were something like blank slates on which new departures could be inscribed.

Arabic numbers – imported from India – made the sophisticated European accounting practices possible in the first place. In fact, nearly every business innovation of the medieval Italians had clear antecedents in the Near East and other parts of Eurasia, including the limited partnership (or the *commenda*), checks, banking, stock markets, insurance, and possibly even double-entry bookkeeping. But even if this latter was a purely European invention, Eurocentric scholars, in Goody's opinion, have made far too much of it. The loaded terms "scientific" and "rational" suggest that European double-entry bookkeeping marked some dramatic leap forward made possible only thanks to apparently unique cultural or mental features of the European people. Far more likely is that all accounting practices derived from procedures arising first in the Near East at least 3,500 years ago and that all have manifested rationalizing tendencies in those who developed and used them. Any such developments were probably made possible by advantageous intellectual and economic circumstances.[6] In other terms, once someone has invented a rational procedure, like accounting, others will naturally develop it further without having to bring in "science" from the outside. Double-entry bookkeeping could have emerged in any one of the highly commercialized cultures and that it did so first in Europe was a mere accident.

Goody devotes two chapters to elucidating commercial developments in India from earliest times when Indian merchants traded regularly with Babylonia and, later, when Roman traders established colonies on the east coast of India in order to acquire cloth, jewels, and spices. When European commercial explorers arrived 1,500 years later, they found thriving craft industries, production for the market, throbbing metropolises, highly capitalized trading ventures, entire villages engaged in weaving, the buying and selling of futures, and a money economy. The wealth of Indian merchants amazed them. Brightly colored Indian cloth took European consumers by storm, which in turn fueled a manufacturing boom in the subcontinent. In fact, only the Europeans' ships and guns gave them an advantage over the locals.

Scholars and observers have presupposed that the Hindu caste system inhibited commercial development in India. Yet Islam, Buddhism, and Jainism also flourished and actually promoted business. In practice, moreover, Hinduism proved entirely compatible with many mercantile activities. Clearly India ran huge trade surpluses with several European countries, leading their governments to impose high tariffs – and in some cases outright bans – on Indian imports, to no avail. The only way European entrepreneurs found to avoid economic colonization was to mechanize textile production. And soon after the beginning of the Industrial Revolution, in 1854, Indian manufacturers began to establish textile mills employing English industrial equipment, so that after 1900 British cloth exports to India declined and Indian exports to Europe soared again.

How could industrialization develop so successfully during these early stages in India, given its eventual economic slump? Goody suggests that the pre-industrial economies of the major European and Asian countries were far more similar than Karl Marx, Max Weber, and most other social theorists imagined. Here he cites the economic historian, Frank Perlin, who contends that India, like Europe, had been developing rapidly both economically and politically since the 1500s, if not longer. One key feature of this development was the emergence of a form of merchant capitalism, similar to that in Europe, thanks to the shared Eurasian environment of social and economic transformations involving intensive monetization of world-wide commerce.[7] Goody adds, in disagreement with Perlin and of course the scholars of dependency theory, that Indian manufacturing declined not because European governments and entrepreneurs actively promoted "underdevelopment" but due to "specific difficulties"[8] faced by Indian commercial interests.

One such difficulty was apparently not the heavy hand of family relations. Our author devotes his next chapter to debunking that assumption, put forward by scholars like Weber. They argued that capitalism could not develop properly in Asia, where enduring influences of caste and clan impeded the emergence of individualism. On the contrary, argues Goody, extended family ties actually promoted business activity and success by making possible long-term commitments of capital, the continuity of family firms, the passing down of commercial knowledge, and the pooling of financial resources among people one knows and trusts. In fact, in such mercantile cultures par excellence as Taiwan and Hong Kong, a huge proportion of all businesses were from the beginning and remain family owned and operated. In such societies, Confucian "familism" may have played a similar pro-business role as Protestant individualism did in the West. Family firms also played a decisive and dynamic role in Japan from before the Meiji Restoration. There were, in other words, distinct, but parallel and equally valid, roads to capitalist development. Indeed, in a later chapter Goody provides abundant instances of the central role family relations often played in successful Western businesses.

Given the fact that so many brilliant social observers and theorists apparently misunderstood the nature of economy development in Asia, Goody suggests that ethnocentrism may have pushed them to overvalue Western achievements and thus to underestimate how similar Eastern practices were to those of the West. Goody suspects that the ramifications of this biased interpretation of Asian society may have gravely warped Western social theory overall.[9] The author sees a key source of such misinterpretations in the division of intellectual labor between an analysis of the modern family by sociologists and of premodern families (kinship in particular) by anthropologists. The result, he argues, is a failure to achieve truly comparative study by either field.

He cites data suggesting that household size was historically not very different in Europe and other parts of the world but that kinship ties were typically far weaker in Europe. Goody attributes this difference in large part to the Western Christian Church, whose leaders aimed to substitute a spiritual kinship for the bonds of "natural kinship." Other evidence indicates that kinship ties are nevertheless not negligible even in contemporary America, despite that country's emphasis on individualism. Therefore, one can assume that kinship ties played an important role in Europe going back to earliest times. Similarly, Goody debunks the widely accepted idea among historical sociologists that strong attachment to one's offspring emerged only in the European Victorian era when parents could count on their children mostly surviving childhood. On the contrary, much scholarship indicates that human beings form such attachments no matter the threat of infant mortality. The same can be said about the alleged birth of conjugal love in modern Europe. In other words, there was nothing fundamentally unique about the European family, parental attitudes, child rearing, courtship, or marriage patterns.

In fact, one can find European countries with sociological and demographic features similar to those in non-Western countries and dissimilar features in some of the most successful non-Western countries. In order to single out features that supposedly enabled the West to give birth to commercial capitalism, the Industrial Revolution, and modern society itself, Marx formulated his conception of an unchanging and inefficient Asian mode of production and Weber emphasized the allegedly traditional nature of Asian societies. Yet since several Asian societies have developed modern social and economic forms, those social scientific analyses – including dependency theory and conceptualizations of family development – must evolve accordingly. Either, for example, the Japanese and Western families always had a similar potential or one must conclude that the features specific to Western families had nothing to do with modern social and economic development.[10] A further irony in Goody's interpretation consists in the dependency theorists and Eurocentrists erring in a similar way: the exploitative colonial past of Chile and Brazil has not prevented their contemporary success, nor have the distinctly non-Western cultures of China and India.

In sum, Goody believes that all of the Eurasian civilizations "were fired in the same crucible and that their differences must be seen as diverging from a common base,"[11] which was laid down in the Bronze Age and included agriculture, urban settlements, literacy, mathematics, relatively sophisticated explanations of natural phenomena, metallurgy, and the wheel. It also included, eventually, a "spirit of capitalism" – risk-taking, entrepreneurship, the desire to acquire and accumulate wealth – that thrived for many centuries throughout Eurasia. Therefore,

> we are well beyond any uniqueness hypothesis which attributes some special "dynamism" to Christian Europe, requiring a "miraculous" concatenation of circumstances to produce the modern world; beyond, too, any notion that such change was rooted in the moral qualities of its entrepreneurs.[12]

Europe did not diverge in the earlier mercantile capitalism but only in the later industrial capitalism that began in the late eighteenth century.

So why did the West rise instead of the East? Goody places the emphasis on "knowledge systems" that began to flourish during the Italian Renaissance, gained momentum in the fifteenth century thanks to the printing revolution, and culminated in the Scientific Revolution and the Enlightenment. Thus, what distinguished the West was a powerful expansion of knowledge thanks in part to catching up to and assimilating earlier Asian achievements and in part to radically improved means of communication. The European Age of Discovery, which superior weaponry and navigational capacities made possible, helped stimulate those advances and of course led to the establishment of huge colonial empires and still more technological and intellectual breakthroughs.[13] In other words, there were no deep structural differences between the European and the other major Eurasian societies, though he believes Europe began significantly to diverge from the rest of Eurasia roughly five hundred years ago.

Moreover, the modern European advances in knowledge were but the most dramatic of the pendulum swings going back to the furthest antiquity, as now one Eurasian culture, now another, excelled at this or that practical or theoretical aspect of learning. Thus, to make sweeping claims about the "birth of mathematics" in medieval Europe, as, according to Goody, even some very serious scholars do, is absurd, since peoples throughout Eurasia and going back to ancient Mesopotamia made impressive advances in this and so many other fields. The author points out that, according to Joseph Needham, China was in advance of Europe from the second to the fifteenth centuries in mathematics, astronomy, and several other sciences.

Goody concludes his book by suggesting that several other allegedly unique features of Western civilization – for example, the rule of law or economic and political freedom – could and should be subjected to similar critical analysis as he applied to rationality, the family, and "scientific" accounting in order to demonstrate that Europe and the wider West developed in ways more similar to Asia than is often admitted by scholars.

The Asian dynamo caused Europe's rise (Andre Gunder Frank)

Andre Gunder Frank agrees but ups the ante. In *Reorient: Global Economy in the Asian Age* (1998), he argues that by 1400 at the latest Asian and Muslim traders dominated a global economy centered on the "Indian Ocean world" (see Map 4.1). Over the subsequent four centuries, Asian countries produced the vast majority of world economic output – and the goods they manufactured were of higher quality and less expensive than those made in Europe. Moreover, few European products enjoyed consumer demand in Asian markets. Only when the European colonial powers seized South America's rich silver and gold deposits could they begin to enter the Asian market on a relatively equal basis. Ultimately, the only way for the European countries to compete with their Asian counterparts was to mechanize production, since their labor costs were high and the more efficient Asian economies kept labor costs low. Europe rose, paradoxically, only because of Asian, especially Chinese, material success. Or, in Frank's own words, "'the Rise of the West' came late and was brief."[14]

He begins by noting that during the sixteenth and seventeenth century admiration and curiosity inspired Europeans to publish hundreds of books about Asia. As late as 1776, Adam Smith, the father of classical liberal economics, described China as far richer than any European country. Only a few decades later, however, European commentators had begun to talk about age-old Chinese backwardness and stagnation. What had changed? The Industrial Revolution enabled Europe to leap out ahead of the rest of Eurasia and thus filled European thinkers with Eurocentric arrogance and bias.

Nearly every recent scholar, according to Frank, has been shortsighted, blinkered by Eurocentrism, or overly specialized and so has seen world history in a merely fragmentary way. Instead, Frank proposes to

> look holistically at the whole global sociocultural, ecological-economic, and cultural system, which itself both offers and limits the "possibilities" of all of us. Since the whole is more than the sum of its parts and itself shapes its constituent parts, no amount of study and/or assemblage of the parts can ever lay bare the structure, functioning, and transformation of the whole world economy/system.[15]

Unfortunately, according to Frank, breaking out of the Eurocentric mindset proved impossible for even the greatest scholars, like Fernand Braudel and Wallerstein. Both – along with so many others, on the left and on the right – erroneously argued that Europe was the center of a unique emerging world economy and slighted the contributions of the rest of Eurasia to its development.

Against the mountains of existing Eurocentric scholarship, Frank puts forth what he considers the first truly global history of the world economy from roughly 1400 to 1800. He claims that,

> contrary to widespread doubts and denials, there was a single global world economy with a worldwide division of labor and multilateral trade from 1500 onward. This world economy had what can be identified as its own systemic character and dynamic, whose roots in Afro-Eurasia extended back for millennia. It was this world political economic structure and its

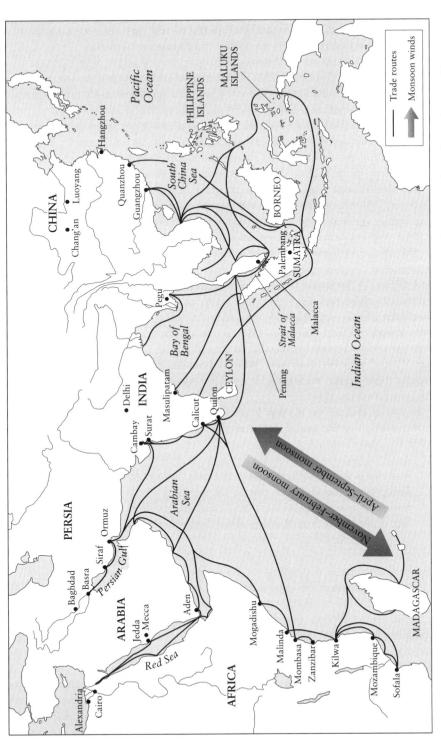

Map 4.1 Major trade routes of the Indian Ocean world: Asia was the great motor of economic development in the early modern world.

dynamic that had motivated Europeans to seek greater access to the economically dominant Asia ever since the European Crusades.[16]

As Frank argues throughout his book, this world economy was centered on
Asia, and indeed Sinocentric. That is, China, by far the world's most dynamic,
productive, competitive, and prosperous economy, stood at its middle.

Since Western scholars have already devoted masses of research to European
economic development in the early modern period, in his chapter on "Global
Trade" Frank devotes less than a page and a half to these developments, but to
the hitherto more neglected Asian economies – 41 and a half pages. He concludes that Europe was a minor participant in the world economy and that its
discovery of precious metals in the Americas alone enabled it to take part in
any significant way. Even then, Europe ran a perpetual trade deficit with the
mature Asian countries. By contrast, all of Asia contributed dynamically to the
world economy, from the Ottoman Empire and Persia and Central Asia to all
the countries of Southeast Asia and Japan and of course most especially India
and China. A series of maps indicating trade routes and the flows of silver
summarize these findings.   Frank seeks to compensate for scholarly neglect in
particular of such regions as Southeast and Central Asia, which he found to be
fully integrated into the Asia-centered world economy. For example, he notes
that Java "was reputed to be the greatest place on earth in the thirteenth century"[17] and that an economic boom commenced throughout Southeast Asia
around 1400 thanks to strong demand for spices and other commodities that
grew in profusion there.

In a brief chapter on money, Frank dissects the role of precious metals in the
world economy. He concludes that the extraction and distribution of silver
from the New World

> was the primary, indeed almost the only, world economic business of the
> Europeans, who were not able to sell anything else – especially of their own
> noncompetitive production – in the thriving markets of Asia. Asians would
> buy nothing else from Europe other than the silver it got out of its colonies
> in the Americas.[18]

Much if not most – depending on the time period – of that silver ended up in
China, in addition to silver produced in other parts of the world, especially
Japan, which also made its way in large quantity to China.

Frank also challenges the view held by scholars from David Hume and Adam
Smith to Wallerstein that precious metals mostly failed to stimulate economic
activity in Asia, and China in particular, at least to the same extent as in Europe,
but instead was hoarded and used mostly for adornment. On the contrary, he
argues, the Asian economies were far better able to absorb the enormous inflows
of bullion and coins than were the European economies, which experienced the
so-called "price revolution," a huge upsurge of inflation beginning in the second
half of the fifteenth century. According to Frank,

The new money which the Europeans brought over from the Americas probably stimulated production and supported population growth *more* in many parts of Asia than it did in Europe itself. This conclusion is supported by at least two observations. One is that the new money drove prices up more in Europe than in Asia, where increased production was better able to keep pace with the growing purchasing power generated by the additional money ... . [A second is that] population grew *more* in Asia, where it rose by about 6 percentage points of the world total, than in Europe where it remained stable (about 20% of the world total). Yet in 1750, Asia's still less than 66 percent of world population produced 80 percent of world GNP.[19]

These facts suggest that the Asian economies were more productive than those of Europe, Africa, and the Americas.

Frank goes on to analyze comparatively nearly every other possible indicator of material success. He presents evidence that throughout the early modern period the populations of Asia – and in particular of the most dynamic countries, like China – grew much faster than those of Europe. Similarly, trade across Asia was flourishing well before the arrival of European merchants. Frank cites, but disputes using other evidence, statistics indicating that European traders dominated world commerce in the eighteenth century. He lauds Joseph Needham's pioneering work on early Chinese science and his claim that as late as 1644 science in China and Western Europe did not significantly differ. He cites other authorities who emphasize continued scientific developments in the early modern Islamic world and India and who argue that science in Europe did not begin to foster technological development until the nineteenth century. Thus, even if it were true that the great ancient civilizations lagged behind Europe in science, then this would not have had any impact on their economic performance.

Other evidence suggests that the gunpowder weaponry, ships, and navigation techniques of the major Asian countries were either equal to or surpassed in efficiency those of Europe. Frank provides data showing that China had developed an excellence in printing, textile manufacturing, metallurgical, and transportation technologies well before the European countries and retained this excellence for centuries. The same could be said in some regards, he shows, of India and countries of the Islamic world. Frank then makes the argument that there was no such thing as European technology. He writes,

In the worldwide division of labor in a competitive world economy, national, regional, or sectoral technological superiority could not be maintained as long as at least some other real or potential competitors had sufficient interest and capacity to acquire such technology as well. That is, technological development was a *world economic process*, which took place in and because of the structure of the world economy/system itself. It is true that this world economy/system was and still is structurally unequal and temporally uneven. However, it is not true that technological or any other "development" was essentially determined either locally, regionally, nationally, or culturally; nor that any one place or people had any essential "monopoly" or even "superiority" within this world economy/system.[20]

Frank cites much evidence suggesting that commercial and financial techniques and institutions were also mutually influencing and relatively equivalent across the major cultures of Eurasia from the early modern into the modern period.

Next Frank addresses the controversy about the "seventeenth century crisis," which saw nearly all of Europe (but not Golden-Age Holland) plunged into a severe economic recession. He cites both scholars arguing that this crisis also gravely affected Asia and others disputing this claim. Frank sides with the deniers, suggesting that their evidence offers further proof that the big Asian economies were more significant and central to global commerce and therefore were independent of European economic trends. The Asian economies suffered from a downturn, but only for a decade or so around 1640, because of a worldwide decline in silver production, not because of any specifically European influences.

Frank presents this discussion within a broader treatment of Kondratiev waves. Named after the Russian economist, Nikolai Kondratiev (1892–1938) who perceived approximately 50-year economic cycles involving allegedly regular upswings and downturns, "K-waves" are proposed by some social scientists (but few economists) to explain long-term historical trends. Some scholars have purported to trace these cycles back hundreds of years. Frank emphasizes that in such analyses Asian countries were the driving forces behind the periods of economic growth in the vast majority of cases. He cites scholars who discern nineteen K-waves beginning in the early Song period in AD 930 and who argue that from 1190 world economic leadership shifted to Europe, yet he rejects this view. He concludes this section with a comparison of the Mongols and Europeans. He writes,

> The structural similarity of the Mongols and the Europeans is that both were peoples in (semi)marginal or peripheral areas who were attracted to and made incursions into the "core" areas and economies, which were principally in East Asia and secondarily in West Asia. Indeed, China was the principal attraction and first target for both … . Significantly in terms of the Gills and Frank analysis of world system-wide temporal long cycles, both the Mongol and the European peripheral incursions into East and West Asia were (relatively and temporarily?) successful during periods of long "B" phase economic decline in these previous economic Asian "cores."[21]

By "B" phase, he means the purported period of decline during a long Kondratiev wave. Here Frank is making an argument similar to that of Abu-Lughod: Europe could rise only because the historical world leader – Asia – was temporarily in a slump.

In addition to Kondratiev waves, Frank also posits longer-term economic cycles – up to six hundred years in duration and divided into periods of expansion and contraction each lasting between two and three centuries. Specifically, the most recent long cycle, he believes, commenced around 1400 throughout much of Asia and then entered the declining "B" phase after 1750. This cyclical decline gave the still-marginal West

> its first real opportunity to improve its relative and absolute position within the world economy and system. Only then could the West go on to achieve a (temporary?) period of dominance.[22]

Frank then compares Europe's rise to the more recent rise of East Asian countries, also "at the 'margin' of the world economy."[23]

Why the major and minor Asian economies declined from the eighteenth century is difficult to establish, concedes Frank. After surveying a wide range of evidence from scholars, he concludes that European advancement and colonial exploitation did not cause the slump, which was apparently already under way *before* major European imperialistic incursions began in the eastern half of Eurasia.

But what enabled the West to rise – to make those incursions? Frank answers this question with a metaphor:

> The answer, literally in a word, is that the Europeans *bought* themselves a seat, and then even a whole railway car, on the Asian train. How were any – literally – poor Europeans able to afford the price of even a third-class ticket to board the Asian economic train? Well, the Europeans somehow found and/or stole, extorted, or earned the money to do so.[24]

Frank adds that they acquired the money from silver mines and sugar plantations in the Americas, from the transatlantic slave trade, from selling in the Americas their manufactured goods, which were uncompetitive and undesired in Asia, and from reselling ubiquitously desirable Asian goods throughout the world.

But again and again, American silver was the source of European prosperity and its eventual rise. Frank notes:

> Without that silver – and, secondarily, without the division of labor and profits it generated in Europe itself – the Europeans would not have had a leg, or even a single toe, to stand on with which to compete in the Asian market. Only their American money, and not any "exceptional" European "qualities," which, as Smith realized even in 1776, had not been even remotely up to Asian standards, permitted the Europeans to buy their ticket on the Asian economic train and/or to take a third-class seat on it.[25]

The availability of almost endless silver to European merchants was their one competitive advantage with respect to their Asian rivals.

Frank argues, rather like Inikori, that Europe's participation in the world economy stimulated the ingenuity of its inventors and entrepreneurs – as the only way to get a piece of the lucrative Asian pie. For example, he quotes James Watt, the business partner of Matthew Boulton, the inventor of an improved steam engine, saying that it was only worth his while to market the device worldwide and not merely in a few countries. Frank also emphasizes the importance to European innovation of the high cost of labor. The agricultural and manufacturing systems of Europe were far less efficient and productive than those of the major Asian countries. Therefore, only by developing labor-saving devices (machinery) could European entrepreneurs hope to compete against their Asian counterparts. The Europeans had lots of capital, thanks to their exploitation of colonial dependencies and the slave trade, and they invested it in mechanization and the switch-over from charcoal to coal.

Europe's rise was facilitated by a new Kondratiev upswing at the start of the nineteenth century, when

> the Napoleonic Wars generated increased investment in and the expansion of these new technologies, including transport equipment, and also led to the incorporation of ever more available but still relatively high-cost labor into the "factory system." Production increased rapidly; real wages and income declined; and the "workshop of the world" conquered foreign markets through "free trade."[26]

In reality, the British government still prohibited the free flow of goods from India, which remained for decades more competitive. Likewise, only the massive export of opium to China reversed the unfavorable balance of trade with that still powerful economy.

Coal and colonies account for the rise (Kenneth Pomeranz)

Frank admits in his book that only one other scholar reached similar conclusions to his – "a minority of two standing against the conventional wisdom"[27] – and that scholar is Kenneth Pomeranz. A historian of modern China at the University of Chicago, Pomeranz seeks to show how Europe managed to rise from a position of inferiority with respect to China thanks in particular to serendipitously big coal deposits in Great Britain and the exploitation of overseas colonial riches, in addition to several other factors, including internal European vitality and innovation.[28]

The world in which Europe rose, Pomeranz argues, was polycentric, without a single dominant economic power. Europe depended, moreover, on such fortuitous global trends, like strong Chinese demand for silver. A key distinction he makes, however, is to compare the leading regions in China – in particular the Yangzi Delta – with the most advanced European countries, since he finds them much closer in economic development than Europe as a whole or China in its entirety.

Like Inikori, he underlines Europe's great benefit from its commercial participation in the Atlantic world. The conquest, depopulation, and development of the New World, in particular using African slave labor, caused enormous resources to flow into Europe at a rate vastly greater than would have been possible within the limits of commercial relations among the Old World countries. This commercial arrangement created a highly advantageous division of labor between raw material extraction west of the Atlantic and the manufacturing of finished goods to its east. Consequently, there emerged the modern world's first "core" and first "periphery," and together they enabled Western Europe to forge a unique commercial system by bringing together already-existing social and economic elements."[29] Like McNeill, therefore, he considers connections and interactions across Eurasia, as well as beyond, to have been of utmost importance.

Pomeranz devotes his first chapter to comparing statistical indices of material well-being in Europe and Asia in the early modern period. Livestock was more abundant in Europe and contributed much protein, he admits, but the manure it provided did not raise crop yields higher than in the main Asian countries. It facilitated land transport, but China had more efficient water transport. Europeans may have enjoyed superior housing, but people in China, Japan, and South East Asia enjoyed far safer drinking water and other public health conditions. People's diet was relatively comparable in the two regions in terms of caloric intake, though Europeans ate more animal protein. People's life expectancy was roughly comparable. He disputes the claim that Europeans consciously had fewer children, though he attributes the Chinese and Japanese achievement in this regard largely to infanticide.

As regards technology and innovation, Pomeranz acknowledges that learned societies and journals probably helped spread knowledge more effectively than the Chinese tradition of public correspondence. Yet he also notes that science and mathematics continued to advance in China and that agricultural and textile manufacturing techniques were more advanced there and in India. Chinese artisans also devised ingeniously efficient wood-burning stoves and specially designed cellars for cotton spinning in the dry months, which both fell into desuetude only with the development of industrial technologies in Europe.

Here the author points to the importance of historical accidents. China's coal-mining and iron-smelting industry a thousand years ago were cutting edge and highly extensive, anticipating British developments in the eighteenth century. Unfortunately, a series of invasions and natural disasters crippled these sectors, which never fully recovered. More curious – but just as accidental – were the differing impediments facing coal-mining in northern China, where most of the deposits lie, and in Great Britain. In China, spontaneous combustion within the mines made them unsafe for workers. Chinese craftsmen therefore devised sophisticated ventilation systems to alleviate the problem. British mines, by contrast, often flood with water, making them unusable. Crafty artisans solved that problem with steam-powered pumps. Of course, ventilators can only move air, whereas steam engines can move mile-long freight trains and therefore could power the Industrial Revolution. Moreover, it really helped British development that big coal and iron-ore deposits lay in close proximity to the main centers of technological advances, unlike in China where they were far removed from the Yangzi Delta.

Pomeranz also takes on the argument put forward by many scholars, including Frank, that the higher wages of European and American workers induced inventors and entrepreneurs to devise labor-saving devices. He counters, on the one hand, that the average wages in China, Japan, and other parts of East Asia were at least as high as those in Europe and, on the other hand, the higher cost of labor can make it harder for entrepreneurs to find the excess capital to invest in untried technologies. Also, he cites studies indicating that the pursuit of new technologies in Europe was often aimed at improving quality and not at driving down labor costs. Pomeranz admits, however, that competing with Asian textile manufacturers who produced high-quality cloth at prices far below anything European entrepreneurs could match was probably the one economic sector in which developing labor-saving devices made the most bottom-line sense. Even so, he argues, had European entrepreneurs not seized a windfall of low-cost raw cotton in the Americas and cheap labor to harvest it – African slaves – then all of the brilliant inventions of the eighteenth century would have been for naught.

An increased understanding of ecology in the eighteenth and nineteenth centuries enabled Europeans to reverse long-term trends of deforestation and environmental destruction that had been afflicting all the regions of the Old World. This knowledge came from advances in Newtonian mechanics – thus, internal European developments – but also from professional experience of scientists and colonial officials in fast-evolving tropical regions and from well-versed Indian and Chinese experts. Again, Europeans made great progress but could not have done so alone.

The one area of European superiority that Pomeranz concedes is in the manufacture of instruments for time-keeping, magnification, and measurement. Though of little wide-scale consumer value at the time, their manufacture habituated European craftsmen to precision engineering that carried over very effectively to the development of steam power and beyond. Even so, he argues, without the large coal deposits in close proximity to one of Europe's biggest concentrations of technical skill, all the brilliant innovations in the world would have been of little value. He writes, "even this energy breakthrough could have been swallowed up by Europe's population boom in the late eighteenth and nineteenth centuries if certain other resource problems had not also been solved," largely because of European conquests across the globe. Neither coal, nor colonies, nor other European technological innovations, taken alone, could have prevented a looming demographic and resource crisis and made possible the emergence of the modern world in which economic growth could continue indefinitely without the input of more and more land.[30] "Coal and colonies," taken together and despite the other factors favoring Europe's rise, were thus in his opinion the crucial ones.

Pomeranz next investigates the nature of economic markets in Europe and East Asia. He concludes that China's agricultural sector was more market driven than Europe's. He concedes that in the Yangzi Delta custom required offering to rent or sell land first to kinfolk or fellow villagers. Yet even there, arable land was generally far more alienable (sellable at will) than in most parts of Europe, including England. True, already in the seventeenth century the land markets in Holland, Lombardy, and Sweden were almost entirely free, yet these comprised small portions of the continent. Thus, by 1800 only a small portion of European cultivators farmed according to the new – and more productive – methods of husbandry. Also, the customary rules concerning such improvements as the draining of swamps and installing of irrigation systems were far more restrictive in most of Europe than in the major Asian countries. Thus, in general, the land markets in Europe were less efficient than those in China or Japan.

How about the labor markets, then? The evidence Pomeranz has sifted through suggests that serfdom and other forms of unfree labor fell away earlier in China for a far larger proportion of the population. Also, mass migration to less populated rural areas was far more extensive in China – and indeed was facilitated by the government – during the early modern period. Europe's guilds generally were able to control manufacturing – especially to shut out rural competition – better than those in China. Moreover, Europe's labor markets seem not to have been better integrated than China's or Japan's, perhaps on the contrary. He concedes, however, that far more Europeans – both male and female – wandered to cities seeking employment, an option made difficult in China by the government and by customs forbidding women to travel alone.

Yet he questions research suggesting that since women could rarely work outside the home, families tended to view their labor as costless or that European families tended to spend more money on household articles so as to free up their womenfolk for home-based manufacturing. He also rejects allegations that comparative analyses of female participation in the workforce prove that Europe was more "revolutionary," and China more "involutionary." For cultural reasons women worked outside the home less in China, yet the products they manufactured within the home were marketed just as much as – if not more than – those produced by European women. Moreover, European cultural norms often compelled women to produce only for the home and not for the market. Such rules "could be at least as hostile to female enterprise as Chinese preferences, which held that women should preferably stay within the family compound but saw nothing wrong with them engaging in market-oriented production there."[31] In fact, Pomeranz points out that the practice of Chinese empresses publicly celebrating women's work – the gathering of mulberries – could not conceivably have had a European counterpart. In other words, the argument that Europe rose thanks to the higher status of women falls flat.

Pomeranz next turns to popular consumption of everyday luxuries – tea, coffee, sugar, cocoa, and other "drug foods." The Chinese as a whole, he finds, consumed more sugar than the Europeans per capita right down to the mid-1800s, and even more tea, though the English consumed more of each several decades earlier. From 1800, however, Chinese consumption per capita declined, because the population soared in poorer regions. As the mouths to feed multiplied, the cultivation of grain squeezed out the drug crops. By contrast, Europeans had vast New World lands in which to plant sugar, coffee, and tobacco.

Similarly, recent scholarship shows that conspicuous consumption of petty luxuries, like books, umbrellas, incense, jewelry, fine clothing, and home furnishings, along with manuals explaining how to acquire and display them, characterized early modern China and Japan as well as Europe, but probably not as much Southeast Asia or the Middle East, though for no region of the world is so much documentation available as for Europe. The better-off Europeans hands down invested more money in their housing, but that was partly because East Asians preferred, for traditional reasons, to build houses out of wood. Homes were more an expression of individual accomplishment and tastes in Europe and of generational solidarity in China, but such distinctions do not necessarily demonstrate a higher standard of living in Europe. Commercialized leisure activities – for example, travel and eating out – proliferated in early modern China and Japan. Such phenomena were also well known in Europe.

One difference scholars have detected between European and East Asian societies concerns the pace of changing fashion. Whereas in China, once the Qing dynasty was well established by around 1700, clothing styles changed much more slowly, in Europe fashion consciousness apparently heightened decade by decade beginning in the early modern period. Pomeranz explains this difference as a function of greater political instability. He argues that the Qing dynasty, by re-legitimizing the state, may have re-empowered trend-setting elites to set strict rules of social status, thus undermining market-directed fashion trends.[32] Why would it work out this way? In part, he argues, because the Chinese government stabilized itself by strengthening the traditional local institutions and kinship networks, which defined people's status and position in society without recourse to consumer-oriented markers. In Europe, by contrast, the opposite occurred: the states weakened kinship ties.

Pomeranz finishes this section by addressing an important point that most scholars take for granted: that the Chinese were uninterested in commodities or manufactured goods from Europe. He notes, to begin with, that in fact there was a market in early modern China for European eyeglasses, some fashion items, and exotic furs, but he asks why no such product had the kind of transformative effect on East Asian cultures like silk or cotton textiles did on European cultures. He rejects the idea, put forward by various scholars, that Europeans were by nature more curious or acquisitive. For one thing, the Chinese imported masses of exotic wares – like sharks' teeth or birds' nests – from Southeast Asia, the Middle East, and the Pacific islands. Yet the quantities of such goods were finite and could not therefore become the objects of fads like sugar or tobacco, which were produced at industrial scale on Caribbean plantations using slave labor. Other scholars make the mistake of considering silver only a medium of exchange. It was in fact, according to Pomeranz, a commodity, a good, which happened to be far more valuable in China than in most other places, so naturally European merchants had no need to find other goods to sell there. This also explains why so many exotic goods flooded into Europe: Europeans coercively controlled the world's biggest supplies of silver.

Next, Pomeranz investigates capital markets, financial institutions, property rights, business firms, wealth accumulation, and public–private commercial ventures at both ends of Eurasia. He found in general that in all the developed societies capital was more abundant than ventures in which to invest it. Also, the longevity of companies may have been more impressive in China than in Europe. Individuals and firms may have been no more prey to government confiscation in China, but their capital apparently was. Yet European merchants who lent far more money to rulers were thus more liable to suffer from government defaults. Also, kinship ties enabled Chinese mercantile families to amass probably as much capital as their European counterparts, even if these ties somewhat restricted how it could be invested.

The key difference between European and East Asian business firms, according to Pomeranz, concerned their deployment for overseas commerce, in which European merchants engaged far more than other peoples. He reasons that larger and more complex business organizations, both partnerships and joint-stock companies, emerged in Europe largely in order to manage vast overseas commercial operations. These bigger firms naturally tended to separate investors and owners and to make possible the pooling of huge volumes of capital.[33] By contrast, Chinese businessmen would travel with their goods in berths they rented from ship owners, because the monsoon winds patterns made it necessary to lay over for months on end at various ports; they could therefore not afford to hire full-time crews to work for them as merchants plying the Atlantic could. Otherwise, Chinese merchants seem to have employed highly refined business techniques, excepting limited liability, which was unnecessary for their ventures.

As Mielants also emphasized (see Chapter 3), Chinese officials interfered less in business activities than their European counterparts but also provided fewer opportunities for merchants to dominate this or that corner of the market. Public–private business operations were more frequent in India, but they seem to have had a smaller impact on the overall economy than in Europe. Chinese officials were probably more involved in business than appeared to the public eye, since they typically concealed such activities in order to avoid appearances of impropriety. In general, our author believes that government interference – or its absence – was probably not a major factor in business success in the early modern or modern periods.

Pomeranz admits that capital markets in Northwestern Europe were probably more efficient than anywhere else in the world, as evidenced by the far lower interest rates for business loans. Yet he adds that collateralized property in China was far more secure than in Europe, where creditors could seize it much more easily in the case of a default. Thus Chinese borrowers might have been willing to pay higher interest rates, since it was highly unlikely that they would lose everything should their investments fail. Our author also admits – though he considers it speculative – that the lower European interest rates may have made it easier to import goods from overseas in riskier shipping ventures. Overall, however, Pomeranz does not believe this difference could have been decisive.

Finally, in this section, Pomeranz analyzes the contributions of overseas extractions of resources and the slave trade to Europe's rise to preeminence. He cites one scholar who calculated that in the late eighteenth century these sources of income constituted only 7 percent of gross business investment. Yet in the conditions of early modern Europe, according to Pomeranz, an increase of that size in capital stock could make a big difference. The Chinese demand for silver, he argues, is what made the Spanish colonies profitable; without it, "the mines of the New World would probably have ceased within a few decades to be able to keep earning a profit while paying the rents that kept the Spanish empire functioning."[34] Indeed, the international silver trade, which was driven by the gigantic silver-based Chinese economy, marked a qualitative and quantitative commercial advancement in global affairs. Still, Pomeranz disagrees with Frank on the question of European demand for Asian goods. Pointing out that Frank seems intent on denying Europe any significant agency in the world economy, Pomeranz admits that the rather extraordinary European consumer demand had to be a significant part of the story.

That demand was filled by what he considers the one truly unique aspect of the early modern European economy: the early government-backed colonial companies. He denies their economic efficiency in general but holds them highly suited for building and running monopolistic commercial empires overseas. These merchant-warriors grew out of a civilization engaged in almost continuous war making.

Pomeranz contests arguments advanced by numerous scholars that armed competition among the European states promoted technological development, economic growth, or the securing of property and political rights. On the first two points, he contends that the ongoing arms race probably diverted resources away from the civilian sectors. As regards the idea that in order to secure revenue for military purposes early modern European governments were forced to grant political and economic concessions to elite members of society, Pomeranz concedes that representative government and property rights often emerged in Europe through this pathway. Freedom of speech and other civil rights, however, were typically gained by other means.

No, the most important feature of the colonial enterprises was those enterprises themselves. They differed markedly from, for example, Chinese endeavors throughout Southeast Asia, which completely lacked government funding and military support and could not attract mass immigration, because of government opposition. Only one large-scale Chinese commercial empire flourished during the early modern period, and only thanks to a Chinese dynastic crisis. (The Chinese state supported territorial expansion into Central Asia but not overseas.)

Why these differences? Since the everyday luxuries like tea, sugar, silk, and tobacco were nearly entirely produced within China, state officials could not slap tariffs on them and thus had no reason to promote their consumption as European officials did. Moreover, the Chinese enjoyed no epidemiological immunity compared to the inhabitants of adjoining regions and so could not take them over as easily as the European conquerors did in the Americas.

It was precisely this advantage – and in general the conquest of far-flung colonial empires – that enabled Europe, which otherwise was not more economically productive or efficient than the other major Eurasian societies – to propel itself into industrialization. Thus, Pomeranz argues that the other advanced economies in the early modern period should not be viewed as "failed Europes." Instead, Western Europe went from being simply one of many developing regions to "a fortunate freak" thanks only to highly unusual circumstances enabling it to break out of historically unavoidable constraints on energy and resources.[35] Here Pomeranz is referring to the huge deposits of coal in Britain that fueled the Industrial Revolution and the vast network of colonies that partly funded it.

In the final section of his book, our author carefully analyzes the ecological and geological constraints that had prevented all the premodern societies from breaking through to modern economic growth. In brief, people had to make do with materials – including fertilizer – derived from very limited supplies of natural substances and with energy derived from water, wind, muscle, wood, and a bit of coal. Land was in short supply in China especially but also in Japan and Europe, and, without major technological advances, demographic catastrophe would have resulted in all three.

In the eighteenth century, the Europeans had far more unused land reserves than the peoples of East Asia and many more improvements in agricultural methods yet to make. Thus they could potentially increase their food output more. In fiber crops, however, Europe was less fortunate than the peoples in the rest of Eurasia, since they could not grow their own cotton, at a time when cotton cloth was becoming very popular. Moreover, none of the Eurasian peoples could readily expand their own supplies of the last two of the Malthusian necessities – fuel and building materials. Most Europeans may have had more abundant supplies of cooking fuel, but the Chinese in particular employed more fuel-efficient means of cooking, and their winters were typically warmer. Coal was a welcome addition to the heating portfolio, but not until after 1850 for most of Europe. And several European regions were down to single-digit forest reserves – far less than many East Asian countries, where trees grow faster because of the warmer weather and people tended to husband their forest resources more efficiently. Overall, however, greater water resources may have given Europe a slight potential edge.

Europe's biggest advantage resulted ironically from its backwardness. Unable to meet its need for food, textile fibers, and fuel through more intensive labor inputs, following the East Asian model, which ultimately would lead to a disastrous dead end, the Europeans began to import these resources. And this made all the difference, argues Pomeranz. Around 1800, China had powerful factors working against it. First, its self-reliance on industrial fibers and lack of colonies from which to import raw materials created an ecological vulnerability. Second, there were very few options for agricultural and infrastructural improvement, since nearly every conceivable one this side of an industrial revolution had already been discovered and implemented. Third, territorial growth was becoming more difficult in the absence of overseas colonization. In view of these difficulties, a rapid economic divergence between China and Europe was probably unavoidable, even though the ecological pressures on Europe were roughly as bad, once one factors in the extraordinary benefits it derived from the exploitation of coal and colonies. Similarly, Pomeranz claims, without a concatenation of positive developments – new technology, learning from Asia, and gaining a windfall from the New World – Europe would almost certainly have ended up in an ecological and developmental dead end like China.[36] Again, coal and especially colonies explain Europe's transformation that led to the "great divergence" of Pomeranz's book title.

The relief could not come from Eastern Europe, despite the tenets of world system analysis, according to Pomeranz, for two reasons. First, custom and landed interests made it difficult to impose on Eastern Europe's peasant laborers the ruthlessly coercive methods used in the West Indian plantations. Second, the region's narrow market for manufactured goods meant that it remained an insubstantial trading partner, and one with which Western Europe ran a trade deficit. In the words of Pomeranz, "Merely finding 'less-advanced' trading partners did not solve any core's problems, at least not for long."[37] No, only the resource windfall of the Americas could break the bottleneck and save Europe from ecological disaster.

Pomeranz subtitles his final chapter "The Americas as a New Kind of Periphery," in which a very large proportion of the labor force was coerced to such an extent that it could not even provide for its own economic subsistence and therefore became a captive market for European manufactured goods – to a far greater extent than the adjacent hinterlands of Asia or Europe could become. In fact the plantation or mine workers specialized completely in producing export commodities, like sugar or silver, that also paid for food cultivated by other European entrepreneurs in the region or for goods from Asia. Such wares as silks, cotton prints, exotic spices, and fine china, which mostly could not have been obtained in any other way, were then traded for slaves in Africa or ended up raising standards of living in Europe. Thus, as Pomeranz argues, the plantation-based economies of the New World colonies constituted a periphery that would maintain a relative balance of trade with the core thanks to a constant exchange of raw materials flowing eastward and finished goods, foodstuffs, and slaves going westward, to say nothing of "(often) more plantation debt, which led to selling more sugar next year, at whatever price."[38] This entire trading system became more and more efficient, as entrepreneurs strived to reduce their costs. Still, the global commercial networks, into which the Europeans attached their own economy, remained polycentric, according to Pomeranz.

Ecological disaster was avoided for Europe also thanks to the importation of specific crops. An acre of sugarcane produces four times more calories and potatoes 9 to 12 times more than wheat. As Europeans consumed more sugar, they could turn more land and especially laborers over to other economic activities. Of course, the higher caloric yield of potatoes was also a New World contribution to European standards of living. Cheaper cloth woven from imported American cotton made it possible for Europeans to dress up against the cold and therefore also to consume fewer calories, something the consumption of tea, coffee, tobacco, and cocoa also made possible.

The customs duties on these and other imported commodities yielded roughly half the increase in the British government's income from 1670 to 1810, most of which went to pay for the bigger military needed in large part to police the colonies and the high seas. And controlling the colonies made it possible to increase imports of sugar elevenfold and of cotton twentyfold during the period 1815–1900 and to compensate for a growing trade deficit with the United States, as it became an export powerhouse. Of course, a vast increase in coal outputs also fueled these developments, not least through steamships.

Thus, the availability of huge coal deposits and the securing of prodigiously fecund overseas colonies can best explain Europe's rise. Like China and other developed Eurasian countries, the European states faced potential socioeconomic and demographic crises until they managed to combine existing labor and capital with "largely extra-European and nonmarket factors" to transform the transatlantic commercial relations into a self-sustaining engine of economic growth. In the absence of those factors, the ongoing but feeble economic expansion might have crashed on several possible bottlenecks, including excessive population increase and quickly mounting costs for raw materials, or might have been avoided only by means of labor-intensive agriculture, which would have made industrial revolution impossible.[39] For Pomeranz, factors external to Europe and historical accidents contributed powerfully to the rise of Europe into the world's dominant and most dynamic economy with by far the highest standard of living.

Nearly all the West's achievements were Eastern in origin (John M. Hobson)

This chapter's final author returns full circle to the previous one. John M. Hobson, a professor of politics and international relations in England, dedicates his *The Eastern Origins of Western Civilization* (2004) in part to his great-grandfather, John A. Hobson, whose *Imperialism* (1902) was a key influence on Lenin's *Imperialism, the Highest Stage of Capitalism*, with which chapter 3 began.

In a volume bolder though built upon a less impressive foundation of research than Pomeranz's, Hobson rejects what he calls the "Eurocentric" or "Orientalist" (terms he uses interchangeably) interpretation of the rise of the West. He claims that these interpretations, starting with those of Marx and

Weber, attribute rationality, dynamism, and ingenuity to the West but irrationality, stagnation, and passivity to the East. Hobson argues that most historical and social scientific interpretations of modern history take these dichotomies for granted and credit them with making possible the West's breakthrough to modern capitalist society.

Yet these scholars, according to Hobson, have the story entirely backwards. What really happened, he argues, was that, first, the East surged forward economically from roughly AD 500; second, it remained the primary engine of international economic relations for well over one thousand years; and, third and most importantly, it played a major role in facilitating the West's ascendancy by making available powerful technologies, institutions, and ideas, which he calls "resource portfolios."[40] Throughout his book, Hobson makes the case that just about every achievement of the West was made possible through the assimilation – either peacefully or by force – of such resource portfolios.

In the first part of his book, Hobson describes what he calls "Islamic and African pioneers" of a global trade network that linked the Afro-Eurasian landmass – from Ummayad North Africa to Tang China – starting in roughly AD 500. The prime movers of this economic system were Muslim traders, in part because the Qur'an and other sacred Islamic texts explicitly promoted commerce, as did the founder of Islam, himself a merchant by trade. Islamic societies flourished across the entire landmass from the Atlantic to the Indian and the Pacific Oceans. They led the world, in other words, in "extensive power." Of this global system of trade, Hobson concludes that "its ultimate significance lay in the fact that oriental globalization was the midwife, if not the mother, of the medieval and modern West."[41] Thanks also to impressive technological, scientific, and industrial developments, the Islamic societies led the world in "intensive power," by which Hobson means the ability to harness and focus human effort for specific purposes. The Muslim world thus dominated in both kinds of power from 650 until around 1100, when the leading edge of intensive power passed to Song China.

Hobson emphasizes the Chinese genius for technological innovation mostly during the Song period (960–1279). (Those achievements discussed earlier in this book will be omitted here.) He begins with the so-called Industrial Revolution of the Northern Song period, during which more iron was produced at lower prices in the eleventh century than in all of Europe before 1700, thanks to early coke-fired blast furnaces and piston bellows, and distributed around the country thanks to extensive canal systems. Chinese society apparently deployed the metal – both wrought and cast – in the widest possible uses, from needles and pins to boilers and suspension bridges. That great Chinese invention, paper, also found myriad uses in Chinese society, from articles of clothing to toilet tissue. Drawing on work by Joseph Needham and other scholars, he describes the world's first military revolution that apparently unfolded in the period between 850 and 1290 and involved wide uses of yet another great Chinese invention, gunpowder, including rocket launchers, firearms, landmines, flamethrowers, grenades, and bombs. The Chinese navy deployed a huge number of enormous ships, some equipped with bomb-hurling catapults and giant battering hammers.

To scholars who dismiss the Song achievements as "an abortive revolution" without further technological advancements, following which the Ming allegedly sealed China off from foreign influences and contacts, Hobson replies that China remained a flourishing economy strongly integrated into global trade networks and with a highly productive agricultural sector. The alleged sealing off of China was in reality, according to Hobson, a fiction that the Ming rulers promoted solely for domestic political reasons. Instead of open trade, they maintained a tribute system, whereby all the other countries of the world were expected to give signs of respect, under the cloak of which vibrant trade proceeded. Hobson explains that the tribute system helped legitimize the Chinese dynasty and state, in part by obligating representatives of the vassal states to prostrate themselves face down before the emperor (the kowtow). This act demonstrated their symbolic acknowledgment of the emperor's Mandate of Heaven.[42] So, while foreign governments pretended to acknowledge Chinese superiority, behind the scenes domestic officials turned a blind eye to trade (often taking bribes to do so), while merchants, smugglers, and pirates kept China connected to the worldwide economic system. As Hobson notes, the proof that China remained part of that system is the fact that it continued to absorb much of the world's silver.

Hobson also presents evidence of highly developed commercial activity in early modern India. In particular, the Gujarati merchants from at least the mid-seventeenth century enjoyed from their rulers both military protection and a relatively laissez-faire administrative environment. He cites the benevolent attitude of one Maratha ruler, Shivaji, who reigned from 1674 to 1680 and considered merchants to be "the ornaments of the kingdom and the glory of the king."[43] At the same time, the central authorities throughout India were typically weak, and the local authorities were often also favorable to commerce. Facing relatively little government interference, Indian merchants developed sophisticated financial institutions and techniques. Business naturally thrived, and some businessmen became fabulously wealthy. Finally, not only was the Indian textile output greater and of a higher quality than Britain's right down to the end of the eighteenth if not into the nineteenth century, but so was its production of steel.

Much the same can be said of South East Asian commerce in the early modern period, according to Hobson. Merchants from the area operated bigger ships than their European counterparts and traded huge quantities of both luxury and bulk goods.

Hobson concludes this part of his book with an overview of the economic dynamism of Japan during the Tokugawa era (1603–1868) – and not just after the Meiji rulers commenced Westernization beginning in 1868. Hobson cites data indicating per capita income growth – and significant growth in agricultural production – for at least the second half if not the entirety of the period. Moreover, like the European absolutist monarchs, the Tokugawa rulers systematically stripped the powerful landholding magnates and territorial over-lords (*daimyo*) and their vassals (samurai) of their autonomy, thus strengthen-ing the position of merchants and other elements of the commons, including the peasantry, who began to produce for the market. With official recognition, numerous banks emerged that deployed sophisticated financial instruments and procedures, involving for example a futures exchange that appeared before any in Frankfurt or London, and whose operations extended into rural areas.

Finally, Hobson denies that Japan's rulers starting in 1639 really intended to wall off their country from foreign commerce and influences – except from China and Holland – as the policy of *sakoku* (meaning "closed country") overtly stated. Rather, they "merely sought to regulate or control foreign trade" and not in fact "to limit trade with the outside world *per se*, but to limit trade only with the Catholic powers of Europe."[44] In reality, commercial relations with a wide variety of foreign partners flourished either openly or in secret.

The next section of the book tackles what Hobson considers "myths" of European leadership from the medieval to the early modern period. The cele-brated medieval agricultural revolution, for example, was made possible by the adaptation of several technologies that developed in Asia, including the horse collar harness, the water mill, and perhaps also the horseshoe and the heavy plow. Similarly, the mounted feudal knights who dominated every European battlefield for several centuries could never have emerged without the invention of the stirrup, which Hobson traces back to China. The supposedly premier medieval European military innovation – the mounted shock cavalry – was first developed by the Persians and the Byzantines. Such apparently quintessential European weapons as the longbow and the lance had Middle Eastern origins. Even the emergence of feudalism, according to Hobson, echoing the Belgian medievalist Henri Pirenne who argued that the Carolingian Empire would have been inconceivable without the threat posed by Islam, was stimulated by attacks from Asian warriors.

Hobson goes further still, arguing that the Western European Christian iden-tity was constructed around an artificial Islamic menace. He argues that the medieval Europeans viewed their own culture as purely good and everything outside that culture, the "other," as evil. Therefore, they needed some imaginary other to despise. Whom did they select? The powerful religious authorities focused European hatred on Islam and constructed it "not just as evil but also as a threat, so that the Europeans could unite against it."[45] The leading European elites then went on to define Western Christendom in direct opposition to the Islamic Middle East. Ironically, however, Christianity was born in the Middle East and not in Europe, and just as ironically, Western Europeans came to think of themselves as the standard-bearers of Christianity throughout the world.

The next "myth" that Hobson seeks to dismantle is that of the "Italian pio-neers" in global commerce. In reality, he argues, all of the technologies and institutions that enabled Italian merchants to forge trans-Eurasian trading net-works were adapted from Asian antecedents, including already existing trading networks. Like Goody and Frank, Hobson points to the wide array of financial instruments and techniques developed by Muslim traders a century or two before the Italians used them. Much the same can be said of technical advances that made Europe's navigational revolution possible. For example, the astrolabe, though invented in ancient Greece, was refined by Muslims. Chinese sailors had first used the compass for navigation in the eleventh century, though Chinese inventors had developed the technology a thousand years earlier. Hobson asserts that Persians or Arabs may have invented the lateen (triangular) sail. Finally, Chinese sailors definitely invented the sternpost rudder and the square hull. In fact, even "the pizza base was first invented in ancient Egypt."[46]

Hobson goes on to catalogue numerous other Asian inventions – either certainly or possibly adapted by European artisans – such as the windmill, the spinning wheel, the textile loom, paper, blast furnaces, and the escapement mechanism for mechanical clocks.

Our author then takes aim at the "myth of the Vasco da Gama epoque." The Portuguese mariners did not embody the modern era of world exploration, he argues, but rather the tail end of the crusading impulse, re-energized because of the Ottoman conquest of Constantinople in 1453 and Athens in 1456. As evidence, he cites papal decrees issued between 1452 and 1456 calling on the Portuguese to overthrow the Muslims and to spread Christianity among them. Hobson admits there were economic motivations for finding a passage to the Indies, but he insists that Christianity justified Portuguese imperialism in Asia from the outset. He also cites sources claiming that one Arab, one Indian (or possibly Chinese), and yet another Chinese mariner had, or possibly had, sailed up the West Coast of Africa before Portuguese explorers sailed in the other direction. Moreover, the riches they found in India awed the Europeans.

The Asians remained more advanced for a long time in navigation and commerce. The European ships were puny compared to those, for example, of Zheng He's treasure fleets (see Map 4.2), and though those voyages were discontinued in 1433, the Chinese navy was strong enough to hold European forces at bay for four more centuries. Ultimately, the Portuguese – and their various European successors – generally triumphed only when they played rival Asian powers against each other. Neither the Portuguese nor the Dutch nor the British established a trading monopoly throughout the Indian Ocean world. Even the famous Portuguese *cartaz*, whereby Asian ships would carry passports and fly Portuguese flags enabling them to avoid higher tariffs in Portuguese ports, was only "protection money" to avoid the economically irrational step of arming their ships against Portuguese naval power. In general, the Europeans had to cooperate with local rulers and merchants and found, in many cases, the greatest profits in the intra-Asian trade.

The next "myth" Hobson seeks to deconstruct is "1492." The sailing of Columbus to the Americas, argues Hobson, was possible only thanks to the borrowing of technology from Asia. He contends that Europe's very economic backwardness gave it an advantage within the highly developed Eurasian context. In other words, the Europeans did not raise themselves on their own, but rather continuously borrowed or imitated the advanced resource portfolios first

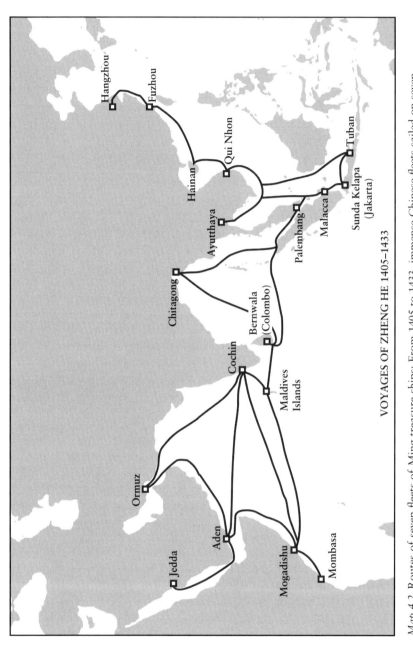

Map 4.2 Routes of seven fleets of Ming treasure ships: From 1405 to 1433, immense Chinese fleets sailed on seven voyages throughout the Indian Ocean world.

developed in the East. It was probably only thanks to these earlier achievements that Columbus was able to cross the Atlantic in the first place.[47]

In fact, Hobson claims that Columbus was at least partly motivated by the medieval Crusader mentality. As evidence, he points out that Columbus wrote in his diary that, if he found much gold in the Indies, it could potentially enable the Spanish kings to conquer the Holy Land. He also obstinately refused for the rest of his life to admit he had not landed in Asia. And the European conquerors nearly all viewed the native peoples – and the Africans they brought in to replace their labor – as inferior, obviously with baleful consequences. At the same time, dominating those peoples enabled the Europeans to construct an identity for themselves as "advanced" and "superior."

In this chapter, Hobson takes on several other "myths" about the alleged greatness of Europe. The Renaissance, he suggests, would have been impossible without the far-reaching and manifold advancements in mathematics, philosophy, science (including scientific method), and the conceptualization of the individual person in the Islamic world. Similarly, since a form of movable-type printing was invented in China in the eleventh century, and a more sophisticated form appeared in Korea around 1400, Hobson considers it highly likely that this technology diffused from East to West and influenced the invention of printing by Gutenberg. Finally, he traces the origins of the European military revolutions to Asia. "Just about every significant technological aspect of the European military revolution," he writes, "was derived from the East." True, by the nineteenth century the Europeans had pushed the technologies to higher levels of effectiveness, yet without the earlier Eastern achievements those European advances would have been impossible.[48] In other words, according to Hobson, some of Europe's most iconic achievements owed almost everything to Asia.

Next, the author sets out to show that British industrialization was similar to the recent Japanese miracle, with the sole difference that British entrepreneurs imitated China instead of the Modern West. He starts with the Enlightenment, which he claims emerged from direct Chinese influences. Intellectuals from Leibniz to Voltaire exulted over Confucius, as an enlightened thinker and pure rationalist, and all things Chinese, especially statecraft and the decorative arts. Early European economists learned the principles of laissez-faire from age-old Chinese state policy. European knowledge transmitted from China began with Franciscan monks returning home in the thirteenth century and continued with Jesuits sent by the dozen from the seventeenth century to report on Chinese technology. As a result of these contacts, several important farming advances – the iron moldboard plow, the rotary winnowing machine, the seed-drill, and modern crop-rotation methods – all probably diffused from China and probably thus made possible the early modern agricultural revolution.

Much the same can be asserted, according to Hobson, about the mechanical technology of the Industrial Revolution. Chinese artisans had invented the blast furnace, a water-powered bellows, a piston-cylinder system, and a co-fusion steel-making process; for textile production they had devised a spinning machine and silk-production mills; and they had also built iron suspension bridges all over China, had used gas lamps to light cities, and had undertaken deep-mining techniques – all centuries before any of these technologies were made successful in Europe. All in all, the greatest claim to fame of the British was not inventiveness per se but only their persevering ability to adapt and improve on Asian breakthroughs, though he adds that "None of this is to say that British industrialization was erected solely on a Chinese foundation."[49]

Hobson next seeks to show that an implicit racist self-identity justified and inspired European imperialism from its origins. He means that a sense of cultural and technological superiority fostered in Europeans a sense of their right and even responsibility to "civilize" other peoples. This outlook was founded on the belief, he writes, that Europe was the birthplace of democracy, while the Asian societies remained mired in despotism. This conceptualization required European thinkers to imagine ancient Greece as their own direct ancestor. Yet Hobson dismisses this idea as incorrect: both ancient and Hellenistic Greece were deeply influenced by Eastern cultures. A second binary outlook, developed by European intellectuals during the enlightenment period, cast Europe as active, self-controlled, and rational and Asia as passive, spontaneous, and irrational. He calls this the "Peter Pan theory of the East," because the peoples of Asia supposedly would never grow up, at least not without Western intervention.

These views, along with the quasi-scientific theory put forward by thinkers like Montesquieu that arid and tropical climates stunted human development, led in the nineteenth century to explicit conceptions of Westerners as racially superior. Charles Darwin's *On the Origin of Species* (1859) and concepts like Herbert Spencer's "the survival of the fittest" helped give birth to allegedly "scientific" theories of racial hierarchy, with Anglo-Saxons or Germans at the top and Africans at the bottom. Although Protestant missionaries rejected concepts of "scientific racism," they spearheaded a powerful effort at "civilizing" the non-European peoples anyway. Hobson concedes that there were purely materialistic reasons for European imperialism, yet he insists that idealistic and other conceptual constructs were probably necessary for it to be carried out in practice.

Like Frank, Inikori, and Pomeranz, Hobson considers British imperialism to have contributed substantially to industrialization. He seeks to debunk yet another "myth," that of British free trade and laissez-faire. On the contrary, he asserts that during the highest period of British imperialism (1688–1815) the British government ran a colossal public debt, imposed a higher level of regressive indirect taxes and higher tariffs than other European countries, intervened heavily in the capital markets and industrial sector, adopted policies to protect domestic industries, granted tax relief to British manufacturers, and negotiated unfair commercial treaties with non-European powers (involving both economic and cultural aspects, like foreign ambassadors refusing to kowtow).[50] In other words, the British government was highly interventionist and not at all laissez-faire. Much of the tax revenues extracted, often from the poorer elements of society, were invested in military might, deployed for example during the Opium Wars, which resulted in the imposition of humiliating commercial treaties on China.

English entrepreneurs, backed by the British military, cultivated vast quantities of tea and opium in India, flooding the Chinese market with the latter and denying profits to China on the former, thus finally reversing the trade deficit they had run for centuries with that country. European merchants systematically transformed many countries around the world into single-crop producers – for example, palm oil and rubber in West Africa. The resultant economies of scale hugely benefited Europe and other Western countries but ultimately impoverished their colonies. Hobson considers of critical importance that the British economic take-off coincided with pronounced government interventionism, militarism, and imperialism.

He dismisses arguments put forward by various scholars, including his great-grandfather, that economic development would have been greater in the absence of empire, into which the British government poured vast resources. On the contrary, he points out, British defense spending was lower than that of any other major country. Thus, since the British paid less taxes than other Europeans, their post-1850 empire could not have imposed a significant fiscal burden on them. Nor could this burden have greatly diminished imperialism's economic windfall for Britain.[51] Moreover, more than half of the wars fought between 1715 and 1815 had nothing to do with the empire. Thus, Hobson concludes that protectionism and imperialism strongly benefited British economic development.

Next, Hobson argues that Europeans were far less rational and democratic during their "breakthrough" period (1500–1900) than Western social scientists have commonly supposed. Thus, the allegedly highly centralized and rationalized absolutist French state was in fact quite weak, deployed a relatively small number of bureaucrats, and collected taxes in an arbitrary manner, leading ultimately to the revolution of 1789. If anything, the Prussian bureaucracy was even more inefficient and arbitrary. Nor did the European governments pursue policies of free trade but rather were highly protectionist, in part because they were too weak to impose progressive income taxation. Nor did most European countries extend the vote even to all adult males until after 1900. In practice many ordinary people continued to face disabilities when trying to exercise their right to vote, and things of course were even worse for blacks in America.

In his concluding chapter, Hobson rejects what he considers the typical "Eurocentric" questions of, what enabled the West to rise? And what prevented the East from rising? He considers these questions nefarious because they imply that the West had to rise and that the East could not. After all, 1,100 years ago no one would have predicted the rise of the West and anyone who viewed the Middle East would have assumed it destined to continue to flourish indefinitely. The same would have been said of China nine hundred years ago. Their dominance was not permanent, nor should we assume the West's to be so. More properly, according to Hobson, one should view the process as continuous and symbiotic with a far more substantial influence from Asia, at least during most of the past millennium. The modern capitalist world and globalization emerged only thanks to a long-term process of economic and cultural developments in which Asia played the major role from AD 500 until recent centuries.[52] Yet he rejects arguments put forth by scholars, such as Abu-Lughod, that the Europeans lacked agency, merely stumbled into preeminence, or rose only because Asia was temporarily weak or because of some global structure.

On the contrary, he argues, the cultural identity and self-perception of the world's peoples contribute strongly to their actions. Thus, China was the world's leading power for a good part of the second millennium, and its leaders integrated into their sense of self a conception of the country lying at the center of the world and of other peoples as owing them tribute. Yet the Chinese never developed an ideology of worldwide imperialism. Such an ideology was precisely developed by the European elites, however, beginning with the Crusades, which they much later carried worldwide thanks to superior economic, military, and technological power. This ideology emerged in part thanks to the conquest of the Americas and the development of the slave trade, which enabled the Europeans to imagine themselves as fundamentally superior to these and other non-European peoples. The Europeans conquered the world, so to speak, thanks not to a "rational restlessness," as Eurocentric scholars often claim, but thanks to a "racist restlessness," in Hobson's words.

Conclusion

The commencement of the West's divergence began as early as the Renaissance, according to one scholar discussed in this chapter, or as late as the nineteenth century, according to others. One denies the Europeans almost every shred of agency, while another claims that a racist ideology of superiority motivated them to conquer much of the globe. Still another concedes an early modern European superiority in scientific instruments, whereas one scholar holds that every important achievement of the West had its origins in the East. On this much they all agree: the cultures of Eurasia borrowed from one another for many centuries if not millennia to great advantage, but Europe came to this synergistic banquet rather late.

Further reading

Chaudhuri, K. N. *Trade and Civilisation in the Indian Ocean: An Economic History from the Rise of Islam to 1750.* Cambridge: Cambridge University Press, 1985.

Chaudhuri, K. N. *Asia Before Europe: Economy and Civilisation of the Indian Ocean from the Rise of Islam to 1750.* Cambridge; New York: Cambridge University Press, 1990.

Elman, Benjamin A. *On Their Own Terms: Science in China, 1550–1900.* Cambridge, Mass.: Harvard University Press, 2005.

Flynn, Dennis O. *World Silver and Monetary History in the 16th and 17th Centuries.* Aldershot, UK: Variorum, 1996.

Lach, Donald R. and Edwin J. Van Kley. *Asia in the Making of Europe.* 3 vols. Chicago: University of Chicago Press, 1965–1993.

Parthasarathi, Prasannan. *Why Europe Grew Rich and Asia Did Not: Global Economic Divergence, 1600–1850*. Cambridge: Cambridge University Press, 2011.

Raj, Kapil. *Relocating Modern Science: Circulation and the Construction of Knowledge in South Asia and Europe, 1650–1900*. Houndmills; New York: Palgrave Macmillan, 2007.

Roman, Colin A. *The Shorter Science and Civilisation in China: An Abridgement of Joseph Needham's Original*. Cambridge; New York: Cambridge University Press, 1978–1995.

Rosenthal, Jean-Laurent and R. Bin Wong. *Before and Beyond Divergence: The Politics of Economic Change in China and Europe*. Cambridge, Mass.: Harvard University Press, 2011.

von Glahn, Richard. *Fountain of Fortune: Money and Monetary Policy in China: 1000–1700*. Berkeley: University of California Press, 1996.

Wong, R. Bin. *China Transformed: Historical Change and the Limits of European Experience*. Ithaca, N.Y.: Cornell University Press, 1998.

Notes

1 Jack Goody, *The Logic of Writing and the Organization of Society* (Cambridge; New York: Cambridge University Press, 1986).
2 Jack Goody, *The East in the West* (Cambridge: Cambridge University Press, 1996), 34–35.
3 Ibid., 47.
4 Ibid., 51.
5 Ibid., 64.
6 Ibid., 80–81.
7 Ibid., 135.
8 Ibid., 136.
9 Ibid., 161.
10 Ibid., 188–89.
11 Ibid., 226.
12 Ibid., 223.
13 Ibid., 224.
14 Andre Gunder Frank, *Reorient: Global Economy in the Asian Age* (Berkeley, Calif.: University of California Press, 1998), xxiv.
15 Ibid., 28.
16 Ibid., 52–53.
17 Ibid., 93.
18 Ibid., 134.
19 Ibid., 164.
20 Ibid., 204–205.
21 Ibid., 256.
22 Ibid., 263.
23 Ibid.
24 Ibid., 277.
25 Ibid., 282.
26 Ibid., 317.
27 Ibid., 50.
28 Kenneth Pomeranz, *The Great Divergence: Europe, China, and the Making of the Modern World Economy* (Princeton, N.J.: Princeton University Press, 2000).

29 Ibid., 24–25.
30 Ibid., 68.
31 Ibid., 99.
32 Ibid., 155.
33 Ibid., 171.
34 Ibid., 190.
35 Ibid., 207.
36 Ibid., 239.
37 Ibid. 262.
38 Ibid., 267.
39 Ibid., 296–297.
40 John M. Hobson, *The Eastern Origins of Western Civilization* (Cambridge: Cambridge University Press, 2004), 5.
41 Ibid., 36.
42 Ibid., 69.
43 Ibid., 80.
44 Ibid., 93, 95.
45 Ibid., 107.
46 Ibid., 132.
47 Ibid., 162.
48 Ibid., 189.
49 Ibid., 217.
50 Hobson refers to the "1873 abolition" of the kowtow (ibid., 262), but the British government certainly lacked the authority to abolish the practice in China in general.
51 Ibid., 279.
52 Ibid., 305.

5 Why not China?

In the last chapter, it was noted that John Hobson deems it inappropriate to pose the question, what prevented the East from rising? Yet China was probably the most inventive and technologically advanced society in premodern times, the longest-lasting great empire in history, and by far the world's richest, most populous, and most powerful country until a couple of centuries ago. The fact that this successful track record did not lead to the kinds of transformations associated with the rise of the West is, to say the least, intriguing. Indeed, dozens of scholars for the past hundred years have wrestled with this conundrum, coming to a variety of conclusions. In fact, there are probably nearly as many "Why not China?" books and sections of books as there are books asking, Why Europe?

Imperial success impeded economic transformation in China (Immanuel Wallerstein)

Let's start with broadly focused studies. Immanuel Wallerstein tackles the question this chapter addresses in Volume One of his study on *The Modern World-System*. He cites evidence that Europeans beginning in the Middle Ages raised far more livestock per capita than the Chinese and thus had more meat for consumption and more beasts of burden. He quotes the French historian Pierre Chaunu: "European man possessed in the fifteenth century a motor, more or less five times as powerful as that possessed by Chinese man, the next most favored in the world at the time of the discoveries."[1] The Chinese apparently did not feel the need to breed more animals, since their agricultural system was pushing them toward more and more intensification of human labor. The Europeans, by contrast, being far less frugal, far more wasteful of their resources, felt a compelling need to seek more territory – more space in which to grow crops – across the seas.

Next, Wallerstein emphasizes the importance of the political makeup of Europe and China. The latter was an empire, while Europe was a budding world economy. Feudalization followed the collapse of the Carolingian Empire in Europe in the ninth century, whereas the imperial structure maintained itself in China by a process that Marx Weber called "prebendalization," in which the

[margin annotations:] ① Food (animals = protein) ↓ drive to find more space

elites shared in the spoils of taxation with a still powerful central authority. Wallerstein elaborates:

> Power and income was distributed in the one case to ever more autonomous landlords, rooted in an area, linked to a given peasantry, and in the other [China] to an empire-wide stratum, deliberately not linked to the local area, semi-universalistic in recruitment but hence dependent upon the favor of the center. To strengthen the center of an empire was a colossal job ... . To create centralized units in smaller areas was impossible as long as the center maintained any coherence, which it did under the Ming and then the successor Manchu dynasty; whereas creating centralized units in a feudal system was, as we know, feasible if difficult.[2]

Moreover, the responsibility of an imperial power is to defend a large territory. Thus, in 1433 the Ming rulers resolved to halt the voyages of the treasure fleets in order to concentrate on defending the country against attacks from the north. Attacks by Turks on the eastern flank of Europe, by a similar logic, might have compelled a European emperor – had there been one – to recall the Portuguese mariners and thus to stop the Age of Discovery before it even began. Also, an empire is supposed to be coterminous with the economy of its territory as a whole. Therefore, an emperor cannot behave like an entrepreneur seeking to increase the wealth of a particular region or state within his empire. But of course that is exactly how the king of Portugal was acting.

Finally, an imperial government has to worry about every kind of armed threat, both external and internal, both foreign invasion and domestic banditry and revolt. But since innovation in military technology could benefit both the official military forces and potential rebels, it probably made sense for China's leaders to impede the development of more and more sophisticated and powerful armaments even at the possible cost of eventual – and surely very distant, given the great power of China – threats to their country's security.

Wallerstein concludes with a paradoxical argument about China ultimately declining because it was more advanced politically and economically than Europe. He writes:

> So China, if anything seemingly better placed prima facie to move forward to capitalism in terms of already having an extensive state bureaucracy, being further advanced in terms of the monetization of the economy and possibly of technology as well, was nonetheless less well placed after all. It was burdened by an Imperial political structure. It was burdened by the "rationality" of its value system which denied the state the leverage for change (had it wished to use it) that European monarchs found in the mysticality of European feudal loyalties.[3]

In his reference to the feudal system, Wallerstein is suggesting that each European monarch or prince could call on the fealty of their subjects to acquiesce in policies that might radically conflict with traditional views and customs, something no Chinese emperor could hope to do.

Chinese technological development stagnated after 1400 (Joel Mokyr)

In his 1990 study on the history of technological innovation, Joel Mokyr goes so far as to claim that:

> The greatest enigma in the history of technology is the failure of China to sustain its technological supremacy. In the centuries before 1400, the Chinese developed an amazing technological momentum, and moved, as far as these matters can be measured, at a rate as fast as or faster than Europe.[4]

He runs through the extraordinary range of technological breakthroughs achieved in China but points out that, when Europe began to grow more innovative in the Renaissance, China grew less so and gradually stagnated. Its economy ceaselessly expanded (but very slowly) thanks to increased domestic trade, growth in the money supply, and migration into the southern territories. Some technologies once utilized were forgotten, and others, being discovered, were not pursued. Mokyr paints a dramatic picture of this development (or rather lack of development) for world history: "The Chinese were, so to speak, within reach of world domination, and then shied away."[5] As their technological edge waned, the Chinese mostly simply ignored this predicament. The population grew century by century, commerce expanded, and agriculture intensified, but there was very little technological advancement.

Mokyr discusses numerous specific cases where Chinese technology stagnated or even lost a lot of ground. Whereas a silk-reeling machine had been in use as early as 1090, by the middle of the nineteenth century all of China's massive crop of raw silk was reeled by hand, and that which was exported to Europe had to be re-reeled to bring it to the desired quality. In those same years, the once formidable Chinese coal industry employed no machinery at all. Although Chinese alchemists invented gunpowder more than a thousand years ago and soon used the substance in rockets and bombs, they had to learn cannon-making from the Europeans. Again, by the middle of the nineteenth century the Chinese army was deploying cannon some three hundred years out of date. Only in the face of the Taiping Rebellion (1851–1864) did government officials commission the purchase of modern Western firearms.

Even Chinese agriculture stagnated from a technological point of view. Chinese farmers adopted the New World wonder crops (potatoes and corn) only very slowly. The Archimedes screw pump and the European piston pump, which might have radically improved irrigation systems, were only sporadically adopted, apparently because of an insufficiency of metal. Mokyr considers this astonishing, given that China had pioneered metallurgical technology hundreds of years before. He cites a historian of Chinese agriculture to the effect that the development of agricultural technology in China slowed down after 1300 and ceased completely after 1700. One major cause of this misfortune must have been the destruction or loss of major treatises on technology in general and on agricultural technology in particular because of government suppression or simple neglect, specific cases of which Mokyr discusses.

Explanations for why innovation in China stalled are considered next. Some scholars argue that the pace of innovation only slowed relative to the rapid European developments or that Chinese agriculture grew far more productive thanks to greater and greater labor intensity. Mokyr retorts, however, that China's technology stagnation is surprising not only in comparison with Europe's advances but also with China's earlier technological prowess. Moreover, the European experience of the gradual acceleration of innovation beginning in the Middle Ages suggests that the step-by-step building on earlier advances is a natural development, yet one that China did not pursue. As for labor intensification in China, Mokyr notes that

> the Europeans did not just save labor and capital, using labor more and more intensively. European inventions were at times labor saving, at times land saving, at times neutral. Their main feature was that they produced more and better goods.[6]

Moreover, whereas in the West agricultural innovation made it possible to produce more and more food, scholars agree that in China keeping up with the alimentary requirements of the people became more and more difficult. This leads Mokyr to speculate that perhaps long-term and widespread malnutrition and parasitic diseases in China "may have devastated the energetic and adaptable labor force required for sustained technological change."[7]

He then proceeds to consider the question of linkages between science and technology. It has been argued that the Chinese technology stagnated in the absence of further scientific breakthroughs. Yet, Mokyr points out, few scholars now believe that scientific advancements directly fostered technological innovation much before the middle of the nineteenth century. Before that time, it seems that technological evolution depended more on trial and error than on systematic methods.

As for social and institutional arguments, Mokyr is skeptical of the claims by various scholars that the low position of the merchantry or the failure of capitalism to develop can explain the Chinese technological stagnation. For one thing, some research suggests that merchants enjoyed improving social status in late Imperial China. For another, it is not at all clear that the rise of merchant capitalism contributed directly to technological innovation in Europe.

Mokyr thinks that Europe's environment of political fragmentation diversified technological options. Thus, if one ruler foolishly sought to suppress a promising invention or refused to fund a proposed venture – like the Portuguese king who turned down Columbus – there was very likely to be another patron available with a different outlook. In China, by contrast, when the Emperor decided to put a halt to the treasure ships sailing periodically throughout the Indian Ocean, that was the end of them.

Moreover, a culturally unified people like the Chinese could also tacitly agree to avoid the social and political disruption invariably caused by technological change by simply resisting such change or refusing to pursue it. Mokyr believes that is what happened. In Europe, he argues, no social groups had anything like as much power as their Chinese counterparts to disrupt an innovative development. For one thing, technological innovation depended largely on private initiative. In fact, only in military technology did state actors play essential or initiative roles at least until the Industrial Revolution. "There was a market for ideas," he writes, "and the government entered these markets as just another customer, or more rarely, another supplier." Furthermore, in the competitive European states system, it was potentially very dangerous for rulers to inhibit innovation and multifaceted experimentation, since any new idea or approach could lead to significant economic and even geopolitical advancement. And since the borders between European states were typically porous, innovators could often relocate if their current place of residence proved unreceptive. Thus, "reactionary societies lost out in the competition for wealth and power."[8]

By contrast, before 1400 the Chinese state played a far greater role in initiating and patronizing technological development – for example in astronomy, which was intimately connected with the legitimacy of the political system, or in agriculture, the foundation of the entire Chinese way of life. At some point, such initiatives ceased – certainly by the Qing dynasty.

So long as state-supported technological innovation continued, great progress could be made, but when it was withdrawn, the progress mostly ceased. In Mokyr's mind, the amazing thing – even "the miracle" – is that it continued so long.

Low wages blocked labor-saving innovation in China (Andre Gunder Frank)

Andre Gunder Frank thinks that the key to understanding the problem is largely demographic and economic. He writes:

> In Europe, higher wages and higher demand, as well as the availability of capital, including that flowing in from abroad, now made investment in labor-saving technology both rational and possible. The analogous argument holds for power-generating equipment. Relatively high prices for charcoal and labor in Britain provided the incentive for the accelerated switch-over to coal and mechanically powered production processes before these also became more economical in areas with even greater surpluses of labor and/or shortages of nonmechanical power, fuel, and capital to develop them.[9]

China and the other East Asian countries indeed had big population surpluses and efficient agricultural systems, which kept labor costs low but also tended to polarize income distribution. And with much wealth at the top of the social pyramid and little at the bottom, aggregate demand for manufacturing output remained low, which again put downward pressure on wages – a vicious circle.

Frank also cites the quantity theory of money, according to which a larger supply of money (in the early modern period one is talking about silver) automatically translates into higher prices, including higher wages. Since Europe had access to a much larger supply of silver in the Americas, its prices and wages rose without necessarily bringing an improved standard of living. Even so, the higher wages – and available supply of surplus money – would tend to justify investments in labor-saving equipment and devices.

Beginning around 1750, however, population growth in East Asia tapered off but increased in Europe. These trends accelerated along the same lines in the first half of the nineteenth century. Apparently, since European entrepreneurs had already embarked upon a concerted effort to develop labor-saving technologies, this population growth gave a strong boost to the economy by providing a large pool of relatively inexpensive labor to operate the expanding manufacturing infrastructure. Moreover, a significant proportion of the increased population migrated to the New World, where they produced raw materials for European industrialization and a captive market for its products. Also, as Asia suffered a long cyclical decline during the same period – a key argument put forward by Frank – European merchants were able to swoop in and seize greater market shares. Naturally, all of this commercial activity stimulated Europe's economic growth and increased the surplus of capital ready for investment in ever-new ventures – a virtuous circle.

The early modern Chinese were closed-minded (David Landes)

David Landes, everybody's favorite Eurocentric historian, because of the sprightliness of his prose, attributes China's decline to culture rather than material forces in his *The Wealth and Poverty of Nations*. He makes much of the awesome treasure fleets that sailed grandly around the Indian Ocean – nearly a century before the Portuguese discovered an ocean path to that body of water. In a mere three-year period (1404–1407), expert Chinese shipwrights crafted or refitted 1,681 ships. "Medieval Europe could not have conceived of such an armada," according to Landes.[10] Yet the treasure ships stimulated little commerce and indeed put heavy pressure on the state budget, already straining under the fabulous cost of moving the capital 800 miles north to Beijing. Landes cites the case of a provincial government official who, having complained about the extra fiscal burden, was paraded in a cage all the way to the capital for interrogation by the emperor.

He points out that the Chinese government not only halted the treasure voyages but also defined as a capital offense the construction of a ship with more than two masts (1500) and criminalized the act of going to sea with such a ship, even for commercial purposes (1551). This closing of society could not have come at a worse time for China, given the extraordinary rise of Europe then commencing. Landes wonders why the Chinese did not take the little extra effort necessary to break out of the Indian Ocean and to open for themselves the high seas and why the first Chinese ships sailed to Europe only in 1851 and only for diplomatic purposes. Landes emphasizes their mindset: "To begin with, the Chinese lacked range, focus, and above all, curiosity. They wanted to show themselves, not to see and learn; to bestow their presence, not to stay; to receive obeisance and tribute, not to buy." They considered their society self-sufficient and perfected and under no necessity to change. They were complacent and not consumed with a passion for innovation.[11] By contrast, the Europeans' greed and passion drove them ceaselessly to improve their military and maritime technology, so that soon after the last treasure ship pulled into its harbor the European merchant warriors could have bested those grand vessels had they but dared to sail out again.

Yet paradoxically, the Chinese believed themselves to live at the center of the universe, ruled by the godlike Chinese emperor, the "Son of Heaven." His officials were minor potentates, smug and haughty in their assurance of superiority, yet who prostrated themselves regularly before the emperor. Landes considers this state of affairs deeply meaningful: "Such cultural triumphalism combined with petty downward tyranny made China a reluctant improver and a bad learner." They avoided improvement and new ideas as threatening to existing conventions and liable to promote disobedience. Their arrogant rejection of foreign ways in reality seems to have stemmed from a fear of the obvious advancements of the "western barbarians." "So Ming China – convinced of its ascendancy – quaked before the challenge of Western technology, which was there for the learning."[12] True, the Chinese emperor and his officials marveled at European mechanical clocks but also trivialized them as objects of amusement or status symbols. Imperial workshops were set up to manufacture them, but in the absence of commercialization and the resultant competition, a clock-making trade failed to develop in China.

Landes quotes European observers down the centuries who despaired at what they considered to be Chinese closed-mindedness and preference for tradition and the established ways. For example, the French Jesuit Louis Le Comte (1655–1728) declared that "They are more fond of the most defective piece of antiquity than of the most perfect of the modern, differing much in that from us, who are in love with nothing but what is new."[13]

The strange thing, however, is that a thousand years ago China was far ahead of the rest of the world in technology, so obviously the culture had not always been inimical to change. So Landes asks why China "failed." He has little patience with scholars who try to soft-pedal this question, for example those who emphasize that China continued to evolve, though more slowly. Right, but why more slowly? Some scholars consider the question unanswerable because supposedly one cannot elucidate a negative, yet one does this all the time in logic and in history. Still others denounce the question as illegitimate, because it proceeds from an assumption of some non-Chinese standard of development. Yet for Landes it all boils down to this: why should one not expect the Chinese to be driven by curiosity about nature? To organize their knowledge and to advance their general understanding of all things? To foster continuous economic development? And to achieve more output with smaller inputs of labor? If China had not previously enjoyed success in each of these areas, these questions would not now be so pressing.[14] In other words, "political correctness" or trying to spare people's feelings is no substitute for meticulous critical thinking.

Landes notes the paradox of Chinese reverence for thinkers and scholars of the past – he mentions an imperial decree of 1734 obliging physicians of the court to perform ritual sacrifices to their deceased predecessors – combined with an unfortunate tendency for past technological advances to be lost or forgotten. He suggests that Chinese advancement developed as "points of light, separated in space and time, unlinked by replication and testing, obfuscated by metaphor and pseudo-profundity … " Since they never developed a method of diffusing knowledge as powerful as European printing, a vast amount of it simply faded away. Moreover, even the language used to refer to inventions was often coined on the spot and then was lost. Thus, scholars today are often reduced to painstaking analysis of ideograms that no longer possess clear meaning.[15] Even the much-vaunted and extraordinarily vast Chinese encyclopedias – one of them ran to 800,000 pages – were for our author more a sign of attempting to fix all of knowledge within overly precise boundaries than efforts to compile useful reference works for the further advancement of knowledge.

Landes rejects the view put forward in recent years by experts on China, according to which China and other developed parts of the early modern world were following their own paths toward the truth and ultimately toward modern science. In their view, there was no primacy of the West or at least they all contributed to the rise of modern science in the West to such an extent that the West does not deserve any special credit. Landes mostly demurs. He acknowledges that Europeans drew upon learning and techniques from throughout Asia as they developed modern science. Yet he insists that the contributions to that development were far from symmetrical. True, in earlier times China and other Asian societies contributed vastly more than Europe. Yet the Europeans, to their immense credit, eagerly absorbed all they could learn from abroad, such that by the seventeenth and eighteenth centuries non-Western scientists and thinkers were nearly incapable of taking part in what we call "scientific revolution," and in practice contributed "just about nothing."[16] Although Landes does not mention our next author by name, he must have had him in mind.

A lack of colonies held China back (Kenneth Pomeranz)

Kenneth Pomeranz devoted nearly the whole of his impressive study, discussed in Chapter 4, to proving that there was relatively little difference between Europe and China as late as the middle of the seventeenth century in terms of economic development. At the end of the book, however, he puts forth some ideas to account for China's decline. Like Frank, he emphasizes economics and demography. The most important factor, he argues, was the gradual shift in the century after 1750 of China's population growth from regions involved in cottage industry to almost exclusively regions focused on agriculture. This change meant that by 1850 the country had become no less agrarian than a century before, and therefore it lacked surplus wage laborers available for factory work (unlike in Britain or the United States). Moreover, the cost of food and all the materials necessary to sustain China's cottage industries increased sharply during this period, driving some handicraft workers (mostly women) back into agriculture. Meanwhile, their families – husbands and children – had to work more intensively in the fields merely to stay afloat. As Pomeranz remarks, this was "not a promising precursor to industrialization."[17]

Nor did China gain a windfall of raw materials, exploitable unfree labor, and captive markets in peripheral overseas colonies. He calls these factors "forces outside the market and conjunctures beyond Europe." These factors, he argues, explain how Western Europe, which was so similar to other developed regions of Eurasia, managed to evolve into "the privileged center of the nineteenth century's new world economy, able to provide a soaring population with an unprecedented standard of living."[18] In other words, if only the Chinese had developed their own colonies they might have achieved similar breakthroughs.

China's elites scorned commerce and scientific discovery (Joseph Needham)

An English biochemist, Joseph Needham devoted most of his life to investigating Chinese scientific development. He became fascinated with everything Chinese when three Chinese researchers (one a young woman with whom he fell in love) visited his laboratory in Cambridge in 1937. He became fluent in their language, and during the Second World War the British government stationed him as a scientific liaison in China. When he returned to England in 1948, he commenced a vast project to research and catalog the entire history of China's scientific past, *Science and Civilisation in China* (1954–2008).[19] To date, 27 volumes have appeared, ranging from physics to alchemy and from botany to metallurgy, many of them not written by Needham.[20]

After a decade or so of demonstrating the glories of Chinese scientific and technological accomplishments from ancient to early modern times, he began to formulate what came to be known as the "Needham question." He stated it thus: "Why did modern science, the mathematization of hypotheses about nature, with all its implications for advanced technology, take its meteoric rise only in the West at the time of Galileo?" At the same time, however, he placed this conundrum in a broader context. "Why," he ponders, "was it that between the second century B.C. and the sixteenth century A.D. East Asian culture was much more efficient than the European West in applying human knowledge of nature to useful purposes?"[21] In other words, why did China's extraordinary élan of innovation and scientific advancement stall? Or why did that long-time world leader fall behind the upstart Europe?

Needham presents a constellation of evidence for China's leading role in science and especially technology from very earliest times. In addition to the extraordinary range of breakthroughs and innovations mentioned in Chapter 4, he discusses the careful records Chinese astronomers from ancient days kept of eclipses, comets, meteors, and sunspots thanks to refined astronomical instruments; sophisticated hydraulic engineering beginning with the Tang dynasty; the use of mineral and animal remedies and not only herbal remedies as in Europe; accurate Chinese speculation about the effects of celestial bodies on the tides beginning in the Song era; an understanding of the hexagonal system of snowflake crystals centuries before European natural philosophers observed it; a calculation of the age of the universe in the tens of millions of years already in AD 724; and from the classical era meticulous studies of the properties of magnetism, including declination.[22] Needham also discusses early Chinese developments in alchemy and protochemistry and their rich influences on Islamic achievements that directly impacted medieval European advances. He makes plain that China's strongest scientific abilities were in the careful recording and cataloguing of data about natural phenomena, often thanks to highly refined scientific instruments.

According to Needham, Chinese science and technology received a boost in early times from a strong centralized state, which patronized the development of what he calls "orthodox" sciences, like astronomy and civil engineering. Government support, for example, made possible the invention of the world's first practical seismograph in AD 130. State-organized scientific expeditions in medieval China – for example, huge geodetic surveys – were mounted on a scale vastly greater than anything possible in the other cultures of the world.

Nor did the low cost of labor in China prevent a precocious development of labor-saving devices, like the wheelbarrow in the third century and the horse collar in the fifth century AD. In fact, unlike in the Mediterranean cultures, where for centuries galley slaves powered most ships, Chinese navigation mostly ran on wind power. Chinese entrepreneurs also harnessed water power for textile production centuries before the Europeans.

Needham observes an interesting feature of human accomplishment. The arts are not cumulative. He writes:

> Where the arts are concerned, there is indeed a certain incommensurability between the civilizations, and little continuous development can be found among them. I suppose there could hardly have been a better sculptor than Pheidias in any age before or since. No poet, either before or after, has outdone Tu Fu or Pai Chu-I, and few playwrights at any time have written decisively better than Shakespeare, but where science, technology, and medicine are concerned, there is a clear increase in man's knowledge and power through the centuries. Nature has remained approximately the same since man began, and we believe that the growth of man's knowledge about nature has been one single epic rise from the beginning until now, and now is not the end.[23]

As far as Needham is concerned, all the great cultures learned from each other, so that none could have risen to any great heights without incorporating advances by its predecessors. China was naturally one of the greatest contributors to these developments.

Paradoxically, however, the extraordinary profusion of innovation throughout the ages in China enabled it to prosper economically and politically but never shook the fabric of society as a few Chinese inventions transformed Europe – for example, the compass, gunpowder, and printing. As Needham expresses the idea,

> That Chinese discoveries and inventions there were, we have long known; that they were transmitted one after the other to Europe we can demonstrate or show to be extremely likely; but the extraordinary paradox arises that while many, even most, of them had earth-shaking effects upon occidental society, Chinese society had a strange capacity for absorbing them and remaining relatively unmoved.[24]

Needham develops his thought metaphorically: China

> had been self-regulating, like a living organism in slowly changing equilibrium, or a thermostat – indeed the concepts of cybernetics could well be applied to a civilization that had held a steady course through every weather, as if equipped with an automatic pilot, a set of feedback mechanisms, restoring the *status quo* after all perturbations, even those produced by fundamental discoveries and inventions. Struck off continually like sparks from a whirling grindstone, they ignited the tinder of the West while the stone continued on its bearings unshaken and unconsumed. In the light of this, how profoundly symbolic it was that the ancestor of all cybernetic machines, the south-pointing carriage, should have been a Chinese device.[25]

There were, therefore, two conundrums that beg resolving: Why did the formidable Chinese capacity for innovation never revolutionize society? And why did that capacity dissipate sometime after the Song dynasty?

As to why Chinese technological innovation did not lead to the transformation of society, Needham points to several factors. Unlike Europe, divided as it was into a congeries of city-states, seaborne principalities, and constantly warring aristocracies drawn toward the outside world in search of riches and exotic commodities, China for more than two thousand years was essentially a unified agrarian empire endowed with almost boundless natural resources, the world's most imposing administrative system, and a formidable cultural tradition. With a few exceptions, the Chinese were mostly content with what they had, feeling little urge to explore the wider world. One might say that the Chinese did everything they needed early in their history and then started to coast. Needham quotes a famous saying that "the Chinese peasant was ploughing with iron ploughs when the European peasant used wood, but that he continued to plough with iron ploughs when the European farmer had begun to use steel ... "[26]

But again, why? Needham considers important the absence of capitalist revolution – or rather ongoing capitalist transmutation. This was true also – and much earlier – of the Chinese development of iron, a metal considered by most historians to have had a democratizing influence compared to far more expensive bronze. The early centralization of the state in China, however, made it possible for the rulers to "nationalize" the iron industry. Here was, perhaps, the biggest impediment to further scientific development also, according to Needham: what he calls the feudal-bureaucratic system at the heart of the centralized state, which aided – or even made possible certain technological and scientific developments – but impeded many others. Most important, the scholar-gentry consistently prevented merchants or other business interests from taking control of the state under the slogan of democracy, which Needham considers an essential precondition of the rise of modern science. He admits that there was democracy of social ability whereby clever peasants could rise to the top of the bureaucracy by means of the civil service examination, but not the revolutionary democracy of entrepreneurs rising to power, dominating local institutions of self-government, and transforming society.

Also, he believes that geography explains the unitary nature of the Chinese state and society. The foundation of the Chinese economy was agriculture, but rainfall was undependable from region to region and year to year. Reliable harvests therefore required huge efforts at irrigation, navigational infrastructure, and water-conservation. Only a centralized state and efficient bureaucracy could manage such organizational tasks, yet these vast works of engineering inevitably cut across the jurisdictions of feudal lords and undermined their authority, which very early in Chinese history became subsumed under the power of the emperor. At the same time, however, in ancient times the lords and rulers possessed only rudimentary armor against peasants armed with crossbows. Thus, there could be no mass slavery, and the rulers needed to persuade the people of their benevolence, whence the importance of the Confucian philosophy. What emerged, socially speaking, was an organic conception of the unitary nature of all things and thorough-going civilian control of political power. The civil servants – mandarins or scholar-officials – who dominated this system strenuously opposed hereditary aristocratic feudalism but also concentrations of wealth and power in the hands of merchants.

Needham develops a further idea by which he purports to account for the failure of modern science to emerge in China. Whereas European thinkers from the time of the Stoics and the early Christians envisaged the universe as obeying laws imposed by a celestial legislator, a concept that many scholars have connected to the formulation of scientific laws in Europe beginning with Kepler, the Chinese conceived of a harmonious cooperation of all beings … [arising] from the fact that they were all parts in a hierarchy of wholes forming a cosmic and organic pattern, and what they obeyed were the internal dictates of their own natures.[27]

Most Chinese thinkers rejected the rigid abstractions of codified law because of unfortunate experiences with the draconian rules of the ancient School of Legalists. The Chinese came to believe in organic forms and customs inhering in all things and apparently felt no need for a Supreme Being acting as a celestial lawgiver for the natural realm or indeed as the creator of that entire realm. As a result, Needham speculates, the Chinese, for all their extraordinary achievements in science and technology, found it difficult to conceptualize regularities and ultimately scientific laws of nature, which European scientists like Newton believed they were "revealing" to the human mind.

A further philosophic twist that Needham perceives as an impediment to the development of modern science in China, was the division between the various schools of thought. He writes:

> The Taoists, though profoundly interested in Nature, distrusted reason and logic. The Mohists and the Logicians fully believed in reason and logic; but if they were interested in Nature it was only for practical reasons. The Legalists and Confucians were not interested in Nature at all. Now this gulf between empirical nature-observers and rationalist thinkers is not found to anything like the same extent in European history, and as [the English philosopher Alfred North] Whitehead has suggested, this was perhaps because European thought was so dominated by the idea of a supreme creator being, whose own rationality was the guarantee of rational intelligibility in his creation.[28]

By contrast, according to Needham, Chinese thinkers had no faith that the "code of nature" could be unveiled and deciphered

> because there was no assurance that a divine being, even more rational than ourselves, had ever formulated such a code capable of being read. One feels, indeed, that the Taoists, for example, would have scorned such an idea as being too naïve to be adequate to the subtlety and complexity of the universe as they intuited it.[29]

Most Chinese thinkers, on the contrary, viewed the universe as one interconnected, organic, and hierarchical whole. The latest science has come to appreciate this wisdom, but probably, according to Needham, the Scientific Revolution could not have broken through to the powerful methods and interpretations of natural phenomena formulated by Kepler and Newton without passing through a theological stage and a mechanistic phase, conceptualizations that were completely alien to Chinese thought.

Centralized authority stifled free inquiry and innovation (Wen-yuan Qian)

Many scholars have criticized the extraordinarily prolific Needham for an almost worshipful interpretation of Chinese scientific and technological accomplishment through the ages. That is the very last accusation one could level at Wen-yuan Qian, a theoretical physicist and historian of science who traveled from China to the United States in 1980, a few years after the Cultural Revolution. Qian, on the contrary, takes a decidedly dim view of Chinese scientific potential. He writes:

> Whenever I read in Needham's works a Chinese passage which talks about the Yin and Yang, or what Needham names as the Pattern, the Order, or resonance that embody the Tao, I knew that he would phrase it as very scientific, very illuminating, but I would frown at the same passage … . How could this essentially pre-modern body of thought become modern without the necessary examination and re-examination, criticism and counter-criticism, formulation and reformulation, mathematisation and re-mathematisation over many generations? Did traditional China at any time offer the necessary politico-ideological conditions to sustain the corresponding degree of intellectual activation and creativity? In other words, I doubt that China has ever provided a social environment that would engender the necessary competition of creative thinking and objective criticism, the constant re-examination through empirical testing and rigorous reasoning.[30]

Qian was not gratuitously bashing China. Instead, as a Chinese patriot, he was expressing frustration with China's apparent inability, at that time, to reach its fuller potential in the modern world.

Qian considers the key factor in preventing experimental and mathematical science from developing China to have been the dominant Chinese philosophy of Confucianism. Because it focused exclusively on political and ethical problems and almost completely neglected the study of nature and, as the official worldview for roughly two thousand years, completely displaced the more wide-ranging schools of Mohism, the Logicians, and the Legalists, Confucianism created a stultifying intellectual environment, in which institutional, economic, and cultural change was strongly inhibited. By contrast, he argues, the absence of a centralized and institutionalized politico-ideological authority after the fall of Rome in Europe made it impossible to prevent a succession of social, political, economic, and cultural movements in Europe from challenging the status quo and broadening the European mind to new ways of thinking and acting – from the Carolingian Renaissance to the Industrial Revolution.

Two other, closely related factors, according to our author, were the political fragmentation of Europe and the weakness of Chinese society. No European rulers ever managed to dominate the entire continent, largely because the

European societies could often hold their own against them. By contrast, the Chinese people could manage no more than repeated rebellions and could never build institutional resistance to central authority. Qian points to the period of decentralization and frequent warfare among the diverse Chinese states, before the establishment of the Qin dynasty in 221 BC, when the Hundred Schools of Thought flourished, as the most fruitful time in Chinese history for intellectual inquiry and advancement. Had this era continued for several hundred more years, he speculates, then Chinese science might have advanced much further. It might have led to something like Europe's Scientific Revolution, in which dozens of innovative scientists hailed from a dozen countries and belonged to numerous denominations of Christianity or even professed Judaism. Intellectual pluralism was fostered in Europe from medieval times in the dozens of universities that sprang up all across the continent. In China, by contrast, there were few institutions of higher learning, and during the six centuries before 1905 most educated men strived only to master the small number of officially sanctioned Confucian classic texts in order to become government officials. China produced many isolated geniuses but no transformational social, political, or cultural movements, no broad networks of scientists, mathematicians, and philosophers all working in concert, stimulating each other.

Qian directly challenges Needham's speculation that under other socio-political circumstances China might have achieved a scientific revolution commencing directly from magnetic field theory rather than from mechanical physics, given the early Chinese understanding of magnetism. Qian counters that the mechanics of Galileo, Kepler, and Newton was mathematically relatively elementary and related to ordinary observations of the movement and actions of objects, compared to the far more highly mathematized electromagnetic theory of Michael Faraday and James Maxwell. In the actual historical development, the principles of Newtonian physics made possible these – and other – later advances, and therefore the opposite progression seems hard to imagine. Moreover, William Gilbert had developed a far more sophisticated understanding of magnetism by 1600 (and his concept of physical forces was an important contribution to the development of modern mechanics to boot) than Chinese thinkers ever had.

Pushing further back in time, Qian points to the early conceptualizations of mechanics by fourteenth-century European thinkers like Jean Buridan, whose theory of impetus was an important advancement toward the dynamics of Galileo and Newton. Since nothing even vaguely approaching such a refined scientific conceptualization was achieved in China for several centuries, Needham's claim that China and Europe diverged scientifically only in the middle of the seventeenth century is necessarily false. It did not help, argues Qian, that Chinese thinkers were mostly uninterested in importing the fruits of Hellenistic science. Euclid's *Elements* may have been translated in the thirteenth century and partially again in the early seventeenth century, but apparently few Chinese mathematicians paid any attention. This was unfortunate, since Euclidean geometry provided an important methodology for the Scientific Revolution in Europe.

Qian speculates that, had Gilbert's *De magnete* (1600) been translated into Chinese, it would have had no greater impact than the *Elements*. He writes:

> It is even less likely that *De magnete* could have attracted a group of readers in seventeenth-century China, and produced any scientific influence which was in any sense comparable to what it did in Western Europe. Western Europe produced *De magnete* because it was the culture that produced a wide circle of potential readers, followers, and innovators.[31]

In fact, Europe was positively buzzing with intellectual ferment, organized professional activity of all kinds, an explosion of learned publications, intensive scientific inquiry, eager and wide-ranging scholarly exchanges, and technological innovation in many fields.

Individual Chinese thinkers made some extraordinary breakthroughs in science and mathematics, but in many cases they did not build upon each other's work. For example, geometrical optics made great progress thanks to Mozi (470–391 BC) and his followers, but when Shen Kua (1031–1095) studied the same topic he had no idea about the accomplishments of his predecessors, nor did Zhao You-qing three centuries later.

Professional continuity was far more assured in mathematics and astronomy, two "official" branches of learning actively promoted by the government, since the development of accurate calendars was one means by which the dynasties legitimized themselves. In the fifth century, for example, when, incidentally, Confucian control was somewhat relaxed, Zu Chong-zhi and his son Zu Geng-zhi carried an analysis of pi to a level not achieved anywhere else in the world until the sixteenth century. These men were members of a five-generation family tradition of mathematical brilliance. Yet that continuity stopped cold. When Jesuits arrived in China in the sixteenth century no Chinese mathematicians had any clear grasp of the field's former glories in their country.

Yet another factor that Qian stresses was the failure of Chinese thinkers to develop rigorous scientific methodology. He writes:

> the great deficiency in old Chinese mathematical thought was the absence of rigorous proof, in particular the absence of a system of deductive geometry. This configuration correlates with the lack of formal logic and the dominance of associative (organicist) thought. From our Sino-European comparison it is clear that the deficiency was not just in mathematics; it hindered the development of modern science as a whole. In other fields of science, the Chinese way of thinking generally lacked accuracy in defining, exactness in formulating, rigor in proving, and logic in explaining.[32]

He then goes on to point out that the great pharmacopeia of the sixteenth century, *Ben Cao Gang Mu*, merely records detailed pharmacological information without critically analyzing the methods by which it was acquired. Similarly, Chinese astronomers carefully recorded their observations for three thousand years, but offered no scientific explanations of the celestial movements or representations of their courses. Chinese cartographers made continuous advancements from pre-Qin times, and Qian approvingly quotes Needham's claim that maps in the Song era were by far the most accurate ever drawn in history until then. Yet, again, when the Jesuits arrived in China, their cartographic knowledge and skill dramatically overshadowed those of their hosts.

Qian cites a striking contrast between explanations for earthquakes put forward by pre-Socratic Greek philosophers (sixth–fifth centuries BC) and an early Chinese theory that apparently enjoyed continuous credence and further development at least until the Song dynasty, toward the end of the thirteenth century. According to this theory, when the Yin represses or hinders the Yang and keeps it from its rightful place, an earthquake occurs, with devastating effects for the kingdom. By contrast, various Greek theories were far more concrete and materialistic. Anaxagoras explained that earthquakes were caused by too much water bursting from upper to lower terrestrial levels. Anaximenes reasoned that huge quantities of earth falling into cavernous regions because of earth undergoing a drying process could cause them. Aristotle – of course no pre-Socratic – suspected that vapor escaping from deep recesses of the earth in response to the drying action of the sun might be the cause. Qian notes that the concepts of the Yin and the Yang were completely undefined and therefore could not in the long run lead to more and more satisfactory explanations of any natural phenomena.

Next, Qian reflects on the hoary yet still widespread conception of China as "timeless" and "quiescent" through the centuries. Nothing, however, could be further from the truth. As he points out,

> no other nation had so many peasant rebellions, was plagued by so many civil wars, and was invaded so often; yet no nation preserved its own characteristic culture so well. A paradoxical situation existed up to 1839: China was often too weak militarily, or politically, to resist invasion, but survived because of [in the words of Joseph Needham] "the extraordinary integrative and absorptive power of Chinese civilization, a power which no invader before modern times was able to withstand."[33]

Very early in their development – more than two thousand years ago – the Chinese evolved an advanced civilization, compared to which all the environing cultures paled. At the same time, they were always surrounded by powerful predatory enemies and threatened by internal strife. The Chinese rulers and elites, therefore, devoted boundless efforts to maintaining their civilization through the constant reinforcement of the Confucian principles of deference to authority and social harmony. Within this framework, artisans were free to devote themselves to technological innovation, but most intellectuals felt discouraged from wide-ranging inquiry.

Our author formulates five questions in order to pursue further the intellectual and institutional preconditions for the emergence of modern science.

In brief, they concern, on the one hand, whether scholars on a wide scale studied and sought rational explanations for natural phenomena and, on the other hand, whether society and government encouraged such efforts. Qian concludes that over time the answers to these questions for China became more and more negative. On the contrary, meticulous preparations for the civil service examinations consumed the efforts of nearly all of China's best minds for many centuries right down to 1905. European society, by contrast, was highly pluralistic, with creative talent divided among diverse religious, political, intellectual, and commercial institutions and pursuits. Only a few eccentric scholars in China devoted themselves to the study of nature, compared to a large proportion of both scholastic and humanistic thinkers in Europe. True, many Chinese scholars organized vast amounts of information in taxonomic compendia and calendrical systems, but they did not build this material into progressive tiers of explanations leading to an ever-greater axiomatic and quantitative understanding.

Qian goes through a litany of what he considers impediments to Chinese progress in science and other fields of endeavor. Chinese culture not only severely restricted communications between members of the opposite sex, it also imposed a strict prohibition on depictions of nudity or the handling of cadavers, which made it impossible to gain a detailed understanding of anatomy, unlike Renaissance European artists and physicians. Traditional Chinese medicine enjoys great respect for its use of acupuncture, but Qian notes that into the nineteenth century practitioners continued to prescribe such folk remedies as "the hide of a broken drum." He also considers it a problem that Confucianism discouraged the practice of primogeniture, which forced younger sons of elite European families into commercial pursuits. In fact, the Confucian scorn for manual labor kept scholars from collaborating with inventors. Even the officially sanctioned sciences like astronomy suffered as a result; Chinese astronomers, who were bureaucrats first and scientists second, studied the stars meticulously but more for finding omens than patterns or regularities.

Japan provides some interesting contrasts with China, despite long centuries of adapting its ideas and values, for example Confucianism and the doctrine of the Yin and Yang. During the Tokugawa period (1603–1868), compulsory urbanization led to far higher rates of literacy and economic development. Competition among feudal warlords (*daimyo*) stimulated innovation in many spheres. Thus, from the beginning of the Meiji Restoration, Japan was ready to embrace change and to adapt the most promising ideas and technology from around the world, including a written constitution, something China had not accomplished at the time when Qian completed his book in 1983 (or indeed even today).

Oppressive social constraints are the reason (Derk Bodde)

A longtime professor of Chinese history at the University of Pennsylvania, Derk Bodde, presents a similarly critical interpretation of Chinese scientific developments. In a wide-ranging study, he seeks to attribute China's "failure to launch" to a variety of cultural elements stemming from ancient times but growing more stultifying through the centuries.[34]

As others have argued, he considers the Chinese to have been more successful in technology than science, partly because of the way in which they tended to compartmentalize the various branches of learning. Of the 36 important Chinese technological innovations – from the crossbow to the magnetic compass – 16 date to the Han dynasty, two thousand years ago, and only two came after the Song dynasty, which itself ended in the thirteenth century. In China before modern times, no intellectual discipline was recognized as autonomous or integrated, including science. Scholars studied many subjects but did not think of them holistically.

Whereas in Europe intellectuals and scholars had to share status and respect with aristocrats, military officers, merchants, bankers, entrepreneurs, and other members of a more and more pluralistic society, in China no one but the emperor surpassed the power and prestige of the scholar-officials. This was perhaps not surprising, according to Bodde, in a society where literacy was so rare, difficult to acquire, and revered – and well it might be, given that an educated Chinese person today or a thousand years ago could command, if with some difficulty, all the nation's great texts going back more than two thousand years. What a powerful tool of cultural integration and continuity. By contrast, a highly educated English speaker today has trouble with Chaucer, who wrote only around six hundred years ago. Since everyone in China for roughly two thousand years studied the same literary language and the same narrow canon of texts, intellectual pluralism was necessarily inhibited.

Bodde considers the Chinese language itself a barrier to clear, scientific thinking. Scholars and thinkers in China throughout the ages typically expressed themselves laconically, an ancient proclivity that often made even authoritative Confucian statements difficult to interpret. Literary Chinese itself lacks both consistent punctuation and many elements of speech serving to modify verbs and nouns. For example, it is often difficult to tell the subject of a given sentence or the object of a given action. In fact, China produced no grammarians at all until the twentieth century. Bodde argues that in China the difficulties of mastering literacy were meant to maintain writing as the preserve of the few and an instrument of power. Otherwise, why would punctuation fail to develop in the country that invented printing? Of course, alphabetization is impossible, given the nature of the Chinese language, but other means of classification – even comparatively modern ones – are highly cumbersome. Moreover, until the introduction of Western printing in the twentieth century, Chinese books lacked continuous pagination, and therefore were cited even by scholars only by chapter or section. Nor were Chinese books equipped with indexes.

The Chinese literary language also invited the wide use of rhetorical devices, such as parallelism, which may have reinforced the ingrained Chinese organicism that Needham found so appealing, and antithesis, which may have strengthened the Chinese tendency to think of reality dialectically (as constantly shifting) rather than categorically (as divisible into meaningful categories). Thus, for example, until very recent times lists were rarely numbered consecutively, apparently because of the Chinese preference for symmetry, which consecutive numbering with one, two, three, or more digits would spoil. Such may also have been the reason for the omission of paragraphs and subtitles. The difficulties these and other features posed to readily accessing desired information made it necessary for Chinese scholars to devote enormous time and effort to learning texts by heart.

Many scholars have suggested that the rote memorization of a small number of classical texts to prepare for the civil service examination and the highly stylized nature of the examination essays inhibited intellectual creativity, pluralism, and freethinking. The examinees in 1487, for example, were given a sentence from Mencius meaning "Delight-in Heaven person, protect Heaven-below" and expected to produce an "eight-legged" essay divided into two parts of four sections each tied together by four sentences and composed in antithetical pairs of ideas. The entire exercise demanded cleverness, memory recall, and the ability to work within rigid norms rather than thinking "outside the box." Bodde elaborates:

> The primary technique traditionally applied to the writing of histories or other significant works of scholarship has been that of scissors-and-paste, or what might be called "composition through compilation." Heavy reliance on lengthy quotations lifted *en bloc* from their original texts and inserted with only minimum discussion and analysis into their new settings exemplifies a conspicuous weakness found in a good deal of traditional Chinese scholarship: its frequent failure to synthesize, generalize, and hypothesize. Even the development of techniques of historical analogism, which could occasionally lead to the formulation of truly analytical hypothetical propositions, failed in the long run to turn the old scholarship significantly away from its overriding concern with particulars rather than systems.[35]

Chinese scholars compounded this problem by continuing to use terminology derived from folk religion, by failing to coin detailed and precise nomenclature, and by codifying no specialized lists of terms. Bodde hastens to add that these disabilities of classical literary Chinese, in his interpretation, impeded its efficient use only for scholarly and scientific purposes and did not preclude awesome achievements of poetic expression.

Bodde considers significant that for over two thousand years and until quite recently, all Chinese thinkers – with the exception of the Mohists – conceived of time and space not as abstract continua, but as discrete periods or areas, such as a particular dynasty or region. Nor for the most part was time thought of as linear; rather, dynasties were viewed as rising and falling in never-ending cycles. Moreover, these conceptions were intimately wedded to a wide range of numerically specific phenomena with important symbolic meanings, like the compass points, the seasons, the "twelve cyclical stems," the Five Elements, and the Yin and the Yang. He quotes Needham:

> Perhaps the entire system of correlative organismic thinking was in one sense the mirror image of Chinese bureaucratic society ... . Both human society and the picture of Nature involve a system of coordinates, a tabulation-framework, a stratified matrix in which everything had its position, connected by the "proper channels" with everything else. On the one hand there were the various ... . Ministries and departments of State (forming one division), and the Nine Ranks of officials ... (forming the other). Over against these were the five elements or the eight trigrams or sixty-four hexagrams (forming one dimension), and all the 10,000 things divided among them and individually responsive to them (forming the other).[36]

Given this manner of thinking, it was presumably difficult for the Chinese to abstract any particular element for analysis or indeed to conceptualize nature in more realistic ways. Also, if everything has its place, and since Confucianism encouraged adhering to the mean, then the Chinese would presumably tend to avoid radical change.

The failure of Chinese scholars to apply quantitative methods to natural phenomena, despite their strength in mathematics, is striking. Bodde cites numerous Chinese thinkers from the age of "feudalism" (before the establishment of the Chinese Empire in 221 BC) bolstering their social and political ideas with metaphors and images drawn from instruments of measurement used by tradesmen, like the carpenter's square and the draftsman's compass. Such rhetorical devices disappeared entirely from literate discourse, however, before the beginning of the Christian era. Moreover, the Taoist philosophers, really the only Chinese thinkers deeply interested in nature, categorically rejected the whole idea of quantification. The Legalists advocated the use of quantitative methods for bureaucratic purposes, an intellectual legacy that continued for centuries in such practices as regular national censuses, yet the Legalist school of thought itself was entirely eradicated. What tended to enjoy great intellectual popularity, by contrast, were rather whimsical itemizations like "the seven physiological kinds of human suffering, the eight kinds of suffering caused by natural disasters, the five kinds based on human relationships," etc.[37] As a result, mathematics never came to play a significant role in the development of scientific conceptualization in China until the most recent times.

Next, Bodde considers the impact of religion in China on intellectual development. From ancient times, China lacked a single institutionalized religion. Buddhism and Taoism maintained a wide network of monasteries, shrines, and clergy, but the Confucian scholar-officials looked askance at them, restricted their liberty, and at times roundly persecuted them. In general, moreover, the cult of ancestor worship held a dearer place in the hearts of most Chinese than did any other faith or practice. Nor did Buddhism or Taoism develop a thoroughgoing political philosophy, probably given their insistent denial of the meaningfulness of earthly things. The most they, or indeed Confucianism, could accomplish socially speaking was to reinforce existing values and institutions, but rarely to challenge them or call for their reform. An interesting exception to this rule, argues Bodde, were the ancient Mohists, who preached an uncompromising, puritanical ethic of constant toil and doing good in the world. This was the only intellectual movement in China to develop a system of logic, systematically to define key terms, and to study such aspects of nature as optics, mechanics, and biology. That this dynamic and innovative intellectual current was stamped out early in Chinese history suggests for Bodde that key features of Chinese development were to some extent already preconditioned at that point.

Political and philosophical orthodoxy, reverence and nostalgia for the past, and deference to authority characterized the outlook of Chinese thinkers from Confucius to the last great Confucian thinker, Zhu Xi (1130–1200), and far beyond. Most of them believed either that the Zhou dynasty (1046–256 BC) provided the most virtuous examples of good governance and harmonious society in all of Chinese history and that every subsequent dynasty fell short by comparison or that the ancient Chinese classics contained the greatest wisdom available to humankind – or both. New ideas, it seems, were to be spurned or at least viewed with suspicion. Bodde notes the complete absence in ancient Chinese philosophy of Socratic dialogues involving rigorous debate aimed at discovering the truth. Instead one encounters brief exchanges in which the master quickly reduces his opponent to silence. In fact, Mencius even lamented that the unharmonious and disputatious times in which he lived required him to engage in debate. Apparently only the later Mohists valued argument and intellectual give and take. The establishment of the neo-Confucian orthodoxy, which endured from the early thirteenth century to the collapse of the empire seven centuries later, reinforced this tendency all the more.

Bodde shows that the viciousness and intensity of intellectual persecution in Europe during the Renaissance and Reformation periods far exceeded anything imposed by Chinese rulers, despite repeated book-burnings and tortures and executions of political dissidents. He interprets this distinction in the following way:

> In short, viewing the situation in Reformation Europe in the light of the Chinese experience, one may conclude that the greater intensity of its persecutions, coupled with a greater resistance these provoked, far from pointing to the effectiveness and totality of thought control, indicates a healthy intellectual diversity and vigor. Such an environment would seem to be particularly favorable to scientific development, provided of course the forces of suppression did not become too strong.[38]

He then goes on to quote from the historian of science, Herbert Butterfield, who suggests that the relatively balanced struggles between the forces of dissent and authority, from the late Middle Ages onward in Europe, have tended to strengthen the individual personality, conscience, and sense of responsibility, with the implication that these faculties developed less vigorously in China.

The official social hierarchy of China from ancient times placed merchants on the very bottom rung, and at the top of the pyramid the Confucian scholar-officials scorned them as materialistic, unconcerned with ethics, and a destabilizing social element. From the mid-Tang period (the 700s), however, their material position gradually improved, and big fortunes were made, often in veiled collaboration with the state. Yet commercial capitalism did not emerge, for which Bodde offers several explanations. First, the absence of primogeniture made it difficult to concentrate wealth. Second, abundant mercantile wealth was diverted toward nonproductive purposes, such as buying offices in the civil service. Third, the government retained ultimate control over some of China's biggest moneymaking ventures, such as the official salt monopoly. And finally, Chinese merchants never devised for themselves what Deirdre McCloskey calls "bourgeois dignity" (see Chapter 1) and instead at every chance sought to ape the scholar-gentry.

The apparently almost unbridgeable gap between intellectuals and artisans in China is striking, according to Bodde. Not a single technological treatise is extant before the Song dynasty, aside from one that deals with government workshops in an imagined bureaucratic utopia. Despite the extraordinary nautical prowess of the Ming Chinese, not a single manual on navigation exists from that period. By contrast, a treatise on agriculture descends to us from Han times over two thousand years ago, indicating the extraordinary importance of agriculture in the Chinese system of values. Similarly, Bodde believes that far fewer artisans down through the centuries are remembered by name – or left any personal statements – in China than in Europe, taking into account the differing population size and length of historical records. Even self-portraits by artists are extremely rare in Chinese art. The main point here is that technical experts and creative minds in China were less individualistic and eccentric, less likely to be in contact with intellectuals, less literate, and over time less innovative than their counterparts in Europe.

Nearly all Chinese thinkers through the ages disdained geographical exploration and expansionism. All but the Legalists strenuously opposed war and violence. They repeatedly heaped scorn on the deeds of explorers, like Zheng He, as extravagant and pointless. Of course, the Chinese rulers increased their imperial sway century by century, but generally this occurred very slowly, without glory-seeking or dramatic invasions. The ethos of simplicity that animated the Confucian literati, and most Taoist philosophers as well, caused them to recoil from such endeavors and, indeed, to express skepticism about innovation and novelties of all kinds.

Bodde also considers significant what he calls the Chinese moralistic view of nature, which anthropomorphizes natural phenomena. Although this tendency was widespread in all ancient societies, it persisted until very recent times among Confucians and other Chinese thinkers. It seems likely that this persistence stemmed from the almost exclusive Confucian preoccupation with ethical matters. Even the obscure, very brief, and unique reference by an unidentified early Confucian to the significance one should attribute to the "investigation of things" never led, even among the neo-Confucians who gave it an important place in their philosophy, to any systematic study of nature. In fact, when the unorthodox neo-Confucian thinker Wang Yang-ming (1472–1529) strived through intensive contemplation for seven days and nights to understand the inner meaning of some bamboo shoots, following what he took to be the method advocated by Zhu Xi, he suffered a short-lived mental breakdown. Presumably, what Zhu Xi had intended was introspection upon mental states and other purely human things. Only a few Chinese scholars, such as Fang Yi-Chih (1611–1671), who apparently fell under the strong influence of Western scientific thought, directed their attention largely to natural phenomena.

The next topic of the book concerns Chinese thought and customs relating to sexuality. To start with, the major Confucian thinkers scarcely mentioned it, except perhaps to warn of its dangers. In fact, Mencius opined that men and women should not so much as touch each other's hands, except in cases of emergency. True, Taoist principles encouraged men to stimulate their female partners to the maximum degree, while themselves abstaining as much as possible from ejaculation, but this was entirely because the Taoists believed these practices would enhance the longevity of men. Anthropological studies made in the 1930s in China, found that it was considered improper for a husband to pay any attention or show any affection to his wife at all until she bore him a child. Even then, public displays of affection were severely frowned upon. Nor has Chinese culture known any tradition – at least since earliest times – of men and women dancing together.

The puritanical attitude to sexuality may have been related to the Chinese culture's tendency to downplay individual self-expression. From earliest times, formal Chinese conversation typically avoided the use of the first person pronouns. So did nearly all Chinese poetry. Another interesting case was biography. Two thousand years ago the recounting of people's lives, including writing about oneself, was rich and detailed. Then gradually, as these genres deepened in the West, they grew more stylized, impersonal, superficial, and stereotyped in China. Similarly, portraiture and self-portraiture were very rare artistic genres in China, especially after a period of flourishing in the Tang era (618–907). Bodde thinks its decline probably correlates directly with a gradual strengthening of social constraints in China, though he briefly discusses a sort of popular eccentricity that flourished among a narrow set of intellectuals during the Ming period. Individualism as such probably did not emerge in China, according to Bodde, citing the historian William De Bary, because of the absence of a host of specifically European pre-conditions, including a vibrant middle class, a capitalist economy, a powerful Church able to contest state power, religious denominations fighting for freedom of conscience, powerful universities, and a free press. Bodde believes these factors also inhibited the development of modern science.

Then there is the question of sports and competition in China. Although a number of competitive sports enjoyed popularity throughout China's history, they differed markedly from such traditions in the West, beginning in ancient

Greece. For one thing, spectator sports were quite rare and small in scale. So was individual competition. The Chinese, it seems, preferred to avoid subjecting individuals to public failure. Also, rarely did various social classes mingle during competitive games, as they often did for example in games of English football. Bodde believes that

> The competitive spirit which had so strongly characterized the earliest stages of Western civilization gained renewed strength as it burst its aristocratic boundaries and poured into the increasingly respectable channels of commerce, industry, and entrepreneurial activity. From this arose the modern society of capitalism, technology, and science.[39]

The one area of Imperial Chinese life in which competition reigned supreme has already been mentioned. It consumed a large portion of the lives of hundreds of thousands of men, exalted to the heights a tiny fraction, and left the vast majority dejected and crushed – the civil service examination. Again, Bodde considers fateful for Chinese civilization that the spirit of competition for many centuries was sublimated into preparations for government service.

In the final section of the book, the author discusses the Chinese conception of nature. Chinese scholars meticulously classified flora, fauna, and other elements of the natural realm from earliest times (though rarely described them with precision like Aristotle), yet only in the eighth century did they begin to observe the social patterns of ants and bees. Thus even Mozi, the ancient Chinese scholar with the apparently most overtly scientific outlook, believed that animals and insects did not have to toil. This misunderstanding may have stemmed from the far greater and earlier focus of Chinese farmers on plants than on animals. Bodde also discusses what he calls the Chinese naturalistic or analytical approach to nature. It posits that man is but a creature among other creatures and is insignificant in the context of the universe. For human beings to claim that nature had been organized for the benefit of humanity by a benevolent Creator was therefore an absurd proposition, as if a louse imagined that its human host had been arranged for it specifically. At the same time, however, apparently all Chinese people, even thinkers, attributed moral qualities to the phenomena of nature. This tendency to animism, according to Bodde, probably made it difficult for any Chinese scholar to conceive of a universal force like gravity.

In conclusion, Bodde puts forward several other factors that he believes inhibited the development of modern science and technology in China. One was a strong disinterest in theorizing and a blind acceptance of ancient theories of numerology, geomancy, and of the yin and the yang. These beliefs may have helped some artisans to achieve such breakthroughs as the mariner's compass and gunpowder, yet they probably impeded innovation in science more broadly. Another was China's geographical isolation, at the extreme eastern end of Eurasia, far from the Middle Eastern heartland of human civilization. Related to this was the Chinese resistance to foreign ideas. The main exception to this tendency was, of course, the enthusiastic adoption of Buddhism by millions, especially during the Tang era. Yet even then, the large number of Indian scholars who settled in China, bringing with them refined knowledge of mathematics and astronomy, seem to have had little impact on science in China. Thus, although early Chinese nautical methods were in advance of Europe's by two or three centuries, they did not achieve mathematical navigation until modern times.

Bodde thinks he may have found the linchpin to explain the far greater success of technology than science in China. He writes:

> The sciences were primarily pursued by learned men whose education was in the classics and whose views of the world stemmed largely from books. The technologies were primarily undertaken by artisans and master craftsman who were often illiterate or semiliterate and whose achievements depended more on practical experience than on abstract theory. This raises the considerable possibility that the intellectual limitations imposed by the yin-yang and Five Elements theories may have been less harmful to the technologies than to the sciences. The same may also have been true of some of the other scientifically unfavorable factors, such as the widespread Chinese tendency to concentrate on discrete details rather than on broad syntheses. In short, we may have a partial explanation here for the fact that so many of China's "firsts" have been in technology and not in science.[40]

Our author considers this trend to have been operative from earliest times in Chinese history and puts forward as proof the failure of the Mohist school, with its central focus on logic and nature, to continue to develop after the second century BC.

A lack of independent institutions was crucial (Nathan Sivin)

Other scholars have viewed the question of the development of science in China quite differently. Nathan Sivin, professor of Chinese culture and of the history of science at the University of Pennsylvania, and Bodde's successor, though now emeritus, denies outright the historical validity of the negative question about the Scientific Revolution not taking place in China. Furthermore, he seeks to show that a scientific revolution did in fact occur in China in the seventeenth century.

In a widely anthologized article, he begins by noting that comparing the whole of science and technology of any two countries in whatever periods of history probably makes little sense before modern times, since their various branches only recently became relatively integrated intellectually and because a lag in one branch might not imply a similar lag in others. Thus, Europe was backward technologically compared to China until at least 1400, yet until modern times astronomers in China were unable to achieve the predictive results of the ancient scholar Ptolemy. At the same time, however, both Chinese and European medicine was pretty dismal as late as 1850.

Next, he writes about the Chinese Renaissance man Shen Kua (1031–1095), an expert on nearly every branch of learning, including knowledge of the natural world, and a government official. This was a time when scholar-officials pursued their interests not only in philosophy, the arts, and literature, as in later times, but also in studies of nature and technology. Su Sung (1020–1101), who devised an extraordinarily sophisticated astronomical clock, was another of the large group of such brilliant polymaths.

As Sivin studied Shen, he discovered that his writings merged together all sorts of topics and ideas without any apparent systematic method. But then so did standard Chinese encyclopedias, which classified under the heading "technical skills" such disparate things as alchemy, painting, and hired assassins. Similarly, Shen organized both medicine and mathematics, as well as architecture and games, under the same rubric. Sivin notes that

> there does not seem to have been a systematic connection between all the sciences in the minds of the people who did them. The sciences were not integrated under the dominion of philosophy, as schools and universities integrated them in Europe and Islam. Chinese had sciences but no science, no single conception or word for the overarching sum of all of them. Words for the level of generalization above that of the individual science were much too broad.[41]

The practitioners of the various arts and sciences in traditional China had nothing to link them together, no philosophers of the Aristotelian sort to systematize their disparate knowledge.

And yet, Sivin argues that these practitioners within their individual spheres passed down interpretations of how their arts fit into the cosmic scheme of things. It's just that these interpretations were never shared among the various arts. Still, thinkers like Shen achieved a profound understanding of Chinese learning and of knowledge in general by intuiting connections among such diverse ways of thinking as intellection and imagination. He and other Chinese thinkers did not need to dichotomize mind and matter or subject and object – an ingrained European tendency descending from the time of Plato.

Sivin contends that the only value in asking why the Scientific Revolution did not occur in China first is heuristic, that is, it may lead to some deeper understanding. Otherwise it is as absurd as asking why one's name did not appear in some issue of the newspaper. He means that it suggests that China should have had a Europe-style scientific revolution just because it was a highly developed society with sophisticated technology and learning. Sivin likewise deplores the presupposition that if Europe achieved the Scientific Revolution then it must have had a deeper understanding of reality than other societies, including China. Yet our author rejects this idea in favor of the conception of Europe as making the great modern scientific breakthrough thanks to the exploitation of nature and the societies it colonized.

Similarly he denies there is any such thing as a universal science. Rather, modern science is infused with European ways of thinking. If modern science were truly universal, then it could coexist with traditional cultural patterns instead of destroying them by means of standardization. Nor is modern science practiced in the same ways everywhere. Of course, Sivin admits that

> It would be foolish to deny that modern science has attained a verifiability, an internal consistency, a taxonomic grasp, a precision in accounting for physical phenomena, and an accuracy in prediction that no other kind of activity shares, and that lay far outside the grasp of early sciences. The rigor that makes these remarkable characteristics possible quickly disappears, however, once the formulation of the law or theory in mathematical equations, matrices of categories, or exactly defined technical concepts and models has been translated into the ordinary language and general discourse of a given culture.[42]

Thus, even modern science was practiced in very different ways, at the time Sivin was writing, in the People's Republic of China and the United States. At the same time, however, he rejects the idea that modern science derives solely from European roots. On the contrary, sources of learning from across Eurasia fed into the stream that gushed forth in the Scientific Revolution.

Likewise, arguments about "inhibiting factors" preventing the Chinese revolution in science can be contested. To those who blame the Chinese scholar-bureaucrats who were uninterested in the study of nature, Sivin points to the immense importance of scholastic thinkers in Europe similarly uninterested in the study of nature. Nor should one dismiss the ancient Chinese text on divination, the Book of Changes, as hopelessly antiquated when, according to Sivin, it is "so powerful in systematically relating broader ranges of human experience than modern science attempts to encompass … "[43] He believes he has zeroed in on two fallacies that Westerners use to deny the Chinese or other non-Western peoples agency in the development of modern science. They work this way: first, if some precondition existed in Europe, then it had to lead to the Scientific Revolution; second, if it existed in China, then it had to inhibit any move toward scientific revolution.

A key causal factor of the Scientific Revolution in Europe, notes Sivin, was the development of a professional orientation by natural philosophers (i.e. early scientists) with institutional structures relatively independent from religious and secular authorities beginning gradually in the late Middle Ages. He remarks also that such institutionalization did not occur in China, largely because the guilds of that country themselves lacked autonomy. Scientific knowledge was pursued and shared by learned amateurs, but the formation of independent corporate bodies was considered socially taboo. Sivin wishes to emphasize that the most brilliant intellectual insights cannot lead to major transformations without the concomitant involvement of social or socioeconomic factors. China may well have had sufficient intellectual ferment of a scientific nature yet may have been prevented from achieving scientific revolution for want of specific institutions.

Sivin concludes with a description of an actual scientific revolution in seventeenth-century China. When Jesuit scholars introduced mathematical astronomy to China from around 1630, numerous Chinese scholars transformed their traditional approach by applying geometry and trigonometry – a radical change. Yet the Chinese thinkers did not go the further step made by Galileo to isolate physical phenomena of all kinds and to quantify them systematically, a development of European science that in any event the Jesuits concealed from their Chinese colleagues. The Chinese astronomers, moreover, carried out a revival of traditional Chinese astronomy and wedded it to the new methods. No transformation of society occurred, however, because the scholars involved were all government officials with everything to lose and nothing to gain from a revolution. Other Chinese advocates of Western astronomy argued that its ancient roots lay in China. These thinkers spawned an entire school of philological study aimed at returning to the original forms of the Chinese classics. Again, not a revolutionary approach.

Many of the same arguments and much of the same evidence marshaled to account for the weakness of scientific developments in premodern China are put forward to explain why commercial or industrial capitalism did not emerge there either. They will not be repeated here. Instead, two other influential explanations will be considered.

Existing efficiency precluded further advances (Mark Elvin)

An important early study by Mark Elvin, a professor emeritus of Chinese history at the Australian National University, blamed China's economic stagnation on a "high equilibrium trap." He meant that the traditional Chinese economy was so efficient as to preclude widespread mechanization and the systematic development of technological improvements.

Having described in detail what he calls the "medieval economic revolution" in China, Elvin tries to understand why the Chinese economy fell into a slump between 1300 and 1500 and why the period of economic growth thereafter was not accompanied by technological innovation. He adduces four causes for the economic decline. First, China had begun to run out of frontier territory for the growing population to settle and develop. Consequently, southern China became overpopulated and could not readily feed itself. Naturally, this also made it difficult to significantly expand cotton output, which made the mechanization of cotton textile production unrewarding. Second, commercial and other contacts with the outside world diminished. A whole series of decrees restricted overseas trade and travel beginning at the start of the 1300s and continued periodically – though from time to time they were eased – over the next several centuries, until in 1842 Great Britain forced China to open their ports to international commerce. The reconstruction in 1411 of the Grand Canal, which linked Beijing in the north with Hangzhou in the south, made it

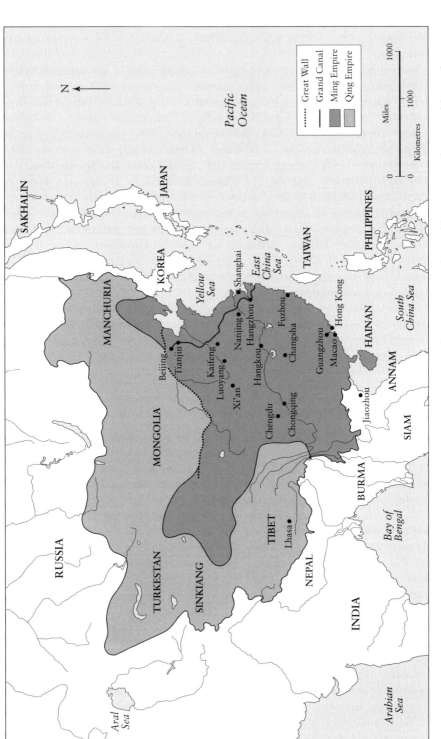

Map 5.1 Apogee of empire: China under the Ming and Qing (until the nineteenth century) was the world's most populous, wealthy, and powerful country.

possible to forgo seaborne transport entirely (see Map 5.1). Elvin suggests this made practical sense also because many Chinese ships were not seaworthy. He also thinks there was a political justification: to prevent the development of alternative centers of power along the coastline.

The third reason for the economic downturn was directly caused by China turning away from foreign trade. The economy depended on silver currency as a means of exchange, yet China produced far too little of the metal to satisfy its needs. The Ming government attempted unsuccessfully to rely instead on paper currency. The reduction in silver imports – and the printing of money that people did not trust – imposed deflationary pressure on the economy. Only the smuggling of bullion into the country prevented a far worse economic crisis.

Finally, Chinese thinkers grew more introspective and less concerned with studies of the natural world. Both painting and philosophy turned away from reality and toward subjectivity and intuition. Elvin cites the case of Fang Yi-chih (1611–1681), whom he considers the best scientific thinker of his time, yet who believed that a spiritual quality infusing objects made their comprehension impossible through purely rational means. Instead, he sought an intuitive means of apprehending reality by responding "to the fine causal stirrings in the World-Mind." The techniques of divination, especially those developed in the *Book of Changes*, played a key role by making it possible "to bring one's subconscious into a suitably responsive state."[44] This outlook, according to Elvin, made it possible to view any anomaly in nature as something intuitively comprehensible and therefore made it unlikely that the sage would be provoked into seeking some new framework for understanding it. The results for Chinese science, he thinks, were catastrophic.

Elvin next proceeds to detail Chinese economic development in the early modern period. During the early Ming times, the holdings of wealthy land-owners increased dramatically in quantity and extent, until by the end of the dynasty in 1644 big landowners in some regions owned more than half of all the farmland. Moreover, in most cases the peasants who worked their land were either fully enserfed or at least personally subordinated. Even hired workers were often treated as servants. By the end of the sixteenth century, however, many rural laborers were growing less docile, so that estate managers found it necessary to treat them more and more with regard. Peasant rebellions were frequent throughout Chinese history, but those on the eve of the collapse of the Ming dynasty called into question the rural social order and in fact pre-cipitated the collapse of serfdom. Elvin believes the main underlying cause for this transformation was the steady expansion of the commercial economy, which increased the class consciousness of peasants, opened up new job opportunities for them especially in the handicraft industries, and tended to undermine the authority of landlords, partly because land itself became a less attractive investment for people with money. Consequently, the large estates fragmented, and anyone with ambition moved to the city.

The end of serfdom had a profound effect on Chinese society. For one thing, it probably led to a doubling of the population in the three centuries down to

1850, because landowners could no longer prevent young peasants (especially females) from marrying and having children. Second, geographical and social mobility increased dramatically. Yet, as landholdings became smaller, peasants struggled to make ends meet or to try to get ahead. Everyone competed desperately, but the broader society did not benefit. "It was a society," he asserts, "that was both egalitarian and riven with mutual jealousies." Since those who exploited labor and those who were exploited were not radically distinguished either economically or ideologically, mutual hostility ensued instead of harmony.[45] Finally, the wealth and influence of merchants increased. They frequently allied themselves with government officials or became government officials by investing in the painstaking preparations for the civil service exam, paying bribes, or simply buying titles or official degrees.

In any event, economic activity expanded rapidly, as rural industry intensified, market towns sprang up, and a commercial network linked producers and sellers across the country. At the same time, however, customs and laws kept key aspects of business, in particular commerce and production, from becoming integrated and therefore more efficient. Technological progress was moreover less robust "than at almost any other previous moment in 2,000 years of Chinese history." Yet this fact merely intensifies an obvious paradox. Why should there have been so little technological innovation during a time (from the later 1500s) of considerable economic development, and therefore why did China not embark on modern economic growth in parallel with Europe?[46] It is to resolve this question that our author devotes his final chapter: "Quantitative growth, qualitative standstill."

He begins by rejecting a number of explanations put forward by scholars to account for China's economic stagnation. To those who have argued for an insufficiency of investment capital in early modern China, he points to many fabulously wealthy merchants willing to invest in productive activities. Nor was the Chinese market too small to make such investments lucrative – on the contrary. Concerning the argument that merchants lacked the political and economic security necessary to justify taking such risks, he retorts that in reality bureaucrats and businessmen often worked together hand in glove. Furthermore, government monetary policy was in general highly constructive or at least laissez-faire. Elvin admits that it was difficult to build large-scale businesses in Imperial China, but it was in fact done. (The families of the branch managers of a major bank were typically held hostage for three to four years to ensure proper behavior, for example.)

Yet the paradox remains – despite impressive commercial and even industrial activity, there was no "take-off." Our author cites descriptions from the late Ming period of huge factories employing thousands of workers and hundreds of water-driven machines and then adds: "Out of so widespread a mastery of the pre-modern mechanical arts it seems strange that no further technological progress should have come … " It seems likely that, had Chinese craftsmen been animated by European-style obsession for technological improvement, they could have developed such devices as spinning machines and steam engines.

This should not have proved impossible for "a people who had been building double-action piston flame-throwers in the Sung dynasty. The critical point is that nobody tried." Except for in the field of agriculture, Chinese technology ceased developing "well before the point at which a lack of basic scientific knowledge had become a serious obstacle."[47] At this point, Elvin puts forward his theory of the "high-level equilibrium trap." In brief, Chinese success itself became an obstacle.

And the Chinese were successful. They adopted New World crops and imitated the simpler firearms and scientific instruments from Europe. Technological improvements were made on a small scale in nearly every walk of life. As already noted, commercial and financial operations expanded and became more sophisticated. Yet the country gradually faced more and more severe shortages of fuel, clothing fibers, draft animals, metals, and especially good farmland – all caused by a rapidly expanding population. The want of resources often made it prohibitively expensive to build even simple wooden machines. China boasted excellent networks of roads, but very little land transport – perhaps because of the lack of draft animals but just as likely because of the excellent water routes, which were so inexpensive that it probably made no financial sense to invest in vehicular technology. Moreover, even improvements in water transport could not make a big difference easily (like the building of the Erie Canal in 1825), because every potential route had already been constructed. The Chinese had in fact achieved what was possible without the steam engine.

The same was true in agriculture: only advanced technologies like chemical fertilizers and mechanized tractors could significantly increase output per laborer and unit of land, which was far higher than in Europe on the eve of the Industrial Revolution. Unfortunately, good farmland in China was in short supply. Yet population growth continued throughout this period, which of course lowered the output per capita and threatened to lead to a demographic crisis, something discerning observers since the time of Adam Smith viewed as the distinctive economic characteristic of China in the 1600s and 1700s.[48] Elvin concludes that the population kept growing relatively rapidly because of highly efficient agricultural techniques, which however barely advanced during the last years of Imperial China, and because of some available lands onto which migrants could settle, in particular in Manchuria.

So why did China fail to continue along its impressive trajectory of innovation and dramatic technological improvements? Elvin suggests a complex explanation. The agricultural surplus, per capita income, labor costs, and per capita demand were all declining. At the same time, farming and transport technologies had already risen to so high a level of sophistication that no modest enhancements were possible, while the vast domestic markets, while static, admitted no obvious bottlenecks. Thus, the most sensible approach for both peasants and merchants, even during times of temporary economic downturns, was to seek not labor-saving machinery but rather frugality in the use of resources and fixed capital. Elvin calls this situation a "high-level equilibrium trap." It emerged thanks to – or perhaps in spite of – the Chinese society's strong commitment to economic rationality, reverence for inventors of the past, and impressive technological achievements throughout its history.[49] China was able to begin to break out of this trap only thanks to the introduction of Western technology in the nineteenth century.

Agricultural interests completely dominated society (Kent G. Deng)

Our last author is Kent G. Deng, who teaches economic history at the London School of Economics. Earlier in his life, at age 15 to be exact, he was sent to a labor camp near the Sino-Soviet border, where he spent six years. In his words,

> I consequently underwent a Stalin-type brain-washing program and was officially recognized as being cleansed of my non-proletarian family background and its related "original sin."[50]

He even officially acquired a quasi-peasant status, which in the age of Mao's Cultural Revolution was the highest status marker possible. His experience, he believes, helped him to understand how social structures and institutions work and, equally important, the nature of peasant life in China, the key to understanding China's development – its successes and failures.

The extremes of its successes and failures are an astonishing enigma to our author. China flourished at a level similar to that of Rome two thousand years ago, and flourishes still. Yet its peaks of development were separated by one thousand years each – first the Han, then the Song, and now the latest times. It is the only great culture of ancient times still going strong and today's only large territorial state founded before the sixteenth century. Making sense of these extraordinary and unique developments constitutes perhaps the modern historian's greatest challenge, aside from explaining the Industrial Revolution.[51]

Deng begins with a survey of 11 social scientific models purported to explain why the West rose and, by extension, China did not. While acknowledging their value for understanding historical development in recent centuries, he pokes holes in all of them. For example, the European city-state was so conducive to economic development, yet why did it flourish for such a brief time? Or, if technological change correlates directly with population growth, why did India and China fail to enjoy sustained technological innovation? Or again, if individual private ownership was a key factor in the emergence of capitalism, why did China not achieve capitalist development two thousand years ago since private ownership of land became the norm in the pre-Qin period? If political fragmentation was so important for the development of human societies, why was China so successful without it for most of its history? And if Confucianism impeded Chinese development, why have a number of countries strongly influenced by Confucianism enjoyed such enormous success in recent decades – Taiwan, Hong Kong, Singapore, South Korea, and Japan?

Deng goes on to propound a multifaceted theory, drawing on the work of previous scholars and especially Mark Elvin's, of "an all-round equilibrium" that may account for both China's amazing cultural and geopolitical longevity and its failure to break through to industrial capitalism.[52] This maintenance of equilibrium centered on agriculture, at which the Chinese excelled from earliest times, in part because China itself has among the best endowed and largest concentrations of arable land on earth. Crops grew so well and so easily that nearly the entire population was drawn into farming. Indeed once they had made this commitment, switching to other occupations grew less and less attractive, unlike in Europe where relatively poorer soils and climates drove comparatively more people into nonagricultural pursuits from as early as the Middle Ages. In China, by contrast, nearly everyone – both rich and poor, elites and commoners – took part for many centuries in a "cult of agriculture," involving shrines, altars, frequent religious observances, and animal sacrifices.

The state itself adopted and enforced laws protecting and promoting private ownership rights for over two thousand years. It also spearheaded vast and steady colonization efforts throughout the Chinese subcontinent – right up to the limits of possible expansion: the Gobi Desert, the Himalayas, and the Indo-Chinese jungles – in order to provide access to land to the ever-increasing Chinese population. Since their custom was to distribute land equally among all male heirs, the Chinese peasants needed a constantly growing fund of arable land. The emergence of multiple forms of landownership, by which several people might have a proprietary interest in a single piece of land, also helped to accommodate the ever-expanding population. Since much of China's land was extremely fertile – three or four crops in a single year from one plot of land were not uncommon – multiple landownership expanded agricultural and investment opportunities without requiring an expansion into new geographical regions.[53] In practice, this approach to landholding and land usage enabled investors and peasants to minimize their tax burden. In any event, Deng reckons that nearly every Chinese family by the late Imperial period owned one right or another to land.

Of course, if nearly everyone in China was invested in land ownership, then landowners must have constituted the only truly significant interest group in the country. That's exactly what Deng has found to be true. For example, a high proportion (39 percent) of the most celebrated and successful participants in the Imperial civil service examination – the "Imperial Examination Champions" – were of very poor socioeconomic background, while (in a separate set of data) the family background of over 75 percent was unknown. Thus, it seems likely that the majority of all Chinese civil servants was of peasant background and was therefore likely to promote the interests of the agrarian community. Deng goes so far as to speak of an "agricultural favoritism in Chinese state politics" by which "to a great extent the Chinese peasantry collectively manipulated state politics."[54]

The agrarian emphasis of Chinese society from top to bottom also tended to confine Chinese society to agricultural pursuits. Few people left the land for occupations in the city full-time. By the same token, Chinese peasants were more likely than those, say, in Europe, who had the safety valve of escaping to urban areas, to band together to rebel against what they considered unjust government. Similarly, Chinese peasants were far more likely than their European counterparts to be entirely self-sufficient economically, which is not to say they did not also participate regularly, though in a more marginal way, in market relations. This resulted in another important impact: since the peasants were so heavily engaged in market economics, they tended to compete with the merchant class, to whom Deng thinks they were a far worse enemy than the state and the ruling elites.

The ruling elites were less hostile to commerce than solicitous toward the promotion of agriculture and ensuring the well-being of rural dwellers, pursuing physiocratic policies many hundreds of years before that philosophy was introduced in France in the early modern period. In fact, Confucian and Taoist thinkers alike argued in favor of social harmony and against political despotism. In such an agrarian society the promotion of agrarian interests was a sensible way to achieve those goals. Thus, Confucian scholars and their pupils for two thousand years, the Chinese emperors, uttered such sage advice as: "Food is the foundation of people's life; people are the foundation of the country; the country is the foundation of the monarch."[55] The vast majority of Chinese people apparently accepted this dictum and was ready to take up arms against any ruler who deviated from it. Confucianism advocated a sort of golden mean: moderation in all things, everything in its place, which naturally included business and trade – just not too much. Confucianism was highly successful in China mostly because it corresponded to the interests of the majority of the population. (By contrast, Legalism, which obviously served the interests of the government above all else, was completely repudiated.)

The same was true of the relatively centralized state: a society composed mostly of free citizens needs a strong central arbiter to adjudicate disputes among them; a feudal or slave-based society does not. Unfortunately, however, a centralized state makes it more difficult to carry new ideas to fruition; thus, much innovative creativity withered on the vine, so to speak.

The key ingredients in the Chinese socioeconomic matrix – "the predominance of agriculture in the economy, the prevailing private individual land ownership, the landowning peasantry as the majority, the physiographic state, the centralized government, and Confucian ideology" – functioned together, according to Deng, in a multifaceted equilibrium built upon a balance of these several elements.[56] The three most important factors were agricultural dominance, the free peasantry, and the physiocratic government, all conditioned by the environment and mediated by Confucianism but also Buddhism and Taoism. The Chinese society's astonishing two-thousand-year success suggests that its failure to engender industrial capitalism stemmed not from a few peculiar elements like governmental inefficiency, the scarcity of land, and the Confucian ideology, but rather from a complex, interconnected framework, involving both "'hardwares' (such as the conditions for the economy, the structure of society, and the function of bureaucracy) and 'softwares' (such as economic policies, values and ideology)."[57] Yet the coming together of all these factors was not inevitable, not caused by some Chinese predisposition to farming or the Chinese land being good only for agriculture.

Instead, it emerged thanks to very specific historical developments starting with the Shang dynasty (1600–1046 BC), which was oriented toward trade and handicrafts far more than toward agriculture. The successor dynasty, the Zhou (1046–256 BC), which replaced the Shang through military conquest, laid the foundations of Imperial Chinese development with an emphasis on agriculture, the protection of landed property rights, and a more sophisticated social structure. A military organization able to keep the menacing nomads to the north at bay was a crucial contributor to their success. Over the centuries, however, competition among numerous states in the region reduced the Zhou to the status of one kingdom among many, until the Qin conquered them all and established the first Chinese Empire. Since several of the competing kingdoms emphasized commerce, the victorious Qin subjected merchants to ritualistic humiliation – a practice that to some extent continued for the next two thousand years. They also undertook extensive reforms aimed at improving agriculture, administrative efficiency, and military prowess. They succeeded in these reforms, thus laying the foundation for what Deng considers China's system of socioeconomic equilibrium.

Deng hastens to argue that there was nothing inevitable about these developments. They resulted from desperate warfare and violent struggle among rivals. Only a ruling group capable of organizing millions of peasants into productive farming and therefore richly contributing fiscal units could triumph in an age of kingdoms founded on mixed economies. The Qin managed to organize their kingdom with a high level of efficiency, but there was nothing inevitable about that.[58]

Throughout the centuries, the Chinese state kept taxes low but frequently mobilized millions of people for big civil-engineering projects like building the Great Wall and the Grand Canal or moving the capital to a new location. In the vast majority of periods, the people called up for these duties obediently complied, again because they presumably believed that the state was looking out for their best interests.

Deng rejects the contention that technological development stagnated beginning in the Ming dynasty era. Innovation, he argues, continued ceaselessly in the agricultural sector, mostly involving more productive seeds and methods of cultivation. As proof, he offers two facts. First, while the population continued to grow rapidly, the amount of land under cultivation slowly shrank. Second, the peasantry continued to feed the increasing number of artisans producing more and more high-quality wares for domestic and international consumption. Nor, according to Deng, does it make sense to blame any alleged technological stagnation on the poor health of the Chinese people, since the extremely high demographic growth rates of the Qing period could only have been achieved by a healthy population.

He also further analyzes the anti-mercantile bias of the Chinese socio-economic system. The peasantry was too committed culturally and economically to farming to seek more than part-time employment in any field other than government service. According to Deng, the dream of every peasant father was for his son to gain an education, pass the civil service examination, and join the ranks of officialdom. At the same time, government officials viewed the peasantry as the main source of new recruits. As a result, "The Chinese bureaucracy was, to a great extent, a group of learned peasant sons, and the peasantry to the same extent formed the supporting majority for the physiocratic party in power."[59] In this context, the merchants were largely squeezed out. In fact, government service and farming functioned like two poles of attraction pulling merchants away from commerce and into the two only truly respectable occupations in Chinese society.

At the same time, those who continued in commercial activity depended far more on government support than their European counterparts. But strangely – from a European perspective – the Chinese state never formed an alliance with the merchants to counterbalance the power of the peasantry, as European rulers often did in order to weaken the position of the nobility. Nor did Chinese merchants develop the kind of relatively independent institutions their European counterparts built up from medieval times, especially autonomous cities as centers primarily of commerce. Chinese cities, by contrast, remained administrative loci serving the interests of the state.

Although China remained extraordinarily stable as a society for over two thousand years, experiencing only four periods of fragmented government and none after AD 1279, the shattering of social harmony by peasant rebellion was frequent. This typically occurred when a combination of factors – official corruption, failure of the Confucian literati to restrain governmental rapaciousness, natural disasters, and economic depression – undermined the legitimacy of the emperor and his bureaucracy in the eyes of the people. Such rebellions were unique in world history. Not only did they occur almost constantly – according to some calculations thousands occurred every year during long periods of time – they also lasted far longer than their counterparts in other countries; a few went on for over forty years. The big ones in China – and Deng calculates 269 of these in the course of 2,106 years – typically involved hundreds of thousands of rebels and sometimes millions.[60] Finally, they also not infrequently resulted in major political change – for example, the overthrow of six of China's main dynasties. Yet the Chinese rebellions had little impact on the socioeconomic system in the country, what Deng calls the trinary structure (agricultural dominance, the free peasantry, and the physiocratic government). Thus, the Chinese peasantry was largely conservative and even reactionary.

By contrast, no peasant rebellion ever succeeded in replacing a government in Europe, India, or Japan. Deng believes they had institutional restraints able to prevent such agrarian actions, whereas China did not. Perhaps that was because in China the main "institution" of the country was the society itself. He even suggests that rebellion became routinized, such that most people expected socioeconomic hardship to provoke mass rebellion.[61] Moreover, the official Confucian ideology at least tacitly condoned and even justified popular rebellion against rulers who failed to maintain social harmony and to promote the common good. In other words, peasant rebellions were a mechanism for maintaining the astonishingly efficient trinary structure. A separate chapter shows that repeated – and often ferocious – nomadic attacks from the north also served to reinforce that social system, since it was the only way to mobilize sufficient resources for defense against them.

Here, Deng suggests, lies the best explanation for China's inability to engender industrial capitalism. In premodern China, the extraordinary success resulting from the interlocking practices and institutions of the trinary equilibrium led both rulers and peasantry to avoid major disruptions and transformations. Not any lack of technology or any ideological commitments motivated this avoidance but rather a practical recognition of the benefits of the enduring socioeconomic patterns to the livelihood of the vast majority of people. This structural equilibrium kept the peasants from leaving the land and thus from providing a flexible labor supply for industrial development and forestalled further growth of the market economy.[62] In this context, the Song dynasty renaissance or "revolution" must be seen as an aberration made possible only by the weakness of the governing authority and to which the trinary Chinese system was entirely antithetical. Thus, it could not be sustained.

In fact, China returned over and over to its state of equilibrium – after invasions, conquests, rebellions, and even periods of intensive innovation and creativity. Therefore, Deng considers it unconvincing to argue that any specific historical misfortunes prevented the development of capitalist industrialization. China during the Han and Song Dynasties came closest to this development but fell short in each case. These periods of flourishing were random occurrences brought about by peculiar circumstances. Deng attributes China's failures to "internal or endogenous deficiencies, mainly structural and institutional."[63]

Yet one can say that China was a "failed society" only from the extraordinarily unusual perspective of a Europe completely transformed by the Industrial Revolution, for until two hundred years ago China was still richer and more powerful and for over two thousand years it had flourished as a culture. At the same time, however, only an external jolt – its wrenching encounter with the modern West – could shatter China's equilibrium and set the country on the path it currently pursues.

Conclusion

China's failure to precipitate the world's first scientific or industrial revolution, despite centuries of technological and commercial leadership, has thus been explained in a variety of ways. Several scholars emphasize political centralization and the stifling cultural hegemony of the scholar-officials. Others blame technological stagnation beginning in the fourteenth century. An extremely efficient agricultural system, which kept wages low and thus inhibited the search for labor-saving inventions, was also considered a key culprit. Others point to the elites' disdain for commerce and scientific discovery and, more generally, an unwillingness to learn or adapt ideas and technologies from abroad. One scholar argues that exploiting colonies in the manner of the early modern Europeans might have enabled China to break through its Malthusian constraints. Another considers a lack of independent institutions to have been detrimental. Finally, two authors attribute China's inability to engender world-changing transformations to its extraordinary success in maintaining a regionally dominant culture for two thousand years. In other words, almost as many explanations have been put forward to answer the "Needham question" as to explain the rise of the West.

Further reading

China in the grand narratives

Braudel, Fernand. *Civilization and Capitalism, 15th–18th Century.* Volume one: *The Structures of Everyday Life: The Limits of the Possible.* Translated by Siân Reynolds. New York: Harper & Row, 1982.
Duchesne, Ricardo. *The Uniqueness of Western Civilization.* Leiden; Boston: Brill, 2011.
Hall, John A. *Powers and Liberties: The Causes and Consequences of the Rise of the West.* Oxford: Basil Blackwell, 1985.
Huff, Toby E. *The Rise of Early Modern Science: Islam, China, and the West.* 2nd ed. Cambridge; New York: Cambridge University Press, 2003.
Jones, Eric. *The European Miracle.* Cambridge: Cambridge University Press, 1987.
Jones, Eric. *Growth Recurring: Economic Change in World History.* Oxford: Clarendon Press, 1988.
North, Douglass C. and Robert Paul Thomas. *The Rise of the Western World: A New Economic History.* Cambridge: Cambridge University Press, 1973.

Interpretations by China experts

Huang, Philip C. C. *The Peasant Family and Rural Development in the Yangzi Delta, 1350–1988.* Stanford: Stanford University Press, 1990.
Marks, Robert B. *Tigers, Rice, Silk, and Silt: Environment and Economy in Late Imperial South China.* Cambridge: Cambridge University Press, 1998.
Wong, R. Bin. *China Transformed: Historical Change and the Limits of European Experience.* Ithaca, N.Y.: Cornell University Press, 1997.

Notes

1 Immanuel Wallerstein, *The Modern World-System I. Capitalist Agriculture and the Origins of the European World-Economy in the Sixteenth Century* (New York: Academic Press, 1974), 56–57.

2 Ibid., 59.

3 Ibid., 63.

4 Joel Mokyr, *The Lever of Riches: Technological Creativity and Economic Progress* (New York: Oxford University Press, 1990), 209.

5 Ibid., 219.

6 Ibid., 224.

7 Ibid., 227.

8 Ibid., 233.

9 Andre Gunder Frank, *Reorient: Global Economy in the Asian Age* (Berkeley, Calif.: University of California Press, 1998), 304.

10 David Landes, *The Wealth and Poverty of Nations: Why Some Are So Rich and Some So Poor* (New York: W. W. Norton, 1998), 95.

11 Ibid., 96.

12 Ibid., 336.

13 Ibid., 342.

14 Ibid., 343.

15 Ibid., 343.

16 Ibid., 348.

17 Kenneth Pomeranz, *The Great Divergence: Europe, China, and the Making of the Modern World Economy* (Princeton, N.J.: Princeton University Press, 2000), 292.

18 Ibid., 297.

19 Simon Winchester's *The Man Who Loved China: The Fantastic Story of the Eccentric Scientist Who Unlocked the Mysteries of the Middle Kingdom* (New York: Harper, 2008) tells his fascinating story.

20 For a scholarly assessment of this monumental work, see Robert Finlay, "China, the West, and World History in Joseph Needham's Science and Civilisation in China," *Journal of World History* 11 (Fall 2000): 265–303.

21 Joseph Needham, *The Grand Titration: Science and Society in East and West* (London: Allen & Unwin, 1969), 16.

22 Needham, *The Grand Titration*; Joseph Needham, *Science in Traditional China: A Comparative Perspective* (Cambridge, Mass.: Harvard University Press; Hong Kong: The Chinese University Press, 1981).

23 Needham, *Science in Traditional China*, 8.

24 Needham, *The Grand Titration*, 61–62.

25 Ibid., 119–120.

26 Ibid., 150.

27 Needham, *The Grand Titration*, 36; see also ibid., 299–330.

28 Ibid., 325–326.

29 Ibid., 327.

30 Wen-yuan Qian, *The Great Inertia: Scientific Stagnation in Traditional China* (London; Dover, N.H.: Croom Helm, 1985), 20–21.

31 Ibid., 81.

32 Ibid., 67.

33 Ibid., 90.

34 Derk Bodde, *Chinese Thought, Society, and Science: The Intellectual and Social Background of Science and Technology in Pre-modern China* (Honolulu: University of Hawaii Press, 1991).

35 Ibid., 92.

36 Ibid., 107. Second set of ellipses in the original.

37 Ibid., 146.

38 Ibid., 190.

39 Ibid., 306.

40 Ibid., 367.

41 Nathan Sivin, "Why the Scientific Revolution Did Not Take Place in China – or Didn't It?" in S*cience in Ancient China: Researches and Reflections* (Aldershot, Great Britain; Brookfield, Vt., USA: Variorum, 1995), 45–66 (here: 48).

42 Ibid., 53.

43 Ibid., 57.

44 Mark Elvin, *The Pattern of the Chinese Past* (Stanford: Stanford University Press, 1973), 233.

45 Ibid., 259.

46 Ibid., 284.

47 Ibid., 286, 297–298.

48 Ibid., 309.

49 Ibid., 314–315.

50 Gang Deng, *The Premodern Chinese Economy: Structural Equilibrium and Capitalist Sterility* (London; New York: Routledge, 1999), xi.

51 Ibid., 5.

52 Ibid., 32.

53 Ibid., 59.

54 Ibid., 83.

55 Ibid., 94.

56 Ibid., 121, 122.

57 Ibid., 127.

58 Ibid., 145.

59 Ibid., 196.

60 In a later publication, Deng tallies 2,106 in just over two thousand years, each lasting seven years and involving 226,000 participants on average. See Kent G. Deng, "Development and Its Deadlock in Imperial China, 221 B.C.–1840 A.D.," *Economic Development and Cultural Change* 51 (Jan., 2003): 479–522 (here: 504).

61 Deng, *The Premodern Chinese Economy*, 245.

62 Ibid., 254.

63 Ibid., 323.

Conclusion

Having surveyed many of the most significant explanations for the rise to pre-eminence of Europe and the wider West, readers may wish to assess which of them is most convincing overall, either singly or in combination. The choice is very broad. At one end of the spectrum is Christopher Dawson, who argues that the melding of ancient Greek and Roman, Judeo-Christian, and Germanic cultural and spiritual traditions yielded the most dynamic, restless, and inventive civilization in history. These qualities, he claims, led to a series of transformations over several centuries that can account for the West's rise. At the other end, John Hobson makes the case that nearly every Western accomplishment was made possible by the imitation and assimilation of prior Asian achievements and by a unique manifestation of exploitative racism. In between these two extremes range a wide variety of interpretations.

Even within the major categories of interpretation one finds rich diversity of thought. Among the scholars who attribute the West's rise largely to features inherent in European culture, Alan Macfarlane traces that apparently key ingredient in Western success – individualism – back to medieval England and, speculatively, to the traditions of ancient Germanic tribes. Deirdre McCloskey, by contrast, holds that a cultural shift enabling the development of modern economic growth occurred rather suddenly in the seventeenth century. Nathan Rosenberg and Douglass North emphasize not culture as attitudes and beliefs but rendered concrete as relatively constant ways to organize people, like governments, businesses, laws, and rights. In their view, Western institutions promoted innovation and prosperity more than those of other cultures. In any event, such scholars as Lynn White and Geoffrey Parker analyze in detail the impressive array of technological innovations brought to life by European inventors beginning in the Middle Ages. Likewise, Joel Mokyr seeks to show that a unique symbiosis between craftsmen and intellectuals, which started in Enlightenment Europe, enabled the West to rise by marrying abstract and practical knowledge and pure and applied science.

William McNeill agrees with Dawson that no civilization in history was as dynamically unstable as the West. He thinks this came about, along with the West's rise, because no other civilization was so open to change and learning from others. In other words, without powerful influences from Asia, Europe's amazing dynamism would have remained little more than "sound and fury." Jared Diamond traces those influences thousands of years back into the past. In his interpretation, nature's bounteous endowment of the Middle East with by far the world's richest assortment of domesticable plants and animals meant that civilization would inevitably emerge first in that region. Europe simply "lucked out" to develop so close to what was for many millennia the world's greatest cradle of innovation. Eric Jones and David Cosandey show in great detail how Europe, once civilization had emerged, enjoyed the natural environments most conducive to prosperity and innovation on the planet. Again, however, Marshall Hodgson points out the immense contributions of the Islamic world in particular to the West's rise. Until then, all of the cultures of Eurasia adapted every valuable new technology or idea that came along. None could gain ascendancy by accelerating the pace of technological change so as to "change the rules of the game" – until the rise of the West. Then technological transformations came so quickly that few cultures could keep up. Hodgson does not, however, blame the West; falling behind for most cultures was simply an unavoidable feature of modern life.

Scholars like Andre Gunder Frank, by contrast, absolutely blame the West. For them, the West was only able to rise by squeezing obscene profits out of colonized regions throughout the globe that were knitted into a hierarchy of exploitation for funneling wealth from the remotest villages toward the richest metropolitan centers in Europe and America. Joseph Inikori provides abundant and meticulously gathered evidence that Africans forcibly settled throughout the Americas contributed vastly more to economic development in England and ultimately to the Industrial Revolution than scholars heretofore have acknowledged. Alfred Crosby shows that not only did European people conquer and settle the Americas and Australia – so also did their plants, animals, diseases, and weeds. The hardier species that had evolved on the massive and heavily populated Eurasian landmass, both flora and fauna, easily overwhelmed native species in every temperate ecosystem where they were introduced. A different kind of ecological imperialism, deploying Western legal concepts to justify the seizure of land, is described in detail by John Weaver.

An entire scholarly approach called world systems analysis, stemming ultimately from Marxist theory, has been put forth by Immanuel Wallerstein and numerous followers. He argues that toward the end of the sixteenth century, a capitalist "world economy" began to emerge in Europe, or rather, centered on Europe and encompassing an ever-expanding hierarchy of peripheral and semi-peripheral lands subordinated in a complex web to the Western core. In his telling, the West rose thanks to this global division of labor. Eric Mielants revises the Wallersteinian model by tracing its historical origins back to the Middle Ages. Andre Gunder Frank and Barry Gills conceive of a global economic development commencing five thousand years ago, and naturally in this picture the West's role is seen as almost insignificant. According to Janet Abu-Lughod, a world economic system emerged in Asia during the heyday of the Mongol

Empire (1200s to early 1300s), and Europe was able to rise only thanks to that prior development and the subsequent stagnation of Asia.

Several scholars in fact seek systematically to poke holes in the "uniqueness of the West" perspective. Jack Goody provides evidence that allegedly great Western achievements – such as superior rationality, unique family structures, and "scientific" accounting – either emerged elsewhere first or were entirely unnecessary for material success in the modern world. According to Andre Gunder Frank, the West actually rose only very late in modern times and only thanks to its coercively obtained windfall of silver from the New World. Kenneth Pomeranz adds to this external factor the blind luck of finding huge deposits of coal and iron ore in relatively close proximity in Great Britain. Only these accidents of history and geography made the West's rise possible. Both of these authors, along with John Hobson, contend that the major Asian cultures enjoyed economic preeminence until at least the early nineteenth century.

Still other scholars wonder, however, why Asia's preeminence did not endure, and in particular why such major transformations of modern times as the Scientific Revolution and the emergence of industrial capitalism did not occur first in China. Numerous authors of synthetic works on the modern world have put forward interpretations. Wallerstein argues that China's imperial rulers, unlike the monarchs of Europe, could not nimbly undertake entrepreneurial ventures or permit their subjects to innovate constantly in military technology, lest they turn their weapons against them. Joel Mokyr emphasizes the near freezing up of technological innovation in China starting in the early modern period because both rulers and people wished to avoid social disruption. Europe, by contrast, was too politically fragmented to permit any social actors to shut down technological change. Andre Gunder Frank blames China's highly efficient agriculture and therefore low overall wages for its failure to develop labor-saving industrial technology. According to David Landes, the Chinese simply lacked the passion and curiosity that drove early modern Europeans to innovate and explore the world. Finally, like Frank, Kenneth Pomeranz stresses material factors. China's huge population demanded ever-greater labor intensification, he argues, but without a windfall made possible by Europe-style colonization, little surplus labor or capital was available for industrialization.

The failure of China, long the most technologically advanced country in the world, to develop modern science has vexed many specialists on Chinese history. Joseph Needham's vast output of research on early Chinese science and technology only sharpens that paradox. In seeking to resolve it, he points to a centralized bureaucratic system ultimately stifling creativity and a lack of interest in discovering abstract regularities in nature. Wen-yuan Qian goes further, blaming Confucianism's almost total rejection of the study of nature, strong aversion to innovation, and disinterest in wide-ranging inquiry. Another scholar, Derk Bodde, attributes what he considers Chinese stagnation to cultural factors, like a devotion to archaic values and attitudes, the extraordinary efforts spent by gifted people on preparations for the civil service exam, the

widespread failure of scholars to generalize, the predominant cyclical conception of time, a disinclination to debate, resistance to foreign ideas, and
ingrained deference to authority. Nathan Sivin, by contrast, denies that the
Chinese failed to develop science; their understanding of nature was simply
more intuitive and less systematic. Still, he concedes, their profound insights
lacked strong institutional means of development in the premodern period.

Finally, two experts on China seek to explain why China experienced no
commercial or industrial revolution in premodern times. According to Mark
Elvin, China stagnated economically because of a "high-level equilibrium trap."
He means that, despite intensive commercial, financial, and industrial activity
and an army of ingenious artisans constantly making minor improvements to
existing technology and infrastructure, the continuously expanding population –
itself a sign of great material success – put heavy pressure on existing resources
and made significant innovation prohibitively expensive, both economically and
psychologically. Yet only major technological breakthroughs could have
enabled China to break out of its trap of relative prosperity. Kent G. Deng
carries this basic argument further, interpreting China's socioeconomic system
as characterized by a multifaceted and extremely long-lived equilibrium,
centered on agriculture, that made possible both its extraordinary successes
through the centuries and its inability to achieve the sort of transformations
leading to the rise of the West. Since the vast majority of Chinese benefited
from this equilibrium, only the tiniest minority was ever willing to advocate
radical change. Innovation continued right down to the fall of imperial China in
1911, especially in agriculture – otherwise how could the population have
grown so spectacularly? – but again radical innovation was eschewed.

Which of these interpretations make the most sense? Are mostly all of them
mutually contradictory, as many indeed seem, or is it possible to combine at
least several of them into more comprehensive and holistic explanations?
For example, is Christopher Dawson's reading of Western culture as uniquely
restless and dynamic compatible with William McNeill's understanding of cultural exchanges as the main driving force of human advancement? Can one
reasonably combine Joseph Inikori's argument that the labor of Africans
contributed substantially to making the Industrial Revolution possible with
Imannuel Wallerstein's claim that efficiencies gained from labor specialization
among various cores and peripheries explain the emergence of capitalism? Do
the geographical accounts of Jared Diamond and David Cosandey work well
together with assertions by Mark Elvin and Kent G. Deng that China's efficient
agricultural system partially determined its historical development? Can
Marshall Hodgson's emphasis on the contribution of Islamic achievements to
the rise of the West be harmonized with Andre Gunder Frank's assertion that
East Asia was determinant in the West's rise?

Probably most readers will have answered "yes" to one or more of these –
and other similar possible – questions. This is because the deepest and most
satisfying interpretations of the rise of the West are typically synthetic,
manifesting a capacious diversity of means of explanation. True, one specific

factor – say, culture or geography – will often seem more determinant than others. Yet my sense is that the professors who write textbooks for courses on Western civilization and world history derive their overall interpretations from a broad reading of the most powerful arguments put forward by a few dozen influential scholars. In writing this book, I have aimed to give their students a glimpse of this fundamental scholarship.

Bibliography

Introduction

Allardyce, Gilbert. "The Rise and Fall of the Western Civilization Course." *The American Historical Review* 87 (Jun., 1982): 695–725.

Costello, Paul. *World Historians and Their Goals: Twentieth-Century Answers to Modernism*. DeKalb, Ill.: Northern Illinois University Press, 1993.

Lockwood, William W. "Adam Smith and Asia." *The Journal of Asian Studies* 23 (May, 1964): 345–355.

Manning, Patrick. *Navigating World History: Historians Create a Global Past*. New York: Palgrave Macmillan, 2003.

Marx, Karl. *Capital: A Critique of Political Economy*. Vol. 1. Introduction by Ernest Mandel. Translated by Ben Fowkes. London: Penguin Books, 1976.

Marx, Karl and Friedrich Engels. *Manifesto of the Communist Party* [1848]. In *The Marx-Engels Reader*. Edited by Robert C. Tucker. 2nd ed. New York: W. W. Norton, 1978.

Mokyr, Joel. "Mobility, Creativity, and Technological Development: David Hume, Immanuel Kant and the Economic Development of Europe." In Günter Abel, ed., *Kreativität. Tagungsband: XX. Deutscher Kongreß für Philosophie*. Hamburg: Felix Meiner Verlag, 2006, 1129–1160.

Montesquieu, M. de Sécondat, baron de. *The Spirit of Laws*. With D'Alembert's analysis of the work. New edition, Revised by J. V. Prichard. Translated from the French by Thomas Nugent. 2 vols. [1752] London: G. Bell, 1914.

Smith, Adam. *An Inquiry into the Nature and Causes of the Wealth of Nations*. Edited by C. J. Bullock. The Harvard Classics. New York: P. F. Collier and Son, 1909.

Spence, Jonathan D. *The Search for Modern China*, 2nd ed. New York; London: W. W. Norton, 1999.

Spengler, Oswald. *The Decline of the West*. Translated by Charles Francis Atkinson. New York: A. A. Knopf, 1926–1928.

Toynbee, Arnold. *A Study of History*. London: Oxford University Press; H. Milford, 1935–1961.

Weber, Max. *The Protestant Ethic and the Spirit of Capitalism*. Translated by Talcott Parsons. Introduction by Anthony Giddens. New York: Charles Scribner's Sons, 1958.

Wells, H. G. *The Outline of History; Being a Plain History of Life and Mankind*. Garden City, N.Y.: Garden City Pub. Co., 1920.

The miracle of the West

Callahan, Daniel, et al. "Christopher Dawson: 12 October 1889–25 May 1970." *The Harvard Theological Review* 66 (Apr., 1973): 161–176.

Cipolla, Carlo. *Guns, Sails, and Empires: Technological Innovation and the Early Phases of European Expansion 1400–1700.* New York: Minerva, 1965.

Costello, Paul. *World Historians and Their Goals: Twentieth-Century Answers to Modernism.* DeKalb, Ill.: Northern Illinois University Press, 1993.

Crosby, Alfred. *The Measure of Reality: Quantification and Western Society, 1250–1600.* Cambridge: Cambridge University Press, 1997.

Dawson, Christopher. *Religion and the Rise of Western Culture.* New York: Sheed and Ward, 1950.

Hall, John A. *Powers and Liberties: The Causes and Consequences of the Rise of the West.* Oxford: Basil Blackwell, 1985.

Landes, David. *The Wealth and Poverty of Nations: Why Some Are So Rich and Some So Poor.* New York: W. W. Norton, 1998.

Macfarlane, Alan. *The Origins of English Individualism. The Family, Property, and Social Transition.* New York: Cambridge University Press, 1978.

——*The Making of the Modern World: Visions from the West and East.* Houndmills; New York: Palgrave, 2002.

McCloskey, Deirdre. *Crossing: A Memoir.* Chicago: University of Chicago Press, 1999.

——*The Bourgeois Virtues: Ethics for an Age of Commerce.* Chicago: University of Chicago Press, 2006.

——*Bourgeois Dignity: Why Economics Can't Explain the Modern World.* Chicago: University of Chicago Press, 2010.

McNeill, William H. *The Pursuit of Power: Technology, Armed Force, and Society since A.D. 1000.* Chicago: University of Chicago Press, 1982.

Mokyr, Joel. *The Lever of Riches: Technological Creativity and Economic Progress.* New York: Oxford University Press, 1990.

——*The Gifts of Athena: Historical Origins of the Knowledge Economy.* Princeton, N.J.: Princeton University Press, 2002.

North, Douglass C. and Robert Paul Thomas. *The Rise of the Western World: A New Economic History.* Cambridge: Cambridge University Press, 1973.

Parker, Geoffrey. *The Military Revolution: Military Innovation and the Rise of the West, 1500–1800.* 2nd ed. Cambridge; New York: Cambridge University Press, 1996.

Pipes, Richard. *Property and Freedom.* New York: Alfred A. Knopf, 1999.

Roberts, Michael. "The Military Revolution, 1560–1660." In Michael Roberts ed., *Essays in Swedish History.* Minneapolis: University of Minnesota Press, 1967, 195–225.

Rosenberg, Nathan and L. E. Birdzell, Jr. *How the West Grew Rich: The Economic Transformation of the Industrial World.* New York: Basic Books, 1986.

White, Lynn, Jr. *Medieval Technology and Social Change.* London: Oxford University Press, 1962.

——*Machina ex Deo; Essays in the Dynamism of Western Culture.* Cambridge, Mass.: MIT Press, 1968.

——*Medieval Religion and Technology: Collected Essays.* Berkeley; Los Angeles; London: University of California Press, 1978.

World history

Chirot, Daniel. *How Societies Change*. Thousand Oaks, Calif.: Pine Forge Press, 1994.

Cosandey, David. *Le Secret de l'Occident: Du miracle passé au marasme présent*. Paris: Arléa, 1997.

Crosby, Alfred. *The Columbian Exchange: Biological and Cultural Consequences of 1492*. Westport, Conn.: Greenwood Press, 1972.

——*Ecological Imperialism: the Biological Expansion of Europe, 900–1900*. Cambridge: Cambridge University Press, 1986.

Diamond, Jared. *Guns, Germs, and Steel: The Fates of Human Societies*. New York: W. W. Norton, 1997.

Hodgson, Marshall G. S. *The Venture of Islam: Conscience and History in a World Civilization*. 3 vols. Chicago: University of Chicago Press, 1974.

——*Rethinking World History: Essays on Europe, Islam, and World History*. Edited by Edmund Burke, III. Cambridge: Cambridge University Press, 1993.

Jones, E. L. *The European Miracle: Environments, Economies, and Geopolitics in the History of Europe and Asia*. London; New York: Cambridge University Press, 1981.

McNeill, William. *The Rise of the West: A History of the Human Community*. Chicago: University of Chicago Press, 1963.

Imperialism and exploitation

Abu-Lughod, Janet L. *Before European Hegemony: The World System A.D. 1250–1350*. New York: Oxford University Press, 1989.

Crosby, Alfred. *Ecological Imperialism: The Biological Expansion of Europe, 900–1900*. Cambridge: Cambridge University Press, 1986.

Eltis, David and Stanley L. Engerman. "The Importance of Slavery and the Slave Trade to Industrializing Britain." *The Journal of Economic History* 60 (March 2000): 123–144.

Frank, Andre Gunder. *Latin America: Underdevelopment or Revolution: Essays on the Development of Underdevelopment and the Immediate Enemy*. London: Monthly Review Press, 1970.

Frank, Andre Gunder and Barry K. Gills, eds. *The World System: Five Hundred Years or Five Thousand?* London; New York: Routledge, 1993.

Inikori, Joseph E. *Africans and the Industrial Revolution in England: A Study in International Trade and Economic Development*. Cambridge: Cambridge University Press, 2002.

Lenin, V. I. *Imperialism, The Highest Stage of Capitalism; a Popular Outline*. New York: International Publishers, 1939.

Mielants, Eric H. *The Origins of Capitalism and the "Rise of the West."* Philadelphia: Temple University Press, 2007.

Wallerstein, Immanuel. *The Modern World-System*. 4 vols. New York: Academic Press, 1974–to date.

——*The Essential Wallerstein*. New York: The New Press, 2000.

Weaver, John C. *The Great Land Rush and the Making of the Modern World, 1650–1900*. Montreal; Kingston: McGill-Queens University Press, 2006.

The greatness of Asia

Frank, Andre Gunder. *Reorient: Global Economy in the Asian Age*. Berkeley, Calif.: University of California Press, 1998.

Goody, Jack. *The Logic of Writing and the Organization of Society*. Cambridge;
New York: Cambridge University Press, 1986.
——*The East in the West*. Cambridge: Cambridge University Press, 1996.
Hobson, John M. *The Eastern Origins of Western Civilization*. Cambridge: Cambridge
University Press, 2004.
Pomeranz, Kenneth. *The Great Divergence: Europe, China, and the Making of the
Modern World Economy*. Princeton, N.J.: Princeton University Press, 2000.

Why not China?

Bodde, Derk. *Chinese Thought, Society, and Science: The Intellectual and Social Back-
ground of Science and Technology in Pre-modern China*. Honolulu: University of
Hawaii Press, 1991.
Deng, Gang. *The Premodern Chinese Economy: Structural Equilibrium and Capitalist
Sterility*. London; New York: Routledge, 1999.
Deng, Kent G. "Development and Its Deadlock in Imperial China, 221 B.C.–1840 A.D."
Economic Development and Cultural Change 51 (Jan., 2003): 479–522.
Elvin, Mark. *The Pattern of the Chinese Past*. Stanford: Stanford University Press, 1973.
Finlay, Robert. "China, the West, and World History in Joseph Needham's Science and
Civilisation in China," *Journal of World History* 11 (Fall 2000): 265–303.
Frank, Andre Gunder. *Reorient: Global Economy in the Asian Age*. Berkeley, Calif.:
University of California Press, 1998.
Landes, David. *The Wealth and Poverty of Nations: Why Some Are So Rich and Some
So Poor*. New York: W. W. Norton, 1998.
Mokyr, Joel. *The Lever of Riches: Technological Creativity and Economic Progress*.
New York: Oxford University Press, 1990.
Needham, Joseph. *The Grand Titration: Science and Society in East and West*. London:
Allen & Unwin, 1969.
——*Science in Traditional China: A Comparative Perspective*. Cambridge, Mass.:
Harvard University Press; Hong Kong: The Chinese University Press, 1981.
Pomeranz, Kenneth. *The Great Divergence: Europe, China, and the Making of the
Modern World Economy*. Princeton, N.J.: Princeton University Press, 2000.
Qian, Wen-yuan. *The Great Inertia: Scientific Stagnation in Traditional China*. London;
Dover, N.H.: Croom Helm, 1985.
Sivin, Nathan. "Why the Scientific Revolution Did Not Take Place in China – or Didn't
It?" In *Science in Ancient China: Researches and Reflections*. Aldershot, Great Britain;
Brookfield, Vt., USA: Variorum, 1995, 45–66.
Wallerstein, Immanuel. *The Modern World-System*. 4 vols. New York: Academic Press,
1974–to date.
Winchester, Simon. *The Man Who Loved China: The Fantastic Story of the Eccentric
Scientist Who Unlocked the Mysteries of the Middle Kingdom*. New York: Harper,
2008.

Index

Abelard, Pierre 21
Abu-Lughod, Janet 91–8, 102, 112, 132, 178
Afro-Eurasia: interaction among cultures 47–9, 61–2, 64; technology dominance within 124; trade throughout 20, 94
agriculture: in China 4, 126, 129, 135, 167, 169–71; in Europe 37, 126, 135; farmers 78, 84, 137, 146, 159; in the Middle East 50–1, 75; new world crops 87, 137, 167; technical advances 29, 167
Alfred the Great 15
America and American tradition 10, 73–5
Anaxagoras 151
Anaxamenes 151
applied science *see* science and technology
Aristotle 103, 151, 169
articulated thalassography *see* geography and waterways
Asia: decline of 94–5, 98; family ties and business 105; superiority over Europe 91, 102, 108, 111, 113
Asia, seventeenth century recession in 112
astronomy and mathematics in China 107, 139, 144, 150, 152, 163; *see also* science and technology
astronomy and mathematics in India 160
authoritarian viewpoint 8

Babylonia 6, 104
Bacon, Roger 25
banking and finance in Europe 32, 73, 93–4, 103–4
banking and finance in India 89, 125
banking and finance in Japan 126
Belgium *see* Flanders, textile industry in
Birdzell, L. E. Jr. 31–4, 38
Black Death *see* disease, role in conquest by Europeans

Bloch, Marc 37
Bodde, Derk 152–60, 179
Boethius 15
Brazil 106
Britain *see* England
Bruges *see* Flanders, textile industry in
Butterfield, Herbert 156

Calvin, John 32
capitalism 5–7, 80–2, 106
Charlemagne 3, 18, 36
Chaucer, Geoffrey 153
Chaunu, Pierre 135
chemical fertilizer *see* agriculture
Chile 106
China 47–8, 96; Book of Changes 162; centralized authority in 53–4, 89, 135–6, 145–6, 149, 156; civil service examinations 152, 154, 159, 166; colonization, expansion or exploration 157, *164*, 169; comparisons to Europe 5, 59, 117–18; cult of agriculture 169; culture of 140–2, 151–3, 157–60; economy, development of 112, 163–6; failure to excel 10, 141, 179–80; feudalism in 135–6, 146, 155; foreign trade restrictions 165; Grand canal 163, *164*, 171; Great Wall *164*, 171; handicrafts and cottage industries 143, 165, 171; high level equilibrium trap 167; language and literature 142, 153–4; manufacturing and technology innovations in 88–9, 124, 129–30; merchants, artisans and entrepreneurs 4, 96–7, 119, 157, 166, 172; naval and maritime technology 97, 127, *128*, 136, 163; population and laborers in 59, 139–40, 142–3, 165, 167, 172; scholar-officials 89, 146, 153, 155, 161,